Tigers

Tigers

Leaders of the new Asia–Pacific

GREG SHERIDAN

ALLEN & UNWIN

Publication of this title was assisted by the Australia Council, the Federal Government's arts funding and advisory body.

First published in 1997 by
Allen & Unwin Pty Ltd
9 Atchison Street, St Leonards, NSW 2065 Australia
Phone: (61 2) 9901 4088
Fax: (61 2) 9906 2218
E-mail: frontdesk@allen-unwin.com.au

National Library of Australia
Cataloguing-in-Publication entry:

Sheridan, Greg. 1956– .
  Tigers: leaders of the new Asia–Pacific.

  Includes index.
  ISBN 1 86448 153 6.

  1. Heads of state—Asia—Biography. 2. Heads of state—
  Pacific Area—Biography. 3. Pacific Area—Politics and
  government. 4. Asia—Politics and government—1945– .
  I. Title.

351.003109225

Set in 10.5/13pt Arrus by DOCUPRO, Sydney
Printed by South Wind Production, Singapore Pte Ltd

10 9 8 7 6 5 4 3 2 1

CONTENTS

I wish to dedicate this book to my wife, Jasbir Kaur Sheridan, with affection and infinite gratitude.

FOREWORD

This is a book about leaders and leadership, in particular the leaders of the Asia–Pacific. It is based around interviews I have had with all the leaders profiled here except President Suharto of Indonesia, President Clinton of the United States, and President Lee Teng-hui of Taiwan. With all the other leaders I have had at least one, and mostly several, interviews in the course of covering the region for the *Australian*. As a frequent traveller in the region over the last decade and more I have been drawn to the experience of hearing from these leaders from their own mouths what they are doing and why. This has given me a privileged vantage point from which to view the region and one I try here to share with the reader. The leaders examined here cover nations of four distinct sub-regions: Northeast Asia, Southeast Asia, Australasia and the United States. Apart from the US, these countries form what one might call the East Asian hemisphere. Although the US is not geographically part of the region it is a major economic and military power in the East Asian hemisphere and you can't really consider the region without considering America's role. Of course, the book is not comprehensive. There are ten nations in Southeast Asia alone, but from Southeast Asia I have written about only Indonesia, the Philippines, Malaysia and Singapore. I am afraid the choice reflects opportunity and experience. It is simply not possible to get access to every single, serving leader in East Asia. This aside, I also decided only to write about countries to which I have been a frequent visitor. This is partly because while the chapters are based on interviews they involve a more general critical evaluation of the careers of the leaders involved and of the political environments in which they operate.

Why leave out Canada when considering North America? Why leave out China? The basic answer is these are the leaders I've had access to, or, in the cases of Presidents Suharto, Lee Teng-hui and Clinton, I have had access to numerous of their Cabinet colleagues and senior officials, have travelled or lived in the countries involved, and consider them too important to leave out. In the case of Japan I have profiled a former leader, Morihiro Hosokowa, but he is the recent prime minister I consider to have been most influential, and most original, in shaping his country's destiny. The biggest gap in the book is China. The Northeast Asian leaders profiled come from Japan, South Korea, Taiwan and Hong Kong. Of course, the Chinese figure in the book. And I write specifically about four ethnically Chinese leaders—Singapore's Lee Kuan Yew and Goh Chok Tong, Taiwan's Lee Teng-hui and Hong Kong's Martin Lee. Martin Lee is not a head of government but he wins the most votes in what is meant to be a semi-democratic system. But mainland China presented me with insurmountable difficulties. The only general secretary of the Chinese Communist Party I ever met in a journalistic capacity was the late Hu Yao Bang and that was too long ago, in 1985, to qualify for this book, which is about the contemporary region. Moreover, China's perverse political system makes its leaders substantially inaccessible and difficult to evaluate as individuals. Perhaps I'll remedy that in a future edition.

Above all this is a journalistic book. No attempt has been made to apply a consistency of approach to the different leaders and their different countries. Nor does each individual chapter make claims to comprehensiveness concerning each leader considered. Rather I've tried to evaluate the contribution each has made to his country, and in Bill Clinton's case to America's interest in Asia (and to Asia's interest in Asia, for that matter). But I have presented the leaders in different ways, reflecting how I came across them and how they struck me and attempting to report some of the individuality of each subject. I certainly don't shy away from making judgments but one of the most useful things a reporter can do is report, and I've tried to do a good deal of that.

Not the least of the psychological demands of politics is that you submit yourself to cross-examination and evaluation not only by the electorate but by scribes and commentators of all kinds. All the leaders in this book have done that to some extent, and they deserve some thanks for that.

ACKNOWLEDGMENTS

This book is substantially based on the access I have had to Asia–Pacific leaders over the last half-dozen years or so. The reason I have had that access has nothing to do with any subtle and otherwise hidden aspects of my personality and everything to do with one piece of overwhelming good fortune I enjoy. I am the foreign editor of one of the region's great daily newspapers—the *Australian*. It is in that capacity that I carried out almost all the interviews which form the basis of this book. As such I would like to record my thanks to the *Australian* for its commitment to covering the Asian story and for giving me the freedom to follow this idea of seeking out the leaders in the most important countries. In particular I should thank the *Australian*'s editor-in-chief, Paul Kelly, whose commitment to getting the story right, and understanding the big trends in our region, is second to none. His support has always been fantastic. Similarly my colleagues at the *Australian* furnish a work enviornment both congenial and stimulating. I would also like to thank a variety of people who helped in specific ways regarding information and interviews in particular regional countries. Among them are: Sadaaki Numaata, Sabam Siagian, Ratih Hardjono, Honesto Isleta, Delia Albert, James Wu, Heng Chen Wing, Jin Park, Byong Kwon, Ashton Calvert, Alan Gyngell, Graham Fortune, Noordin Sopiee, Rohana Mahmoud, Frank Lavin and Rich Armitage. Within Australia I would particularly like to thank Phil Scanlan, Dick Woolcott, Stephen Matchett, Michael Marx, Stephen FitzGerald and John McCarthy for an endless informal seminar on regional issues. Also I should record my thanks to the officers of the Australian Department of Foreign Affairs and Trade who answer queries of all kinds from journalists with courtesy and skill. Thanks are also due to John Iremonger of Allen & Unwin. He has provided editorial advice, enthusiasm for the project and friendly support in every way. Finally I should thank my wife, Jasbir, whose patience and inspiration are magnificent. Of course, nobody mentioned above is in any way responsible for the opinions expressed in this book, or its mistakes.

INTRODUCTION: TIGERS ON THE PROWL

As an Australian journalist I have for a long time thought there was only really one story to be interested in. That story is the re-emergence of East Asia onto the main stage of global history. To have chosen any other story ahead of this, it seemed to me, especially for an Australian, would be to earn the rebuke once directed at Henry James (who left America for England), that as a novelist he gave up the opportunity to witness the emergence of the most powerful nation the world had ever seen in order to eavesdrop at European dinner parties.

And so for the last decade and a half I have been primarily interested in trying to work out what is happening in East Asia. Everybody now can tell that something extraordinary is afoot, something that is going to change the world, that has already changed the world. The economic growth rates that we are all familiar with tell the story. South Korea, Malaysia, Indonesia, Singapore, Taiwan, southern China and Thailand have all averaged more than 7 per cent growth per year for the last six years. Malaysia has grown at better than 8 per cent a year for a decade. Southern China's growth has seen an explosion of economic activity, frequently soaring into double-digit growth rates in the last half decade.

East Asia has witnessed the greatest number of people exiting poverty in the shortest time in the history of the world. After the Korean War, the people of South Korea had a per capita income of less than $US80 per year. Now it is more than

$US10 000. After the Chinese Civil War the people of Taiwan were running essentially a subsistence economy. Now their per capita income is greater than $US10 000. Hong Kong and Singapore have per capita incomes well above a number of European countries inside the European Union.

We are all familiar with figures such as these, but less so with the dramatic, sweeping social and psychological changes they have brought in their wake. A revolution has swept across East Asia, and in the last twenty years it has predominantly been a peaceful revolution. What is utterly astonishing is that there has been so little dislocation in the face of such rocketing social and economic change. It really is beside the point to say that great inequalities of wealth still persist, or that there are structural problems in the Korean or Japanese economies. All that is true enough but it pales into insignificance compared with the magnitude of economic and social success and the new patterns of global power that must flow from this.

Noordin Sopiee of the Malaysian Institute of Strategic and International Studies has argued that future historians will look back and see three decisive periods of change in the twentieth century. The first was 1914 to 1918, which saw the outbreak of the first European civil war, the first global war and the establishment of the first communist state. The second was 1939 to 1949, which saw the second European civil war, the second global war and the outbreak of the Cold War. And the third will be the period from 1989, which saw the overthrow of communism in Europe, the end of the Cold War, and possibly more important than either of those, the rise of the East Asian economic miracle.

This economic miracle has already transformed the world we live in. The popular term globalisation has really so far predominantly meant Asian competition. East Asia finances American debt. East Asia sets the benchmark of global standards in many industrial products. East Asia also offers the sense of hope to South Asia, to Latin America and to Africa, that there is a way out of poverty, that economic development can be rapid and consistent with civil peace. No one now wants to embrace the communist model. A substantial, but probably declining, number are still attracted to Islamism as a political system, along the lines of Iran. But throughout the developing world policy makers are studying the experience of Japan, of South Korea, of Malaysia, of Singapore, of Hong Kong. What is the secret? How is it done?

There has been a substantial debate about whether there is any secret at all. Paul Krugman has argued that it is all factor accumulation—more labour, more capital and that it is just like the early Soviet industrialisation. This is an inherently ridiculous thesis. As Lee Kuan Yew has tartly riposted, is Singapore Airlines just like the old Aeroflot? And how can the industrialisation be inefficient when so much of it has to meet global best-practice by earning its keep in exports?

The World Bank, and lots of others, have tried to unravel the secret. Is it to be found in the highly interventionist state in Japan, or the laissez-faire practices of Hong Kong? Does it reside in encouraging huge corporations, as in Korea, or in the unbridled flourishing of countless small and medium-sized firms in southern China and Taiwan? Has aid been a factor, as in Indonesia? Has it all been based on preferential access to the American market? If so, how come the early results from Vietnam, which does not enjoy such access, are so encouraging?

Is democracy part of the formula for success, as in Japan, and more recently, South Korea, Thailand and Taiwan? Or is partial democracy better, as in Malaysia and Singapore? Or autocracy, as in Indonesia and China, or benevolent colonial rule, as in Hong Kong?

One of the few things that can be said about the region with confidence is that it is extraordinarily diverse. Economists have settled on some things which seem important in most cases of economic success, namely sound money, the avoidance of the welfare state, emphasis on education and training, emphasis on the family in social relations, high savings rates, deferred consumption, high investment rates, heavy reliance on exports to enforce global standards, emphasis on the interests of the producer rather than the consumer, and a stable rule of at least commerical law. Even the last requirement is hardly universal when you consider China or Indonesia.

But perhaps the missing ingredient from most of the analyses is leadership. After all there is nothing inevitable about East Asian economic success. Plenty of East Asian societies have failed. The Philippines under Marcos was one. Its prospects looked so bright in the 1950s and '60s. It was richly endowed with natural resources, had a large English-speaking population, had by regional standards a well-educated population, had democracy and the rule of law and intimate links with the United States. Yet under Marcos it fell apart and its people saw nothing of the aid or loans that were advanced to it. Nor did they see much indigenous economic development. Myanmar (Burma) under the predecessors of the State Law and Order Restoration Council chose the so-called 'Burmese Way', the way of isolation and rejection of the west. It found that this way led to poverty and misery. Even China, before the market reforms of Deng Xiaoping, produced periods of mass starvation and social chaos. Vietnam, after beating off the Americans, embraced the worst economic policies anyone could possibly imagine and was driven to market reform by complete failure of the old system.

The East Asian societies that have been successful, which includes all the East Asian societies considered in this book, have had extremely pragmatic leaderships. Very often they have had long, stable periods of leadership by the one party, or even one individual, as in the cases of Malaysia, Singapore and Indonesia. In others, such as Japan, and to a lesser extent South Korea, the policy stability has been provided by a powerful and effective bureaucracy. In the Philippines economic success only arrived after the advent of an extremely pragmatic president in Fidel Ramos.

All the old political patterns in East Asia are undergoing serious change as a result of the economic and social developments of the last decade. One of the most important developments is regionalism. Intra East Asian trade is growing more rapidly than trade between East Asia and any outside region. But the American market is still absolutely fundamental to the success of East Asia. The net wealth transfer from the United States to East Asia each year is of the order of $US100 billion. Perhaps even more fundamental is the continued US military role. There is no indigenous military balance in East Asia. Without the US, hegemony must be exercised by either China or Japan, or some combination of them. Perhaps later a more natural regional balance will emerge. At this stage the US is absolutely essential.

Can we really talk then of an East Asian miracle, or even an

East Asian region, without including the US? Several dynamics of regionalism are at work in the East Asian hemisphere. Not only the US but also Australia are vital to these processes. First, consider the building blocks of the region. There is Northeast Asia. This consists of China, Taiwan, Hong Kong, Korea and Japan. All of these are Confucian-derived societies and they all use a similar type of character-based writing. Their cultural similarity is real and readily observable.

Then there is Southeast Asia. This is a much more diverse region and consists of Indonesia, Malaysia, Singapore, Brunei, Thailand, the Philippines, Vietnam, Laos, Cambodia and Myanmar. These ten nations embrace many of the world's religions, including Islam, Buddhism, and Christianity. However, since 1967 there has existed the Association of South-East Asian Nations, which now includes seven of the ten (Laos, Cambodia and Myanmar are not yet members but will be by 2000). The development of ASEAN should be a great source of comfort for developing nations everywhere, because it demonstrates that it is possible for what were poor and unstable nations (in 1967) to come together and control their own destinies. The success of ASEAN is the success of endless consultation and pragmatism in international affairs. This success has been so great that it is now not unreasonable to talk of an emerging Southeast Asian identity. Indeed ASEAN has taken a giant step towards cementing that identity by deciding to move towards an ASEAN Free Trade Area, an ASEAN common market.

At the same time in both Northeast Asia and Southeast Asia, while they have been experiencing such stupendous economic success, the US has been a critical partner. At a less intense level Australia and New Zealand have also been important. The encounter with the west has been the great challenge of modernisation for Asia. In the long run this will be no less a challenge for the west. But to Asia in the short term modernisation has meant deep involvement with the west.

Enter Australia. Australia and New Zealand are the bit of the west nearest to East Asia. They are big enough to count but small enough not to be threatening. They have been an important source of training for East Asia, and also of political dialogue. When the United States to some extent dropped the ball on regional leadership as the Cold War was ending Australia produced the blueprint for and founded the Asia Pacific Economic Cooperation (APEC) forum.

Australia is important to East Asian regionalism in another way. As Kazuo Ogura, the former deputy foreign minister of Japan, has argued, the presence of Australia can de-ethnicise East Asian regionalism. Eventually the big powers of East Asia will need to offer global leadership. Including Australia and New Zealand in regional structures can symbolically and substantially demonstrate that these regional structures are not based on any nasty notion of racial exclusivism.

And so there are four elements to what is a new Asia–Pacific regionalism: Northeast Asia, Southeast Asia, the United States and Australasia. Two other dynamics are acutely important. Southeast Asia and Northeast Asia have discovered each other once more. Japan, Korea and Taiwan have become important investors in Southeast Asia. Southeast Asian nations have become important investors in each other. Trade between Northeast and Southeast Asia is booming.

At the same time, culturally, a certain Asia–Pacific fusion is taking place. As George Yeo, a minister in the Singapore government, has argued, East Asia needs the liberalism of the west to soften its sometimes harsh authoritarian streaks. As he was perhaps too polite to argue, western societies could do with some of the economic drive and social discipline of many East Asian societies in recent times to help recover both economic competitiveness and social morale, especially in the inner cities of America and in other distressed areas.

The Asia–Europe summits inaugurated in 1996 show that, certainly, East Asia can do some things without America. But the China–Taiwan crisis in the same year demonstrates America's absolute centrality when push comes to shove. The best kind of East Asian regionalism in a globalising world is Asia–Pacific regionalism.

But for any regionalism to really work the national leaders have to win the policy debates within their own countries. They have to understand the fundamental issues and provide effective leadership.

Because it often eschews universal pretensions and dramatic

rhetoric much East Asian leadership is underestimated internationally. This is a book about Asia–Pacific leaders, leaders from
Northeast Asia, Southeast Asia, the United States and Australasia. They are not all unqualified successes but they have been
at the helm when extraordinary changes, in their countries and
throughout the Asia–Pacific, are taking place. I have been lucky
to have privileged access to these leaders. Their stories tell us
much about what is happening to this Asia–Pacific of ours and
why. It is a story worth telling.

1

KIM YOUNG-SAM AND THE CRUCIBLE OF KOREAN POLITICS

Panmunjom is the village at the intersection of South Korea and North Korea, the Republic of Korea and the Democratic People's Republic of Korea. It is the last military flashpoint of the Cold War, it is the world's most dangerous point of nuclear confrontation. On the day I first visited Panmunjom, in August 1994, the village was more than usually tense. It was the eighteenth anniversary of the day in 1976 when a group of North Korean soldiers used their axes to hack to death two United States servicemen trimming some overgrown poplar trees. It took four minutes and it nearly caused a war.

I had gone to Korea to interview President Kim Young-sam, South Korea's first civilian president in more than 30 years. But inevitably I was drawn to Panmunjom, there to observe the inescapable strategic reality which confronts the Republic of Korea. Panmunjom is 40 km north of the capital, Seoul, with its 12 million inhabitants. In the rolling hills and deceptively gentle mountains to the north of Panmunjom, battery upon battery of North Korean artillery nestle. Almost all of these could reach Seoul. If hostilities ever should break out, with or without the use of a nuclear weapon, North Korea could raze Seoul in an hour, causing unimaginable loss of life and material destruction. I wonder if this reality is given enough weight in explaining South Korea's frenetic drive to modernisation, its fierce and seemingly single-minded quest for production and meeting national targets, along with the other more commonly cited aspects of Korean culture.

On the day I visited Panmunjom I saw two Korean soldiers facing each other in classic military confrontation, barely 10 m apart, one from the north, one from the south, their bodies rigid and their faces taut. The North Koreans like to annoy their southern counterparts by flashing mirrors in their eyes. So the South Korean soldier wears sunglasses. He also stands with his body half concealed by the Military Affairs Council meeting hut. He does this in case he is fired upon. His orders then are to take cover and return fire.

These orders are no joke. In the last 40 years, dozens of soldiers from both sides have been killed in incidents in the laughably misnamed Demilitarised Zone. Before the axe murders of the US servicemen in 1976 allied policy was not to react to North Korean provocations. But since then the orders have been much tougher. Any show of force will be met with a decisive response. At the same time, allied commanders do not want to let incidents escalate out of control. This paradox, letting the enemy know he will pay for any provocation, but never offering him an excuse for wider confrontation, is one of the countless practical difficulties the South Korean and American soldiers face. The tension in the place is palpable. Civilians living in the area must be indoors and accounted for by 9 p.m. All the South Korean soldiers who serve at Panmunjom and surrounding districts must be above average height and body size and have extra martial arts training. The Americans there fairly bristle with muscle and military alertness.

Yet Panmunjom seems a fantastically inappropriate symbol for modern South Korea. For the Republic of Korea is not fundamentally a militaristic society. Certainly, aspects of military culture have been important in the broader culture. Certainly, until the diminutive Kim Young-sam won the 1992 presidential election the country had been ruled by a succession of military strongmen. Certainly, reunification, its immense positive possibilities but also its many terrors, is a perennial preoccupation of South Korean life. But from numerous trips there and conversations with many Korean friends the impression I get is not of a society obsessed with military security, like Israel, nor overwhelmed by the domestic presence of its own security forces, like the old South Africa. Instead you get a very familiar impression of an East Asian society determined to achieve a respected place at the international table of nations, and determined equally to be among the winners in the global economy. Of all the East Asian economic miracles, South Korea's is probably the most miraculous. Just after the devastating Korean War, South Koreans had a per capita income of less than $US80. Now it is more than $US10 000. That is as astonishing, and in quantitative terms as great, as any economic transformation anywhere in the world at any time in history.

Although the threat from the north has been something of a motivator in this success, you get the feeling in Korea that comparisons with other East Asian success stories, with Taiwan, Hong Kong and Singapore, but most particularly with Japan, are among the most important motivating factors. Despite the cruelty and tragedy of the Korean War, and despite the long, undemocratic periods in South Korea's postwar history, the country also benefited, as did so many East Asian societies, hugely from its association with the United States.

But the quest to become a fully developed society means much more than just economics. As Korean intellectuals will readily tell you, being a developed society entails a whole panoply of attitudes and aspirations, a world view embracing democracy, prosperity, social progress and amenity. It's not that these qualities are tightly defined or prescribed in their content for developed societies, but rather the realisation that becoming a modern, developed society is a huge psychological challenge for Koreans as well as an economic challenge.

If a single figure symbolises all the struggle involved in this transformation, it is Kim Young-sam. A little like Yitzhak Rabin for Israel, his life history holds up a direct mirror to the great struggles of his nation. But unlike Rabin he was not a leader in government for most of his republic's turbulent history, but rather a leader of the Opposition. Yet in his way Kim has been central to Korean politics and national life for decades. With his famous rival and occasional ally, Kim Dae-jung, he is one of only two modern giants Korean politics has thrown up. All the former presidents have been discredited after their terms in office, some have gone to jail, one was assassinated, another went into exile. Kim Young-sam's dramatic career could have no greater conclusion than an honourable retirement. He may prove to be the most important and successful politician his country has ever seen, notwithstanding the trials, metaphoric and literal, which beset his country in the middle of his presidential term. Of course, the contribution of the previous military leadership, corrupt and undemocratic as it mostly was, in bringing about the Korean economic miracle should not be underestimated. Even there, however, Kim has often influenced the shape of policy even from Opposition.

To talk to, Kim is easy-going and straightforward. In a society renowned for its hierarchy in social matters, its pervasive sense of formality, ritual and deference to proper procedure, interviewing him is a surprisingly relaxed and free-flowing business. As with most East Asian leaders, there is a requirement to submit a list of questions in advance. The president's advisers kindly supply me with a list of written answers to the questions, answers which I can use however I like. This allows the face-to-face interview to range more freely in uncharted territory and Kim, and his large retinue, are completely relaxed about this.

Kim Young-sam has been the complete politician, all his adult life. Indeed seemingly all his conscious life he has been absorbed in the great political struggles of his society. He was pre-eminently possessed of what Koreans call *daetongryong byung*, or 'presidential disease', the overwhelming hunger for the highest office. Indeed his critics sometimes hold his obvious ambition against him, but which successful politician was not ambitious? Political ambition is a good, indeed a necessary, quality in a democracy. You won't have a democracy without ambitious politicians. Political ambition, provided it is balanced against fundamental ethical imperatives, is nothing to be ashamed of. Moreover, Kim's ambition was always linked to authentic political ideals, above all the struggle for democracy in South Korea.

Kim was born in Koje-gun, in South Kyongsang, on December 20, 1927. This was one of countless strokes of good fortune for Kim. As South Korean politics became more democratic it was dominated for a time by regionalism and extended family structures. The region from which Kim Young-sam came, South

Kyongsang, was, with its large capital city, Pusan, far more populous than the region, namely South and North Cholla, which gave loyalty to the man who was to prove to be his rival over many decades, Kim Dae-jung. Although Kim Young-sam proved himself the superior politician to Kim Dae-jung, merely coming from a more populous region, and therefore being able to count on its support in a national election, was to prove a huge benefit to Kim Young-sam in the 1992 presidential election, where he definitively defeated Kim Dae-jung. Thus is democracy shaped by many accidents.

Coming from South Kyongsang benefited Kim in other ways as well. His three predecessors, Roh Tae-woo, Chun Doo-hwan and Park Chung-hee, also all came from the Kyongsang region. Although Kim was opposed to these men, when he eventually came to join the ruling party in the 1990s, and form a temporary alliance with Roh, his regional background made this a more comfortable operation than it otherwise would have been.

Kim Young-sam's parents were, like so many in Confucian Korea, obsessed with education. Although Kim was not an exceptional student in his early years at school the family moved to Pusan so he could attend the high-class Kyongnam High School. Like many men who later go on to high office Kim had political ambitions even when at school. During his middle school period, when in photographs he looks extremely sombre and serious, he wrote out a poster bearing the inscription: 'Kim Young-sam: Future President' and stuck it up on the wall of his room. After school he attended the Seoul National University, the best of Korea's universities. He graduated in 1952, having majored in philosophy and political science.

His studies had been temporarily interrupted by the Korean War, when North Korean soldiers invaded the south. Kim worked for a while for the South Korean government during this period but still managed to complete his studies before the war finished in 1953. After university he went to work for the government. He had been a good student and a keen debater. In 1954, at the positively precocious age (in the Korean context) of 26 he was elected to the National Assembly, representing the ruling Liberal Party. But he quickly became disenchanted with the increasingly high-handed and undemocratic behaviour of the president,

Syngman Rhee, and his government. Kim established himself as a rebel and left the ruling party in 1955 when the president had the constitution changed so that he could run for president again.

Having left the government party Kim quickly became an important figure in the Opposition, forming the Democratic Party. Political parties in postwar Korea have been extremely fluid. As in some other East Asian societies, the party structure is weak and malleable, with politics dominated by individuals, regional loyalties, which have remained hugely important, and evolving interest groups. Between the party and the individual leader, the individual leader is stronger. Even the formal institutions of the state have generally not been strong enough to contain the powerful personalities who have run Korean politics. In 1961 General Park Chung-hee took over in a bloodless coup and Kim was among the leaders of those outraged by this undemocratic transfer of power. Throughout the 1960s Kim came to increasing prominence as one of the leading parliamentarians in the New Democratic Party. He would later declare: 'My political career has been formed through parliamentary activities. I believe in parliamentarianism.' By the late 1960s he was urging the Opposition leaders to choose younger candidates, in their 40s, to more effectively oppose military rule.

As Kim's officials point out, his life is resplendent with political records. He was the youngest citizen ever elected to parliament, he was the representative elected most often (nine times), the person most often elected Opposition floor leader (five times) and the man most often elected leader of an Opposition party (four times). What this bald recitation of records discloses is a simply astonishing stamina for the marathon of South Korean politics. Kim Young-sam has the credibility of persistence, and this too was to be crucial in his ultimate presidential success in 1992.

In 1971 Kim, in his early 40s, took his first shot at the presidency. He stood for his party's nomination for the presidential race. He was defeated by the man with whom he was to dance a seemingly endless political minuet, Kim Dae-jung, who subsequently lost to Park in the general election. The voting pattern in the general election was revealing, and to be repeated many times subsequently. The Opposition carried the intellectuals and much of the emerging middle class in Seoul, but the countryside was far more conservative and voted overwhelmingly for the ruling party. In 1972 Park declared martial law which the two Kims opposed bitterly. Park's rule became far more autocratic, personalised and undemocratic, with the Opposition and the press being particular targets for restrictions and harassment.

Kim Young-sam became leader of the New Democratic Party in late 1974 and energetically pushed a liberal agenda, demanding Park's resignation, a new constitution and the release of dissidents. Kim had been in jail several times under the Park regime but he continued to defy its numerous restrictions on criticism and the free expression of political opinion. It was in these years that Kim solidified his reputation as a politician of courage with an impeccable commitment to democracy. The 1978 National Assembly election was a turning point. The New Democratic Party, led by Kim Young-sam, for the first time ever received more votes than the ruling party, although this did not translate into a majority within the assembly because a large number of assemblymen were appointed by the government. The ruling party took severe harassing action against Kim and other oppositionists. Kim finally declared Park's government 'a minority dictatorial regime' and was expelled from the National Assembly as a result. But, in an incident in its way typical of Kim's ability to galvanise the Opposition around his own personality, the rest of the Opposition members of the assembly also walked out to express solidarity with Kim and opposition to the government's high-handedness.

Kim's speech on being expelled from the National Assembly was full of high-flown, florid rhetoric, which may seem over the top to some western ears but has been extremely effective in Korea. On October 4, 1979, he declared:

> Today the Democratic Republican Party [the ruling party]
> turned the National Assembly into a handmaiden of the ruling
> power and made it serve as the cat's paw of terrorist politics
> by coercively expelling the leader of the major opposition party
> from the National Assembly. Since I was elected leader of the
> New Democratic Party last May 30, the ruling power has
> continuously resorted to acts of political repression by
> mobilising the administrative, judiciary and legislative branches.
> All these acts have proved to our people and the world that

democracy is not practised in any major way in our country. In
the past 100 days the politics of repression have been rife. At
one time hoodlums were mobilised to attack the New
Democratic Party headquarters in Seoul. Barging into the party
headquarters, they indiscriminately beat up party members,
including National Assemblymen, and reporters who were
covering party activities there. In another act of terrorism,
political hooligans raided and dragged a female worker out from
her living quarters, causing her death. Scores of party members
were inexplicably arrested.

South Korea was in uproar. It was not yet a democratic society
but nor was it a society complacent about violent government
repression. There was no real consensus on how politics should
be conducted but a huge segment of the population disapproved
of the government's heavy-handedness. The ruling military
powers were themselves bitterly divided over how to handle Kim's
brilliant challenge to their legitimacy and their power. In October
1979, President Park was assassinated by the head of the South
Korean Central Intelligence Agency, Kim Jae-kyu. In May 1980
the government declared martial law and the two Kims, along
with hundreds of others, were thrown into jail. The crackdown
was widespread and tough. All political activity was banned.
Newspapers and radio stations were closed down or censored.
Universities and colleges were closed. About a year later, Chun
Doo-hwan, a retired general, was the only candidate for the
presidency and was thus installed by the electoral college. Kim
was in and out of jail, and house arrest, over the next few years.
Chun was as punitive and repressive as any of his predecessors,
if anything worse. Kim's NDP was prevented from participating
in National Assembly elections and the ruling Democratic Justice
Party thus swept into a majority position in the assembly.

In May 1980, in protest against the government crackdown,
there had been a massive pro-democracy uprising in the city of
Kwangju. It was put down by government troops acting with
barbaric ferocity. Some 250 protesters, mainly students, were
killed by the soldiers. Kwangju, in South Cholla, had long been
a centre of protest and resistance. South Cholla, unlike neighbouring South Kyongsan, had been substantially bypassed in South
Korea's postwar development. It felt that it had been discrimi-

nated against, that it had a grievance, on top of all the grievances of all the pro-democracy forces. Whatever the reason, the Kwangju massacre was an act of great barbarity in modern Korea and has had permanent, and to this day unresolved, embittering effects on Korean politics.

Finally, in May 1983, on the third anniversary of the Kwangju massacre, Kim, while still in custody, took one of the most dangerous and dramatic steps of his career; he went on hunger strike, demanding that democratic rules be implemented for politics, dissidents be released, direct elections be held and restrictions on freedom of expression lifted. He stayed on hunger strike for 23 days and very nearly died. It was a galvanising event for the nation. Once again Kim, in effective pursuit of his political ideals, had also projected his own personality over all of the Korean political scene. He had once again made himself the central focus of dissent, more than that, the central focus of Korean life and politics. It is no disrespect to Kim's idealism, nor to his courage, to note also the astuteness of a populist politician. Again, the government did not know how to react. Fearful that he might die in custody, with uncontrollable domestic and inter-national consequences, they set him free. But he went to a hospital and continued his hunger strike. Finally, after 23 days, and dangerously weak—according to some reports very near death—Kim ended his hunger strike. His demands had not been met but he had utterly transformed the political situation. He had gained intense international attention. There was no feeling that he had ignominiously backed down but rather a renewed and deepened respect for the tenacity of his campaign for democracy.

Again, the remarks he made on ending his hunger strike, on June 9, 1983, were an important event in themselves. Again they were florid and dramatic. Again they galvanised the Opposition forces and intensified the political situation. Kim said in part:

> Today, with profound sadness and an aching heart, I announce that I am discontinuing the fast I began in protest. I have been surrounded by an intrigue staged to try to bring my fast to a halt. I deeply appreciate all my fellow citizens who, during my more than twenty days of fasting, wholeheartedly encouraged me, enthusiastically supported my demand for democratisation and were profoundly concerned about my health and safety.

Their encouragement and love gave me the strength I needed
to endure the painful ordeal of my lone fast, protected my life
from the threat of autocratic power and reaffirmed my belief in
our people's desire and ability to realise democracy in our land.
I am deeply convinced of the common bond linking the people
and myself in the call for democratisation. Fellow citizens, I am
halting my fast not because I want to live even in shame. I am
doing so because I would rather continue to fight for
democracy to the end than allow myself to die in vain.

After the hunger strike, Kim's political position was strengthened. The Opposition forces generally were reinvigorated in their
determination to fight for democracy, and temporarily willing to
put aside their own internal differences. Kim Young-sam and Kim
Dae-jung joined together to chair the Council for the Promotion
of Democracy. More Opposition figures were released from jail.
Eventually the two Kims were involved in forming the New
Korean Democratic Party. The political situation was an
inherently unstable stand-off. The authorities were still repressive
but had to yield to some of the Opposition's demands. Most
importantly they allowed free elections for the legislative assembly in early 1985 and the NKDP won almost 30 per cent of the
vote, emerging as the largest single party in the assembly.
    The next two years were taken up with complex political
manoeuvring. The Opposition wanted above all electoral reform.
It felt, with considerable justice, that only a direct presidential
election would ever give it a chance to take real power. The
government conceded that electoral reform was necessary but
favoured a Westminister-style system. The Opposition party split,
as usual. Kim Dae-jung was sent back to jail and Kim Young-sam
formed the Reunification Democratic Party. Finally, a form of
constitutional reform was agreed upon which, crucially, included
direct nationwide election of the president to a single, five-year
term. The presidential election held at the end of 1987 was the
Opposition's best chance to achieve real power. There were mass
rallies, the governing party used the organs of government to put
pressure on civil servants to vote for the government candidate,
but in general the election was clean. What stopped the Opposition from winning, and handed the election to the ruling
regime's candidate, Roh Tae-woo, was the inevitable split between

the two Kims. Kim Young-sam delcared in October that he would be a candidate for the presidency. A little while later, Kim Dae-jung declared his presidential candidacy on behalf of the Peace and Democracy Party, another newly created, temporary creature on the Korean political scene. As it turned out the two Kims got 55 per cent of the vote between them but Roh won with 36 per cent.

This is perhaps the worst episode in both the Kims' careers. Had either been prepared to throw his support behind the other, Roh would very likely have been defeated, and a civilian president with impeccable democratic credentials would have been elected. Was Kim Young-sam wrong to insist on running? Certainly both Kims probably suffered a decline in their standing because of their behaviour. But the case for Kim Young-sam's running was considerable. He came second, demonstrating that he had more popular support than Kim Dae-jung. He also had always been more centrist and less radical than Kim Dae-jung, and this radicalism frightened some Korean voters. It is perhaps not absolutely certain that even with Kim Young-sam's support, Kim Dae-jung would have won the election. If he had won, what sort of president would he have made? Would he have been main-stream enough? Would he have been tough enough with the North Koreans? Would the South Korean military have tolerated a Kim Dae-jung victory? All of these are of course unanswerable questions. But it was legitimate for Kim Young-sam to be influenced by them, as well as by his own ambitions, in making up his own mind as to his own course of action. It is perhaps sufficient to suggest that both Kims let ambition stand in the way of democratic change.

Nonetheless, Roh had his problems as a result of the election as well. He had won a legitimate democratic election but he did not have the confidence of the majority of the people. In 1989 National Assembly elections Roh became the first South Korean president to lose a majority. But Kim Young-sam had also been somewhat humiliated by the events of 1987 and beyond. He had come second to Roh and his party had been reduced to being the second largest Opposition party. He needed a dramatic new initiative to revive his own standing as heir apparent. Roh's administration had been democratically elected. Kim felt that an alliance with Roh, in part to secure the succession, would be justified. So, with another Opposition party, he merged his forces with the ruling party to form the Democratic Liberals, which, just after the merger, commanded a huge majority in the National Assembly. Kim justified this astonishing move on the basis of new political thinking.

Plenty of political observers have seen in it a fairly crude power trade. Kim gave Roh the numbers to secure overwhelming support in the National Assembly in exchange for Roh's agreeing to support Kim for the subsequent presidential election. It was by no means clear, however, that Roh had made such a promise. However, Kim played the succession game brilliantly. Many of his bitterest long-term enemies were members of Roh's party. They did not want to give Kim the presidential nomination. But once the merger of the parties had been effected Kim basically had them over a barrel. He could, and frequently did, threaten to leave the ruling party, splitting it in the parliament and effectively blowing up its national organisation. There was a presumption that he would be the ruling party's candidate. As the jockeying for the nomination in the lead-up to the 1992 presidential election intensified, Kim's supporters would frequently make the claim that Roh was actively supporting his nomination. Even if this were not quite true, Roh, whose interests were concerned with the health of his own government much more than with the succession issue, did not feel inclined to contradict this assertion publicly.

Kim's tactical manoeuvring throughout all of this period was nothing short of brilliant. It showed his superiority to all his rivals purely as a politician. His rivals within the ruling party were tainted by their past association with military regimes. Kim Dae-jung, on the other hand, always looked fiery and radical compared with Kim Young-sam, who positioned himself as the perfect compromise, the candidate who had simultaneously the mantle of incumbency and the standing of democratic opposition. It was, however, not inconceivable that had the hardliners in the DJP forced him out he would once again have collaborated with Kim Dae-jung. This effectively stayed their hand. At the same time, he courted enough of the progressive elements of the old ruling party to isolate and weaken his most bitter foes. It was an adroit if dangerous game, but Kim Young-sam by 1990 was a master of brinkmanship. These moves were as second nature to him.

Eventually Kim Young-sam was selected as the ruling party's candidate for the 1992 election. But relations between Kim and Roh had soured very badly. This was partly caused by a typical piece of corporate insider behaviour in the intersection between politics and business. The government had awarded a contract for the second mobile phone project to a company headed by a relative of Roh's. In the context of the wider scandals of Korean corporate life this was pretty small potatoes. But Kim felt, correctly, that it would damage him in the presidential election. He campaigned to have the decision reversed and was successful. Subsequently Roh stayed officially neutral in the presidential election itself. This greatly angered Kim at the time but, given the scandals that were later to engulf Roh, was a long-term blessing in disguise as it meant Kim's eventual election was not tarnished by association with Roh.

The 1992 election was the most peaceful, calm and democratic that Korea had known. Mass rallies were out of vogue, there was no great attempt to influence civil servants to vote for the ruling party candidates, there was no violence, no allegations of electoral fraud. Kim's opponents were, inevitably, Kim Dae-jung, and, most surprisingly, the founder of Hyundai, Chung Ju-yung, whose eccentric candidacy drew compairsons with that of Ross Perot in the United States. Kim Young-sam won 42 per cent of the vote but in a three-way contest this was a convincing win. Kim Dae-jung won 33 per cent, a clear second and a clear loser, but still a tantalisingly substantial support base. Chung Ju-yung, who had ruthlessly mobilised the vast Hyundai *chaebol* to support him, won 16 per cent of the vote, in some ways a surprisingly good result but not substantial enough to justify the muddying of the choice which his candidacy had involved, or indeed the troubles it later caused the Hyundai group.

Kim Young-sam had campaigned on a promise to end the 'Korean disease', namely corruption, lawlessness and a lack of legitimate authority. As is so often and so paradoxically the case in his country, in which the strength of culture is overwhelming, he promised a 'new Korea'. However, in substance he did offer

Koreans the combination they wanted: the promise of reform and the guarantee of stability. In a straight, head-to-head contest with Kim Dae-jung his margin would probably have been greater. He won everywhere except in Kim Dae-jung's home province of South Cholla and in Seoul, where he trailed the other Kim by just a whisker, thus nonetheless repeating the traditional ruling party formula of losing in Seoul but winning in the countryside. He won overwhelmingly in his own home province of South Kyongsang and in the two southern cities of Pusan and Taegu. Other demographic voter breakdowns were enlightening as well. Older voters overwhelmingly preferred the less radical Kim Young-sam, but voters in their twenties were split evenly between the two Kims.

The election victory was the crowning achievement of Kim Young-sam's career. His image as a clean and decent politician had been engraved in the Korean consciousness over 30 years of relentless activism and campaigning for democracy. It was also a crowning achievement for Korean democracy, ending decades of governmental and societal crisis, of a crisis ultimately of legitimacy in Korean society. Tear gas and riots and violent confrontation ceased to characterise South Korean life. The Republic of Korea in 1992 took an enormous leap towards becoming a normal country in a normal time.

It would be wrong to class Roh's presidency as, in general terms, a failure, although the later revelation of the slush fund scandal must be held as a further huge negative. Nonetheless, he is more fairly to be credited with three main successes—democratisation, inter-Korean dialogue and the 'northern policy' (that is, essentially, the policy of seeking diplomatic relations with China). Roh may have been a reluctant democrat but he did nonetheless act as an effective transition from autocratic military rule to basic democracy. Secondly, he pushed dialogue with North Korea much further than it had gone before and, for a military leader, showed considerable flexibility. Thirdly, his government pursued diplomatic relations with most of the communist world—all of North Korea's former allies and supporters. This was what was called the 'northern policy'. Most important of all these was achieving diplomatic relations with China, which is of immense strategic and economic importance to Korea. This effectively left

North Korea isolated, for it did not pursue any similarly successful policy towards South Korea's allies, such as the United States.
Moreover, the South Korea–China relationship has become hugely
profitable economically for South Korea and was important in
allowing the South Korean economy to keep growing during the
Japanese recession of the 1990s. South Korea in 1991 also joined
the United Nations.

All of this gave Kim Young-sam a stable and predictable
foundation for his presidency in 1993 and beyond. Any sensible
South Korean president would have maintained a great deal of
continuity with these successful policies. However, Kim surprised
his countrymen by turning out to be a bolder reformer than most
people expected.

One of his most important reform efforts was an attempt to
change the culture of corruption which has dominated Korea for
so long. He voluntarily declared his personal assets, thus putting
pressure on others to do the same. Later he sponsored legislation
to make this compulsory. He said he would not play golf while
in office, as golf had become a symbol of corporate–government
cronyism and the exchange of corrupt gifts. (This effectively
meant his senior officials were deprived of the pleasure of golf
as well.) He appointed senior people from business, from universities and from politics to his Cabinet, rather than military
figures. He appointed some women. He took a range of symbolic
steps, acutely important in a society such as Korea, among them
opening up the road in front of the Blue House, the presidential
office and residence complex, to the public. He declared that
while in office he would not accept a single penny in donations
from business figures.

On August 12, 1993, he undertook one of the most important
reforms of all. He issued a presidential decree requiring people
to use their real names for all financial transactions, especially
bank accounts. The anonymous or false-name account had
been the backbone of the black economy and massive fraud,
corruption and tax evasion schemes. These practices were hardly
ended by this measure but it made them much more difficult,
and it was a significant step in changing the culture of business
life in Korea.

Kim argued to his countrymen that an end to corruption was

not only an ethical priority but a necessary part of modernising Korea's economy, ensuring, for example, that there was real competition in the domestic economy. In November 1994, on a visit to Australia, he first outlined his *Segyehwa*, or globalisation, policy. *Segyehwa* would come to be a central theme of Kim's presidency. It certainly meant globalisation of the Korean economy, the drive for world's best practice standards, for global competitiveness, for high quality growth rather than the former emphasis of the quantity of growth alone. But it was also a psychological challenge to Koreans, a challenge of self-conception, to identify modernisation of society with internationalisation of outlook. In some ways Korea had been one of the most isolated and culturally self-sufficient societies in the world. A conscious drive to internationalisation represented a profound change in direction, even if the results were not dramatic at first.

I first met Kim Young-sam face to face in late 1994. It was a crisp autumn morning—cool, clear and brilliant. We drove down the vast, sprawling Taepyongno Road, Seoul's main drag, around past the old palace grounds and into the foothills that edge this huge city. The golden autumn leaves, fallen but not yet decayed, formed a thick carpet on the footpaths. We passed a series of checkpoints and arrived at the Blue House compound, Kim Young-sam's office and residence. Entry to the Blue House is a rare prize in South Korean society and it's not hard to see why. The garden at the front of the majestic, blue-roofed building is as perfect as you'll see. Less ornate than Japanese or Chinese gardens, it achieves its breathtaking effect almost through understatement, through the deployment of space, and an asymmetry of design only a hair's breadth removed from a symmetry that would be too neat.

Architecturally, the Blue House is massive and shaped along traditional Korean pagoda lines. But its bulk and design are deceptive. It is only a few years old. The previous Blue House had been built by the Japanese and, as such, had to come down. No country in Asia, not even China, bears more scars from its modern encounter with Japan than does Korea. There are no Japanese cars on these Seoul streets, nor does Japanese pop music play on the radio. While much of the rest of Asia, albeit at times reluctantly, has embraced much of popular Japanese culture, this is not true of Korea. Similarly, while most of the rest of the region worries over the challenge resurgent Chinese power will pose in the decades ahead, Korean strategic thinkers are preoccupied, as ever, with how they will contain Japan.

I interview President Kim in a modest, upstairs meeting room that could easily accommodate 500. We are each sunk in a voluptuous sofa. He is accompanied only by a couple of advisers and a brilliant press secretary acting as interpreter, and the conversation flows. Kim is a small, trim, fit-looking man who jogs every morning and seems full of physical energy. He reminds me physically of the former Australian prime minister, Bob Hawke, not least because he obviously pays attention to his hair. Years ago it was streaked with grey, now it is jet black. When I interview him again in 1996, he has abandoned this vanity—his hair is once more flecked with grey.

One question is more important than any other. Is he satisfied that his country has fully made the transition to democracy, and will stay democratic? He replies:

> Though it has been less than 50 years since Korea was liberated from colonial rule, our nation has already become democratised to a significant degree while recording remarkable growth. This can be considered a miraculous development with few parallels in world history. This process was not easy, however. It involved fierce struggles and numerous sacrifices. I myself experienced all manner of hardships while fighting for democracy for decades as an opposition politician. I am convinced that Korean democracy is now on the right track. The past political dichotomy between those trying to maintain authoritarian rule and the advocates of democracy is now gone. Democratisation is no longer a political issue. All the basic elements of democracy, especially the freedoms of speech and the press, the political neutrality of the military and the protection of human rights, have materialised. The further maturation of Korean democracy in the future is assured by the country's economic strength, the existence of a large middle class and the keen political awareness of the general public—all mainstays of democracy.

Kim is also enthusiastic about an even grander project for democracy—bringing it to North Korea, a process for which, at that time, he outlines an ambitious timetable:

My goal is to form a Korean Commonwealth during my
remaining term of office. This proposed entity is designed to
promote the peaceful coexistence and shared prosperity of both
Koreas by developing a single economic and social community
to bring the south and the north together. If this is done it will
be possible to become fully unified before the present century
is out. A unified Korea should be a single, democratic state
that guarantees all its citizens freedom, well-being and human
dignity.

That timetable came to look more and more unrealistic. And
yet reunification does appear as near to inevitable as a thing can
be. If reunification does occur Korea will move to assume its
rightful place as a major global economy and a significant,
regional military power—a nation of 70 million hard-working,
disciplined, Confucian people at the hub of Northeast Asia. 'We
will be another Germany,' as one senior official put it to me.

In my discussion with Kim the problem of North Korea
loomed large, as it did when I interviewed him again a year later,
although then there was less cause for optimism. In our first
interview there was plenty of cause for optimism as what
appeared to be a breakthrough agreement with the north had
recently been concluded. It was essentially an agreement between
the United States and North Korea but it offered South Korea
much that it wanted from the situation.

In August 1994, Washington and Pyongyang made a deal in
Geneva, designed above all else to prevent North Korea acquiring
and proliferating nuclear weapons. The North Koreans agreed to
freeze their existing nuclear program, to seal off their main
research facility, shut down their existing graphite reactor, which
produced weapons-grade plutonium, and not proceed with the
development of yet more and bigger reactors of this type. The
Americans for their part agreed to move towards full diplomatic
relations and to facilitate international economic aid. As well they
would oversee the construction of light-water nuclear power
stations, from which it is more difficult to extract weapons-grade
plutonium. One of the controversial elements of the deal was
that North Korea would not need to submit to special inspections
of certain facilities, which would determine whether it had

extracted enough plutonium to make nuclear weapons in the past, for five years.

In the course of all this deal-making, contact between Washington and Seoul was intense. President Clinton and President Kim took to having fairly frequent phone conversations, a kind of long distance summitry that was important in the attempt by both South Korea and the United States to make sure that Pyongyang did not succeed in dividing the two allies. For in this business Washington and Seoul did not have exactly identical interests. Exploiting and widening any difference between them was a primary objective of North Korean policy. For Washington the overwhelming priority was to avoid nuclear proliferation. For Seoul, even allowing North Korea to keep a single nuclear weapon would be unacceptable, even if its production of further weapons was stymied. Similarly, the North's strategy was always to try to negotiate directly with Washington, rather than involving South Korea. The North always gave the impression it would give more concessions if it could deal directly and exclusively with Washington, thus cutting Seoul out of the play, diminishing Seoul's status and diminishing the growing sense that the North Korean regime was one day going to collapse and the failed communist state be absorbed back into the Republic of Korea. But any split between South Korea and the United States would have been disastrous for Washington in the long run. This was one problem where President Clinton, though still liable to flip flop on issues of substance, did understand that he had to give it attention, and where his schmoozing style with international leaders was of some benefit. Simply picking up the phone to talk to Kim was a constructive move.

Straight after the deal between the Americans and the North Koreans was concluded, Kim offered to build the light-water reactors for Pyongyang. The Americans would supervise the operation but the South Koreans, with a significant contribution from the Japanese and some others, would pay the bulk of the costs. This was both a generous and a self-interested suggestion by Kim. It was generous because it involved South Korea paying a lot of money to help North Korea. It was self-interested not only because South Korea would be the main beneficiary of reduced military tension on the Korean peninsula, but because

South Korea would almost certainly inherit the reactors when reunification took place, itself almost a certainty. The question of whether the reactors would be built by the South Koreans became a major point of contention with the North as the subsequent months wore on. There were many other points of contention as well. But the agreement did appear to serve its basic purposes—reducing the chances of proliferation and the military tension on the peninsula.

Notwithstanding all this, Kim had to put a little daylight between himself and Washington in order not to look, to his own people, like an American cypher. This delicate balancing requirement was evident when I asked him about the Geneva Agreement between North Korea and the United States. He expressed unhappiness with aspects of the deal, while saying he supported it overall. He said,

> Of course there cannot be 100 per cent satisfaction for a negotiating party in any negotiation, whether it be a nation or a person. But I think because we have reached the final results of the negotiation through close cooperation between the United States and the Republic of Korea we support the Geneva Agreement entirely. However, I must say that the period from now on is much more important than what has gone before in the sense that we must make sure that North Korea faithfully implements the contents of the Geneva Agreement. I think the Geneva Agreement at least made it possible that North Korea has actually introduced a freeze on nuclear development. The fact that special inspections have been delayed does not disturb the basis of the agreement.

According to Kim, the agreement would help maintain peace and stability on the peninsula while freezing North Korea's nuclear activities. He told me:

> With the basis for the resolution of the North Korean nuclear issue now in place, it can be expected that inter-Korean dialogue will be resumed before long. The agreement to support construction of safer light-water nuclear reactors in the north, a multi-billion-dollar project in which the Republic of Korea is to play the central role, should boost substantive inter-Korean cooperation. In the long run, all of this should contribute to

the opening and reform of North Korea, now a tightly controlled society.

Because some of the specifics were not entirely satisfactory, the nuclear agreement was not exactly the best possible solution, Kim said. 'All things considered, however, we evaluate it as the next best alternative that is in line with our basic policy goals.' I asked Kim whether he was confident that North Korea would honour its part of the agreement. He replied:

> Whether North Korea will faithfully keep its promises to the letter and spirit of the agreement we have to wait and see. We can't be sure at the moment. As for the new leadership in North Korea my impression is that there are not any competent opposition groups that may challenge the practical leadership of the new leader, Kim Jong Il. [Kim Jong Il was presumed to have succeeded to leadership in North Korea following the death of his father, long-time communist dictator Kim Il Sung.]
> Somehow there isn't official top leadership in North Korea, which is something rather difficult to understand. With regard to the leadership transfer in North Korea we will have to wait and see what will emerge out of this transition process. If a normal leadership in North Korea emerges, then it is very natural that the two Koreas should enter into dialogue.

Kim's carefully chosen, delicately balanced words reflected considerable uncertainty even within the highest ranks of South Korea's government as to what was actually happening in North Korea.

In numerous visits to Korea in 1994, '95 and '96, I was informed by South Korean intelligence analysts that a number believed Kim Jong Il was suffering from a debilitating psychological or physical illness. That, they believed, was the only possible explanation for his apparent unwillingness to make speeches at public functions and his continued failure to take formal positions of state leadership, following his father's death on 8 July. If true, this could have serious, even profound, consequences for peace and security on the Korean peninsula. Kim Jong Il, known to his countrymen as the 'dear leader' was groomed for decades by his father, Kim Il Sung, known as the 'great leader', to take over the North's leadership. But month after month went by after his father's death and he took no formal position nor did he make any public speeches. There was increasingly a view that the North Korean military was the effective power, and Kim the younger their stooge, an interpretation lent weight by the vast increase in resources, in a society on the brink of widespread starvation in early 1996, that the army received.

Doubts about Kim junior's capabilities were further borne out by the Chinese, who say privately they have been unable to have a satisfactory meeting with Kim Jong Il for years. The political consequences of this could be serious. For one thing it makes a Korean summit all but impossible. Kim Il Sung had agreed to a summit with Kim Young-sam. This would have pushed Korean dialogue to new levels and made possible the kind of cooperation necessary to normalise relations between the Koreas after the nuclear deal was struck.

If Kim Jong Il does suffer from a debilitating problem, the obvious solution would be for the North to replace him, but this may be impossible given the internal dynamics of the North's politics. Kim Il Sung was elevated to the status of a living god in the North. It was a bizarre, quasi-religious cult of personality. All North Koreans wore Kim badges on their lapels. Their identities were moulded by their metaphysical relationship with the 'great leader'. The death of Kim senior thus posed an obvious identity crisis for North Korea, quite apart from the international collapse of communism. Thus the only shred of legitimacy the regime in Pyongyang had was its dynastic connection, through the person of Kim Jong Il, to Kim Il Sung. So Kim the younger, even if he is impaired, is indispensable.

Consistent testimony from defectors from the North suggests that the Democratic People's Republic of Korea may have been the most successful of all communist societies in brainwashing its people. I lived for a good part of 1985 in China and never came across a single person, not even in the Institute of Marxism–Leninism–Mao Zedong Thought, who actually believed there was a single word of truth in the whole crazy metaphysical and historical grab-bag of communist ideology. Similarly, I've never met a single Vietnamese, in any capacity, who did not regard communism as either an abject failure or a cruel joke. But North Koreans, according to many defectors, have an extremely limited knowledge of the outside world. This is one reason, so long as the nuclear deal holds, that Kim Young-sam is keen to normalise relations and open the North to outside influences through joint business ventures. This would appear to be an essential step along the path to normalising the North Korean population.

In mid-1996 I interviewed Kim again. In April, in a summit with Bill Clinton, Kim had proposed four-party peace talks between the two Koreas and the United States and China to try to produce a durable peace on the Korean peninsula and nor-malise relations between the two Koreas.

When I spoke to him at the Blue House, Kim was still perplexedly waiting for an official North Korean response to this proposal. He said:

> The Republic of Korea made clear its willingness to hold South–North Korea talks at the government level without any preconditions. I believe that the four-party meeting is a most realistic and rational formula that amply takes North Korea's position into consideration. I expect that North Korea will respond positively to the proposal since it is the one that would benefit the most from it. The realisation of the four-party meeting would not only help improve South–North relations but also contribute greatly to peace in Northeast Asia. North Korea's economy has been making negative growth every year since 1990. It is in dire straits and is unable to satisfy the very minimum requirements of its people because of the shortages of food, energy and raw materials.

North Korea will eventually provide a low-cost, highly disci-plined labour force in the heart of Northeast Asia. South Korea is determined that it, and it alone, will take the lead in the North's development. That is why Kim Young-sam announced a policy of promoting economic cooperation with the North (although the North did not respond positively). He was acutely aware that by 1994 some 100 Japanese companies were active in the North. But more than that Kim, like other South Koreans, believes the North Korean system cannot possibly survive sus-tained exposure to the outside world. Indeed, one line of analysis in South Korea involved encouraging North Korea's military to emulate the Chinese People's Liberation Army—getting deeply involved in business activities, enriching its senior officer cadre and developing a taste for the good life. This would give the real power brokers in North Korea a personal interest in continuing a policy of economic liberalisation and opening to the world. Graft and corruption after all have been effective in killing communist commitment in many countries.

But the years following the signing of the nuclear agreement were, once again, disappointing for South Korea and her friends. North Korea slipped badly economically and seemed anxious to place obstacles in the path of cooperation at every point. It poured an increasing slice of its declining resources into the military. It constantly went back and forth over details of implementing the Geneva Agreement. Everything of substance was stalled. The only real plus, but admittedly it was a huge plus, was that the nuclear freeze appeared to hold. In any event, when I interviewed Kim a second time, in late November 1995, a little over a year after our first interview, he was distinctly more pessimistic about the outlook regarding North Korea. He said:

> North Korea has implemented none of the agreements it made so far with the Republic [South Korea] on political reconciliation, non-aggreesion, economic and cultural exchanges and cooperation and denuclearisation. Instead, North Korea has destabilised the situation on the Korean peninsula by refusing to dispel suspicions about its nuclear capabilities, while also snubbing the Korean armistice setup.

This last remark referred to Pyongyang's repeated wish to negotiate a formal treaty with the United States, which did not include South Korea. South Korea and North Korea are not technically at peace but merely observing the terms of the armistice which ended the Korean War. So the North's desire to negotiate a treaty directly with the United States is designed as a deliberate snub to Seoul. Kim continued:

> Moreover, even during the time when our republic was shipping to the north $US250 million worth of free rice, North Korea was infiltrating its armed agents into the South, thus heightening military tension on the peninsula. This attitude is very disappointing. However, in view of the strong determination and resolve of the people and the government of our republic to defend and preserve peace, as well as current international developments, I am certain that North Korea's

hostile policy will not pay off. When the North Korean authorities realise the futility of their intransigent stance and move toward South–North cooperation, relations between us will rapidly improve. Then the people of the South and North will build through democratic means a reunified Korea where freedom and human rights are guaranteed.

The grandiloquent phrases in Kim's interviews, as in his speeches, are partly the result of the distorting processes of translation. But they are also partly an accurate rendition of what is a formal and at times grandiloquent culture, and a formal and at times grandiloquent language.

The other preoccupying subject in our first discussion in 1994 was the Asia Pacific Economic Cooperation forum. Perhaps only Australia in all the East Asian hemisphere has equalled South Korea's enthusiasm for APEC. Indeed the two countries have developed a significant diplomatic partnership on APEC. Kim sees APEC as offering immense benefits to South Korea, and to the region generally. When I interviewed him in November 1994, he was about to go to the historic APEC leaders' meeting at Bogor, Indonesia, which committed APEC to achieving full free trade by 2020, and for the developed nation members of APEC, by 2010. I spoke to him about a week before he went to Bogor. The proposal for a free trade commitment was being widely discussed in the region. Kim chose our interview to make his first public commitment to supporting such a declaration, a move which, given Korea's heavily protected agricultural sector and the role of protection in some other sectors of the South Korean economy, was an act of some political bravery. Kim said, 'I will support the recommendation to complete free trade by 2020 in Bogor.' Kim also took the then mildly controversial position of committing Korea to supporting APEC trade liberalisation on a non-discriminatory basis—that is, extending the benefits of APEC trade liberalisation to countries which are not members of APEC. There had been considerable debate, much of it led by the American economist, Fred Bergsten (chairman of the APEC Eminent Persons' Group), about this, with some Americans pushing for APEC to become a preferential or discriminatory trade bloc along the lines of the European Union or the North American Free Trade Agreement. Kim's determined rejection of this option was important in APEC's development. Kim said: 'It wouldn't be desirable to introduce a sort of discriminatory treatment into the free trading system. I think the best option is to maintain multilateralism.'

Kim was also prepared to be more ambitious, perhaps more visionary, for APEC than any other Northeast Asian leader had been. He told me that he believed APEC could become 'a model for multilateral cooperation in the twenty-first century', and went on to say that Korea was 'trying to create a kind of common living sphere in the APEC region'. This would take place through 'encouraging more visits by people living in the area such as businessmen and students, and encouraging more cultural contacts and exchanges between the countries belonging to the APEC organisation, thereby pursuing common values systems within the area'. This was perhaps the most ambitious statement of APEC's purpose so far by any significant Asian leader.

Kim also spoke effusively of his diplomatic partnership with Australia's then prime minister, Paul Keating, in APEC, claiming a joint credit for himself and Keating in engineering both the first APEC leaders' meeting in Seattle in 1993 and the second in Bogor in 1994.

> There were some countries that were not very enthusiastic about holding an APEC leaders' meeting but Prime Minister Keating and I discussed the matter deeply and exchanged our opinions very fully on how to make the APEC leaders' forum possible. This produced the APEC leaders' meeting in Seattle. We are very satisfied and proud of our joint efforts to produce such a good result. I think that by now all the participating countries have become very positive towards the goal of APEC. In that sense I estimate Prime Minister Keating's efforts and his vision very highly. So I can say to you, based upon such active support for the APEC development, Australia has in fact become a full partner in the East Asian region.

Kim also claimed the same joint credit for making the second APEC leaders' meeting happen in Bogor: 'At the first APEC leaders' forum in Seattle last year Prime Minister Keating and I played a leading role in making this second APEC leaders' meeting possible.' Similarly he was remarkably fulsome in endorsing Canberra's push to have Australia considered a full partner in the East Asian region:

> Over the years the Australian government has made strong and sincere efforts to integrate Australia into the Asia–Pacific region by not only allowing many Asian immigrants into the country, but also by endeavouring to increase its understanding of the region. I fully believe that the Australian government's endeavours have greatly helped to dispel the East Asians' perception of Australia as a different world. I hope that the Australian government will continue to persevere in its efforts to expand exchanges and to interact positively within the region.

This was certainly as fulsome an endorsement as Australia has ever received for its desire to be part of the East Asian picture.

A year later, in November 1995, the situation for Kim in APEC had changed slightly. I interviewed Kim in 1995 in the run-up to the Osaka APEC leaders' meeting. He was, publicly at least, holding out for agriculture to be given special treatment within the plan for an APEC free trade target. At the same time he still stressed the importance of APEC to Korea, but he had to speak with more sense of the domestic political difficulties the APEC free trade plan could hold for him. It was perhaps also a sign of APEC's maturing—both that the sense of pioneering excitement had dimmed a little, and that hard decisions about hard commitments, under the APEC rubric, had to be taken. As it turned out the Osaka meeting did not compromise the principle of 'comprehensiveness' to accommodate special treatment for agriculture, which is what Korea, Japan, China and Taiwan had publicly called for. Kim's very Confucian political persona allowed, indeed dictated, that he support contradictory principles—comprehensive liberalisation and special treatement for agriculture—at the same time.

His words are a case study in the elegant East Asian habit of holding contradictory positions simultaneously. He said:

> APEC member countries account for 60 per cent of the world's gross product and 46 per cent of the world's trade volume. Their combined share of our republic's external trade amounts roughly to as much as 70 per cent. Thus APEC carries very great importance to our economy. With the ongoing dynamic growth of the APEC member nations, the APEC region is

taking on increasingly crucial importance relative to the world.
It is the hope of our republic that APEC activities, by linking
the economic sphere of North America with that of East Asia,
will contribute positively to strengthening the multilateral trade
regime through open regionalism.

We expect that by accelerating the economic development
of the Asia–Pacific countries and strengthening the basis for
their mutual trust, the APEC forum will play a decisive role in
enhancing the stability and prosperity of the Asia–Pacific
region. In particular, our republic will do its utmost under its
Segyehwa, or globalisation, policy to fulfil a leading role in the
liberalisation of trade and investment in the APEC region, and
will at the same time exert active efforts to promote close cooperative relations among the APEC member countries.

Our republic supports comprehensiveness as the principle of
liberalisation in the APEC region. However, since the APEC
member countries are diverse in terms of both the degree of
economic development and culture, this diversity should be
fully reflected in the process of liberalisation. In this context it
is our republic's basic position that unlike the manufacturing
sector, such particularly sensitive sectors as agriculture must be
given adequate consideration according to the peculiar situation
of each member country.

Both the Republic of Korea and Australia are working for
the APEC forum to move toward open regionalism. I believe
that our two countries share the view that the APEC forum is
an organisation meant for consultation, not for negotiation.
With regard to APEC's pursuit of trade and investment
liberalisation, our republic's position is that in deference to the
basic principle of cooperation—a principle that has been upheld
by the APEC forum since its inception—APEC must fully
reflect the diverse situation of each country of the Asia–Pacific
region.

As it turned out there was no concession made to exempting
agriculture at the APEC leaders' meeting and it is hard to know
what the intense horse-trading sessions preceding the Osaka
meeting were if they were not negotiations. But these circumlo-
cutions, the verbal curlicues and arabesques, are part of the stuff
of APEC, indeed part of the stuff of Asian diplomacy. Kim is a
practised exponent of such arts.

I then asked Kim about the three major powers whose interests intersect on the Korean peninsula—Japan, China and the United States. The contrast in particular between the surprising warmth of his remarks on China and the cold hostility of his remarks on Japan was especially enlightening. Japan and South Korea are both democracies, both intimately linked to the United States in security alliances, they are two of the most similar societies in the world, at the formal level they have greatly improved relations in recent years. Yet the truth is a deep antipathy persists. More than anyone else in Asia the Koreans are suspicious that the Japanese have not taken to their hearts the lessons of the Second World War, of the colonial period when Korea was ruled by Japan and of centuries of aggression and conflict before then. On the other hand, China is a giant power which is still nominally communist, whose troops poured into Korea to assist South Korea's mortal foes, the North Korean army, during the Korean War. You would expect Seoul to be suspicious of China. Yet China has become the crowning glory of Korea's 'northern policy'. The bilateral economic relationship has become so successful and substantial that Seoul now probably has greater leverage over Beijing than Pyongyang does. The first time I interviewed Kim he was fresh from a meeting with the Chinese premier, Li Peng. South Korean *chaebol* have invested billions of dollars in mainland China ventures. These investments, and exports to China, have become a fundamental engine of growth for the Korean economy. These diverging impulses were clear in Kim's responses to my questions about China and Japan. However, by mid-1996 things had changed somewhat. Kim had had a successful summit with Japan's prime minister, Ryutaro Hashimoto, who said all the right things about World War II. And South Korea and Japan had agreed to jointly host soccer's World Cup in 2002.

In the 1995 interview I asked Kim if he was at all concerned about China's recent assertiveness in the region. He replied:

Bolstered by its successful push for reform, if this trend
continues China's role in the Asia–Pacific region and in the
world community is certain to be further strengthened. We
expect that the heightened status of a reformed and more open
China will contribute to the stability and economic
development of this region, rather than pose a threat. China

needs stability in the region and in the international community at large so that it can carry on its reforms and economic development. Therefore, China is expected to continue to pursue stable external relations in the area of both international politics and military security.

Japan, on the other hand, had been recently annoying Kim. A Japanese minister had been reported as saying that the period of Japanese colonialism in Korea, regarded by most Koreans as a nightmare of unrelieved brutality and national humiliation, had had some good features. He had been forced to resign but the episode had obviously left a sour taste in Kim's mouth. I asked Kim about the propensity of Japanese leaders for making unsuitable remarks about the past. He replied:

> On the 50th anniversary of the end of World War II, we expected the Japanese government to take a thorough look at the truths of history and make efforts to set the historic record right. In this regard, the fact that Japanese government leaders have continuously made preposterous remarks is a matter of great disappointment. It is an irresponsible thing, influencing even the future of Korea–Japan relations. It is unfortunate that Japan refuses to acknowledge its past aggression against Korea, China and many other Asian nations. If its leaders continue to make such preposterous remarks, world suspicion against it would rise and anti-Japanese sentiment deepen. I hope that Japan will not invite such a misfortune on itself and will reflect on the best way to win world respect. Only if Japanese political leaders first have a correct understanding of history will there be a basis for genuine trust and friendly, future-oriented cooperation between the two countries.

These were tough words from the normally diplomatic Kim, but they reflected no more, indeed much less, than the feelings of his countrymen. On the other hand, like the Japanese, he regards an American military presence as absolutely essential to the stability of the entire region, and speaks about America accordingly, despite America's poor handling of East Asian relations throughout the '90s. He said:

> It is our belief that the maintenance of smooth relations between the United States and Japan and between the United States and China can only contribute to the stability and peace

of this region and of the world. In this respect, it is fortunate
that US–Japan and US–China relations, which have experienced
some tension recently, have begun to show signs of an amicable
solution.

Notwithstanding Kim's determination to be positive about the
US, he could not fail to acknowledge, politely, the mess the US
had made of its relations with China and Japan. Nonetheless, as
would any Korean leader, he acknowledged the importance of the
American alliance:

> Our republic and the United States are basically upholding
> solid ties as allies, working toward balanced bilateral trade and
> commerce and maintaining in general close relations of
> friendship and cooperation. In particular, we are satisfied with
> the fact that Seoul and Washington have been coordinating
> very closely with each other over the North Korean nuclear
> issue. Given the current unstable security situation in East Asia,
> we think it important for the United States to continue to play
> the role of a balance between different forces in the region.

Interviews like this with East Asian leaders tend not to be
very personal. But I asked Kim what had motivated him through
his long decades of activism and struggle in Korean politics. He
replied:

> In the course of struggling for democracy my life was
> threatened several times and I suffered many other hardships
> including imprisonment and house arrest, as well as a 23-day
> hunger strike. Nevertheless, I have ceaselessly struggled with
> the conviction that genuine democracy must be realised to
> guarantee the basic rights of the people and to develop the
> nation.

He was particularly enthusiastic about the international
dimension of his policies:

> With foreign trade contributing more than 50 per cent to our
> gross national product, Korea has no other choice but to adopt
> a strategy of outward-oriented economic development. Therefore
> any change in international circumstances becomes a very
> important consideration for us. In particular, as national borders
> begin to dissolve and new information, communication and
> transportation technologies are introduced, the world is turning

into a global village where all are united in a single market economy. Not only people, money and natural resources, but also knowledge, information and culture move freely across national borders, indicating changes in human civilisation. In recognition of these facts the Korean government, with the support of the people, is actively pushing a *segyehwa*, or globalisation, policy. I am confident that the *segyehwa* policy will provide Korea with an opportunity to take another leap into the world and at the same time will help create a more open cultural environment at home.

At the time of our interview Korea was rocked by a scandal surrounding former president, Roh Tae-woo. State prosecutors had revealed that Roh during his time as president had accumulated a private slush fund of $US600 million, of which some $200 million remained in his personal bank accounts. It was also revealed that Kim Dae-jung had taken $2 million from Roh for his presidential campaign in 1992, badly denting his image as an absolute political cleanskin. Kim Dae-jung accused Kim Young-sam of also taking money from Roh, but the president insisted that while Roh's money in the past had been used to run the party he had not personally taken a cent from Roh. It was a huge scandal in Korean politics, involving not only the charging of a former president but accusations against those *chaebol*, or conglomerate, figures who had allegedly given him the money.

I was told in advance that this would be a very sensitive matter to raise with Kim Young-sam. He would only speak generally on the subject, avoiding specific details of the scandal, and saying this:

> Since assuming the presidency, I have worked to root out graft and corruption and have initiated institutional reforms to sever the collusive links between politics and business, especially by implementing the real-name financial transaction system and promulgating the Public Officials Ethics Act, requiring the public disclosure of the personal assets of high-ranking officials. In particular I pushed for a comprehensive Election Law so that a fair and honest election climate would take root in the country, while working to institute political reforms, including the revival of local autonomy which was interrupted by the military coup d'état 34 years ago.
>
> What I wanted to accomplish through such political

reforms is to firmly establish the rule of law, which is the basis for democracy. Political culture cannot be changed in an instant, but I think change will be steadily realised in the days ahead because of the people's high political consciousness as well as the institutional reforms continually being carried out since the launching of the civilian government.

The severance of the collusive link between politics and business by the civilian government's reform program is creating a business climate which guarantees transparent, healthy and fair competition. This is the most important factor in building a strong economy.

Given the depth of corruption revealed by the Roh scandal this last statement must be regarded as an aspiration rather than an achievement. But the Roh scandal will play a role in strengthening the dynamic for reform, and change of the old culture in Korea. That is partly Kim's aim, to use the scandal to further reform.

The Roh scandal was followed by the charging of another former president, Chun Doo-hwan, with treason and murder for his part in the 1979 coup that led to the Kwangju massacre. It is still too early to say what the final judgement on Kim's handling of these scandals will be. Certainly South Koreans are unforgiving about the Kwangju massacre and the arrest of Chun seemed to do Kim no harm politically. Indeed the charging of both Roh and Chun, while highly traumatic, can also be seen as part of a perhaps necessary catharsis and cleansing in Korea's political evolution. Provided the basis of South Korea's democracy remains secure, no future president will ever be tempted to behave like either Chun or Roh for fear of the consequences, the possibility of prosecution after leaving office. Evolution from military dictatorship to fully fledged democracy, from backward agrarian society to wealthy fully developed OECD member, is bound to be traumatic. But it is reasonable to see the Chun and Roh prosecutions in that light.

Certainly, while Kim's own standing was somewhat damaged by his past association with Roh, he had made the fundamental strategic decision to turn necessity into a virtue in the way he prosecuted the Roh and Chun affairs. It demonstrated once again his consummate skill as a politician. This was a period approaching crisis for South Korea—two former presidents thrown in jail, the entire Cabinet resigned and a new prime minister appointed, and continuing menacing military build-up in the north. Yet apart from a few street demonstrations, to be in Korea at this time was not to observe any real instability. All these problems were to be handled through the political and legal mechanisms of the Republic of Korea, not at the point of a bayonet or the crushing rumble of a tank.

By mid-1996 when I interviewed Kim again he was much more relaxed about the subject of the two former presidents and their trials and spoke more openly about the subject. He said:

> The two former presidents are on trial on charges of destroying the constitutional order by staging a coup d'état and causing bloodshed and also amassing enormous illegitimate wealth by using their political power. They gained both political power and personal fortunes through illegitimate methods and that was the ultimate source of all the maladies that have plagued Korean society. Although belated, their trial by law is being held to shed light on what really happened and mete out punishment accordingly. This is intended and necessary to dispel once and for all the spectre of coups d'état from our land, completely eliminate the pattern of political-military collusion bred by past military regimes and thus help establish a sound sense of ethics in our society. The trial of the former presidents thus represents a necessary effort to right the wrongs of our constitutional history; place the process of our national history on the right track and set our nation and our future into the right direction.

Kim was damaged by the revelation that his personal aide, Chang Hak-ro, was to be indicted for allegedly taking bribes of $1 million. Although Kim was not directly implicated the stench was starting to get very near to the heart of his administration. Kim's popularity fell. A crucial political test came in April 1996, with National Assembly elections, to be followed shortly by a visit from President Clinton. Astonishingly, North Korea declared that it was 'suspending' the armistice that had kept the peace on the Korean peninsula for 40 years and wanted direct negoti- ations with the US. It broke the terms of the armistice by moving unauthorised numbers of troops, with unauthorised arms, into the Demilitarised Zone. Although most analysts thought this was bluff and bluster rather than a prelude to war no one could afford to miscalculate. In any event the North played into Kim's hands. He argued strongly that a time of military tension needed unified national leadership. Despite suffering some losses, he managed to keep effective control of the National Assembly, a remarkable result given the difficulties of the previous year.

Kim's astonishing career and life can be regarded as the ultimate triumph of the professional politician. Democracies need professional politicians. Abraham Lincoln was a politician. Almost any politician anywhere who achieves anything worthwhile is a mixture of motivations. Kim certainly has his egotistical and self-centred side. Certainly he has been a master manipulator. Certainly, like many politicians, he has felt most comfortable when he personally is the centre of attention. Yet his commitment to democracy was clearly genuine and involved taking great personal risks over a long period of time. More than that, he not only put his life on the line, he was always willing to put his political position on the line by facing the voters. Kim has never been scared of a popular election. He will be seen eventually as a transitional figure for Korea but his contribution will be judged by history to have been enormous. The constant campaigning for democracy, the successful election as president, the anti-corruption measures, the globalisation policies, the reinstitution of local government and local elections, the painful steps towards economic liberalisation—these are giant steps for Korea.

Probably the area in which he has been least successful is in reforming the economy to diminish the influence of the giant *chaebol*, or conglomerates, which dominate Korean economic life. These were engineered originally by the state to give Korean firms the size and clout to compete internationally. Having done their job they have become something of a roadblock to wide-ranging liberalisation within Korea. But now they are so big that they are seemingly impossible to dislodge from the commanding heights of the Korean economy. On the other hand, because they are so export oriented they have achieved high standards of efficiency. They are not the worst problem for an economy to have. The forces of globalisation, and the rising consciousness of the Korean consumer, will force more changes on them over time.

Overall the Korean economy has continued to show strong growth during Kim's presidency.

But this is really a footnote to Kim's giant career. He does have claims to being considered his country's most successful politician ever. This diminutive figure—relentlessly jogging every morning, paying filial respects to his own parents, traditional and modern, sometimes democratic and at other times haughty, egocentric but self-sacrificing—demonstrates the force of the individual in history. The Korean peninsula would be a very different place today had the young Kim Young-sam not decided politics was his vocation.

2

'STEADY EDDIE' RAMOS: PEOPLE POWER MARK II

 We drove up to Manila's vast Malacañang Palace in a modest white mini-van. The group of us in the van was feeling a little like the weather—saturated, hot, baking, wet, slow, drowsy. I was accompanied by a little troupe of Australian and Filipino officials on my way to meet 'Steady Eddie' Ramos, president of the Republic of the Philippines. Malacañang itself is an imposing sight. Vast, pristine, white and strikingly elegant, it is a marvellous symbol of the cacophonously discordant strands of the Philippines cultural past and present. It was built in the eighteenth century by the Spanish and used subsequently by the Japanese and the Americans. On the day in May 1994 when I am to have my first formal interview with Fidel Ramos it basks in a triumphal sun, surrounded by beautifully tended, exquisitely lush gardens. First stop is the office of Honesto Isleta, the president's deputy press secretary, who carries an anomalous military rank from years in public relations for former regimes. His office is a modest little cupboard with a huge colour television set playing in the corner near the ceiling. As I wander through office after office in Malacañang I discover that senior Filipino officials like to keep in touch with the outside world, while they work, via the ubiquitous TV. On this day all the sets are tuned into the same program. In Honesto's office, and in all the offices I visit, eyes constantly dart towards the TV, distracted from the matters at hand.

For a telecast of central relevance to the Philippines cultural consciousness is taking place, a program which through its vast, popular appeal demonstrates the true cultural unity of the nation. It is the Knicks versus the Pacers, the eastern conference finals of the United States basketball play-offs that pervades Malacañang that day. That's the Philippines—where you watch American basketball in a vast Spanish palace.

Ramos does not live in Malacañang. Nor did his predecessor, Cory Aquino. Probably no president of the Philippines will live there again. Remarkably it is not so much its Spanish, Japanese and American colonial associations which make it distasteful as a residence for a modern democratic president but its now eternal association with Ferdinand and Imelda Marcos and the excesses and crony capitalism they oversaw. Wandering around Malacañang is slightly spooky. The heavy, overly ornate Spanish touch is everywhere, despite 50 years of American rule and 50 years of independence. Part of Malacañang has become a museum to the Marcos excesses. Anything to do with the outrageous Mrs Marcos is a potent tourist attraction. A glimpse at the sumptuous lavishness of the Marcos era is a drawcard for many Filipinos and foreigners.

It is right of course that Filipinos should be both fascinated and revolted by the Marcoses. But Malacañang is a symbol too of all the other diverse and strange cultural influences on this strange nation. A portrait of the Filipino wartime president, Jose Laurel, adorns the Malacañang walls as do the portraits of other past presidents. But Laurel collaborated whole-heartedly with the Japanese while his countrymen provided one of the most coura- geous and strongest anti-Japanese resistance movements anywhere in Asia. In other countries he would be reviled as a traitor, not honoured as a past leader. Of course, after the war the Americans did not attempt to dismantle the collaborationist oligarchy and its power structures in the Philippines. But the confusion of fervent Catholicism; hundreds of years of brutal Spanish colo- nialism which involved extensive racial hierarchy as well as extensive racial inter marriage; a strange burst of American colonialism; savage Japanese occupation; a postwar independence tarnished by the oligarchy's continued influence; decades of extravagant kleptocracy by Marcos; and the exhilaration of the 'people power' revolution of 1986 which swept Mrs Aquino into power, followed by the acute disappointments of Cory's actual presidency, have left Filipinos—as David Steinberg put it in his brilliant book, *The Philippines*—in search of a 'useable past'. While the super human powers of forgiveness of Filipinos have allowed them to acknowledge all the influences of their past there are few episodes which are not somehow compromised by an association of colonialism or corruption.

These confusions and contradictions have left the Philippines with a somewhat confused sense of identity. When I first went there in the mid–1980s, at the very end of the Marcos depredations, it didn't feel like Southeast Asia. It even had a different look to it. The flat board trucks with rural workers aboard, the signs in the bank in the Manila Hilton asking patrons not to bring their guns into the bank, the macho male culture, the strutting policemen, the florid religiosity, the vast Romanesque cathedral, the Catholic churches everywhere—it all reminded me more than anywhere else of El Salvador.

No one has been more aware of these contradictions than Filipinos themselves. Benigno Aquino, Cory's martyred husband, once wrote that Filipinos were 'an Asian people not Asian in the eyes of their fellow Asians, not western in the eyes of the west'. There are a million jokes along these lines, the most famous being that the Philippines was understandably schizophrenic after 400 years in a Spanish convent followed by 50 years in Hollywood (or 50 years in a brothel if the joke teller is a little more risque). One government official told me that the Filipino feels like a Spaniard, thinks like an American and acts like an Asian. Certainly the feel of the Philippines in the 1980s was Latin, in both good and bad senses. As one wag put it: America is rich, optimistic and its people sad whereas the Philippines is poor, pessimistic but its people happy.

In truth Filipinos were wrong to let others define them, especially others in Asia who didn't much like their democratic ways and had an interest in defining their society, and therefore their democracy, as somehow or other unAsian. It is the mission of Eddie Ramos to transform this feeling of being the odd man out in Southeast Asia, especially but not only in terms of economic performance. Although of course he would be deeply affronted were any suggestion to be made that he is not culturally in sympathy with his countrymen, it nonetheless is one of the modest ironies of history that in this overwhelmingly Catholic country it should be the republic's first Protestant president who is attempting to instil what Max Weber regarded as the quintessentially Protestant virtues (or now in East Asia are often classified as Confucian virtues) of industry, thrift, diligence, productivity, predictability and above all profit and success. 'The Philippines', Ramos's promotional literature everywhere declares, 'is back in business in the heart of Asia.'

Ramos is an unlikely and undramatic democratic hero but he is staking a claim to being his country's most successful leader ever. This is in its way as weird and unlikely a story of personal as well as national triumph as any within Asia. Ramos was born in 1928 in the province of Pangasinan, north of Manila. His family was part of the elite, of the ruling oligarchy, although his own family was middle class rather than ostentatiously wealthy. Philippine politics often seems even these days to be a business conducted essentially by a few dozen highly influential families. Ramos was a cousin of Ferdinand Marcos. Throughout the 1970s and '80s he often appeared, in general's uniform, standing behind Marcos on platforms and in photographs, a potent reminder of martial law. Ramos was a career soldier, who early on showed outstanding abilities. He was chosen to study at the US Army academy at West Point. As the former US secretary of state, George Shultz, makes abundantly clear in his memoirs, the US military always liked Ramos, whereas they found most of the Philippine military unreliable, ineffective or corrupt. Indeed Ramos's good standing with the US would be crucial in the tumultuous people power revolution of 1986. After graduating from West Point Ramos went on to the University of Illinois where he obtained a master's degree in civil engineering. In recent years he has played up the image of himself as an engineer, almost a technocrat, focused on solving real-world problems. But Ramos is a man of almost as many diverse influences as the nation he leads. The American connection has remained critical for him, but he has also tried to Asianise the Philippines, to get it on the inside of the East Asian success story. As president he visited first the fellow nations of the Association of Southeast Asian Nations (ASEAN), and then the key Northeast Asian nations, Japan, Korea, China.

The image of Ramos as an engineer making the trains run on time is also designed to help neutralise other aspects of his personality and his past. He was one of the first Philippine soldiers to undertake special-forces training and holds a master's degree in national security administration from the Philippine National Defence College. He also managed to squeeze in a Master of Business Administration, giving him three masters in all. Ramos rose quickly in his country's military and saw active service in Korea and Vietnam, experiences which further entrenched his American connection. From 1970 to 1986 Ramos headed up the Philippine Constabulary, which has occasionally had a paramilitary role. He also in the early '70s became a member of the 'Rolex Twelve', who earned their name because of the Rolex gold watches that Marcos gave each of them. They were an important group of advisers to Marcos. But it is important to remember that Marcos in his early years as leader was not the decrepit and vindictive dictator he became. Rather, early on he appeared a vigorous and successful leader.

Critics of Ramos, and especially those who opposed his election in 1992, point to two aspects of the constabulary in Ramos's years. One, corruption was very widespread in the constabulary throughout this period. Two, the constabulary was responsible for many human rights abuses.

But in 1972, after he declared martial law, Marcos placed the constabulary under the control of the Philippines Armed Forces, a move which greatly diminished Ramos's control. Fabian Ver, one of the most hated figures of the Marcos years, was commander-in-chief of the Philippines Armed Services for much of this period. In his defence Ramos has said that Ver appointed people to the constabulary who did not report to Ramos, who were effectively outside the chain of command. Moreover, no one has pinned any specific dirty deed on Ramos. By and large he kept himself remarkably clean in what must have been a hugely difficult task for a patriotic soldier of serving a regime which began with much promise and only gradually deteriorated into a corrupt, incompetent and vicious beast. Similarly for much of the time that Ramos was a soldier the Philippines was confronting a deadly serious, and just plain deadly, insurgency movement from the ultra-extremist, Marxist New People's Army. During the

1992 presidential campaign Ramos also defended his record by pointing out that his position within the Marcos administration allowed him to exercise a moderating influence, in particular in getting political prisoners' sentences reduced. Ramos intervened to get Benigno Aquino's time in jail reduced and Aquino, not long before his death in 1983, commented of Ramos: 'The good guys are behind him. But I don't think Ramos will prevail.' Happily, Aquino was wrong.

Ramos's most dramatic public moment came after the 1986 presidential election, which Marcos, in a huge miscalculation which demonstrated how out of touch he had become, called a year early to try to outsmart his opponents and re-establish his legitimacy. International observers, including an American congressional team, reported widespread vote fraud as Marcos declared himself the winner. Corazon Aquino also claimed victory. The country was poised on the brink of civil war. Ramos, and then defence minister Juan Ponce Enrile, holed up with loyal troops in Camp Aguinaldo on the outskirts of Manila and demanded Marcos turn over power to Aquino. Marcos tried to get his troops to storm Aguinaldo but Mrs Aquino, Catholic Church leaders, and Ramos and Enrile themselves called the civilian population into the streets to prevent the Marcos troops from reaching Aguinaldo.

It was at this point that Ramos's friendships in the US were critical. The American National Security Council monitored events in Aguinaldo on a minute by minute basis. By now the Americans, despite the deep personal reluctance of President Reagan to ditch a long time US ally, were telling Marcos he had to go. Earlier rumours that Marcos had been going to sack the reform-minded Ramos had led to sharp exchanges between Marcos and the Americans who told Marcos that this would be unacceptable. Thus, partly through American influence, Ramos was still in a position to play a decisive role in Mrs Aquino's victory.

It was at this moment too that the Philippines dominated international news coverage. Ramos and Enrile and Cory Aquino became household names as television flashed their heroic struggle around the world. The Aguinaldo rebels were successful and Mrs Aquino, and the entire Philippine nation, were hugely grateful to the military defectors. Befitting his caution, and the dilemmas of any decent soldier serving a government which has run out of control, Ramos is said to have agonised up to the last possible second before deciding to move against Marcos. Mrs Aquino's relationship with Enrile soon soured but she was to draw ever closer to Ramos, promoting him from chief of the armed forces to defence minister. If he established his democratic credentials in 1986 he consolidated them over the next six years by protecting Mrs Aquino's government from seven military coup attempts. Mrs Aquino more than once said the Philippines owed its democracy to Ramos. She is said to believe that she personally owes him her life.

It was a debt she would to some extent repay in the 1992 elections. She teased Ramos, and the nation, about whom she would support. Ramon Mitra ultimately became the ruling party candidate. Miriam Defensor Santiago, a fierce anti-corruption campaigner, came from nowhere to be a formidable contender. Marcos crony and millionaire Eduardo Cojuanco ran, as did Marcos's widow, Imelda, and Aquino's vice-president, Salvador Laurel. Ramos looked to have many disadvantages in this contest. He had never run for elective office. He was reported to be taking singing lessons so he could participate in the endless Filipino ritual of public singing, and to enliven his relatively austere personality. As a Protestant, he was opposed by the nation's powerful Catholic hierarchy, especially Manila's Cardinal Jaime Sin. But eventually Mrs Aquino did endorse Ramos which was crucial in his getting over the line. And his very lack of conventional charisma seemed to be a big plus. He looked reliable rather than flamboyant and that's what people seemed to want. Nonetheless his win was anything but convincing. In a seven-sided contest he scraped home with a bare plurality of 24 per cent of the vote.

What has happened since then has been nothing short of revolutionary. The auguries did not look good for the Ramos presidency. He did not have control in Congress, his mandate was attenuated at best, there was no reason to believe he had great hitherto hidden political skills, the economy was a mess. This was the worst of his problems—the economy. International investor confidence was very low after the series of coup attempts against the Aquino government and Aquino's generally ineffective administration. It had been an incompetent, internally divided and frequently paralysed government. Despite her popularity Aquino could not implement effective economic reform. The Philippines, after World War 11, had looked the Asian economy most likely to grow rapidly. At that stage it was ahead of Japan on numerous economic indicators. In the 1960s it had been economically well ahead of neighbours such as Indonesia, Thailand and Malaysia. It had high rates of English speakers and a culture which emphasised education. It looked set fair to be an Asian success story. And indeed there were periods of success. For much of the 1970s Marcos, before he went off the rails, oversaw growth in the Philippines economy of 7 per cent a year. But in the last years of Marcos the economy actually declined by 15 per cent. Then came the ineffectual Aquino years. All this Ramos inherited, as well as the economic damage of the withdrawal of the two huge American military bases and a series of natural disasters, including the after-effects of the devastating eruption of Mount Pinatubo and the Ormoc flood and the earthquake of 1990. Throw in continuing communist and Muslim insurgencies, as well as unrest in the military, and in all you could not imagine a more daunting set of circumstances.

Yet Ramos, to everyone's amazement, confronted all the challenges head on and succeeded to the extent that by the mid-point of his presidential term the Philippines was back on a high-growth trajectory, the political situation had been stabilised and one of the most acute investment analysts in Asia, a woman based in Singapore, told me she would recommend the Philippines as the most attractive investment destination in Southeast Asia. Why? Because you would be getting in early in the growth cycle and compared to other Southeast Asian nations the Philippines had a comprehensible and moderately reliable commercial legal system.

His first 60 days were crucial to Ramos. He identified a top priority as being the power shortages, the famous brown-outs, which had plagued Manila. Not only did they inconvenience industry they were devastating for morale, civilian morale and commercial morale. He sought and got special congressional approval to tackle the problem and simply started building power stations. Ramos also announced his intention to pursue an amnesty approach to the insurgents, to all the insurgents, to the communists, the Muslim separatists and the right-wing army coup plotters. The purpose of this was to draw them in and normalise them in political life (and by so doing, of course, to marginalise them).

In all, the president was a happy man when I met him at Malacañang in May 1994. The setting was the typical Philippines mixture of formality and informality. I sat, with two Filipino officials and an Australian friend of my own nomination, at right angles across a vast desk from the president, while a bevy of other Filipinos lurked in a friendly fashion at the other end of the room, palace photographers snapped away and a TV crew recorded our handshake for posterity. In other circumstances, with other leaders, it would have seemed a daunting prospect. But in conversation the president could not have been more relaxed. He comes across as a man very comfortable in his own skin. He fondled and generally played with a giant cigar during the course of the interview but did not actually light it up. This is Ramos's compromise way of giving up smoking.

Ramos's good humour that day was no mystery. The first-quarter economic statistics were outstanding, polls were registering his approval ratings in the mid 60 per cent range, the power problems that plagued Manila industry the previous year had been vanquished and a raft of international news magazines—in particular *Newsweek*—was hailing his administration as the most effective the Philippines had had in decades. He had also, through encouraging defections and building coalitions, established an effective majority in the lower house of Congress. The following year, in 1995, he would establish a similar position in the Senate. The Philippines political system, loosely modelled as it is on the American system, does include all manner of frustrating checks and balances. But like most presidential systems it confers enormous power on the president himself. This power, if used shrewdly, ought to be enough for effective government to proceed.

The week before he met me he had finally got past the Congress a new amnesty law as well. 'The amnesty is very important,' he told me. 'It is really a process of reconciliation, unification and healing that we want to see happen.' His new amnesty law tidied up the amnesty to political opponents outside the political process which Mrs Aquino had extended. The amnesty approach has been fundamental to Ramos's attempts to marginalise the extremes in Philippines politics. 'The communists are legal now but they get a tiny percentage of the vote,' he said. The new amnesty law 'also extends amnesty to soldiers and politicians so long as their offences do not involve gross abuses of human rights,' he explained. This is very much the Ramos way—open the tent for almost everyone and have a fair democratic contest once they're all inside. And it has worked.

Ramos has in effect if not killed at least greatly weakened the insurgencies with kindness. The Communist Party is legal and attracts a dismal following. The New People's Army is down to perhaps 8000 or fewer followers and much or perhaps all of its activity is indistinguishable from straight forward banditry. Peace talks have waxed and waned but the peace process has drawn the teeth of the communists, as has, more importantly, economic growth. As well, the NPA has been subject to devastating internal splits. A similar fate has befallen the Muslim insurgents in the south who have also been drawn into the peace process. A more radical variant of Muslim separatism has emerged which is capable of sickening terrorism and it is probably now a bigger security headache than the NPA. But overall the situation is infinitely improved from the Marcos and even the Aquino years. In late 1996 a formal peace was signed with the main Muslim insurgents in Mindanao.

Similarly Ramos was successful in neutralising the Reform the Armed Forces Movement or RAM, the chief right-wing military coup plotters. Ramos is in many ways the president from central casting for this task. He is now a staunch democrat with solid democratic credentials but he is also a West Point career military man, a former chief of the armed forces and former defence minister, drawn from the very heart of the Philippines military. Very few senior soldiers have been tempted to dream of deposing Ramos to impose a military regime in his place.

Ramos is also trying to turn the Philippines into a player once more in regional politics and he offered me that day a *tour d'horizon* of the issues he thought most important in the region. Washington's then recently announced decision to back down from its threat to withdraw China's Most Favoured Nation trading status would be a turning point, he predicted, in America's relations with Asia. Also, somewhat to my surprise, he gave very strong support to the proposal by Malaysia's prime minister, Dr Mahathir Mohamed, for an East Asian Economic Caucus, a proposal which has been strongly opposed by Australia, at the same time calling for Australia to play a greater role in the region and for Australia and the Philippines to make more of their shared World War 11 experience.

On the US relationship with China he said: 'Trade and politics should not be combined. We strongly recommended renewing China's MFN status. We see that decision as also being favourable to us.' He also thought the decision could be a turning point, 'considering that President Clinton during the election campaign was saying something else'.

On the proposed EAEC, which Canberra had consistently opposed because it excludes Australia and the United States and because Canberra believed its development would tend to divide the Pacific and detract from APEC, the president was very upbeat: 'The cooperation that can be generated within the EAEC will be very, very helpful to us.' He also said the consensus view, to which he subscribed, was that the EAEC should 'remain as a forum which will be supportive, although also a little independent, of the bigger groupings such as APEC.' However, Ramos was also very positive about APEC itself: 'APEC was the spark plug that enabled the US to come up with the hard decision to go for the conclusion of the Uruguay Round [of the world GATT trade negotiations].' At the first APEC summit at Seattle the Philippines 'backed up President Clinton very strongly as APEC members'.

He was also wholly positive about Australia's increased role in the region: 'The pronouncements by your prime minister [Keating] that Australia really belongs to Asia is a most welcome pronouncement to us here. We welcome Australia's greater role in Asia.' However, he was at this stage cautious about Keating's proposal to link the ASEAN Free Trade Area with the Closer Economic Relations agreement between Australia and New Zealand:

> I really haven't given very much thought to it. We would have to be very sure because of the differences in the levels of

development. The ones who can't immediately bring tariffs
down, like us, must also be given consideration. This is the
problem in AFTA now. Indonesia and the Philippines are seen
as the slowest to reduce the number of tariff items, or items
that are protected by quantitative restrictions. The more there
are in the trading area the better the trading area would be in
the end but we have to take care of that transition period very
carefully.

Naturally as a military man he also suggested that Australia and
the Philippines devote more energy to celebrating their shared
World War II heritage: 'We are very well aware of your outstanding military traditions.'

On another occasion Ramos would stress to me also the
common democratic ideals of the Philippines and Australia. In
the meantime, however, the Philippines' raucous democracy is
one of the things that sets it apart from its Southeast Asian
neighbours, and particularly its ASEAN brothers. ASEAN now
consists of two democracies—the Philippines and Thailand; two
semi-democracies with some authoritarian features, Malaysia and
Singapore; one rough authoritarian regime with a developing civic
space—Indonesia; one absolute monarchy—Brunei; and one communist dictatorship—Vietnam; with communist Laos, authoritarian Myanmar and ramshackle Cambodia set to join before the
end of the decade. This will pose problems for Australia, because
the weight within ASEAN is now reinforced with non-democracies.

It will also cause serious problems within ASEAN itself. These
problems will likely be most acute for the Philippines. Thailand's
democracy can be pretty raucous at times, too, but it occurs
mostly in the Thai language. This is especially true of the most
outspoken political comment, which appears in Thai-language
newspapers. But in the Philippines much of the public discourse
is in English. And the Philippines has without doubt the most
voluble, high-spirited and dedicatedly irreverent press anywhere.
It seems at times a nation of 60 million newspaper columnists.
It is quite likely that the Philippines' democratic culture will
increasingly place it in conflict with its neighbours.

This has already happened in two high-profile cases. One was
the 1995 execution in Singapore of the Filipino maid, Flor

Contemplación, for the murder of her boss's four-year-old son and another maid. This case and its handling by the Singapore authorities was in no sense of course a crime against democracy. But the strength of the Philippine government response, which involved cancelling a trip by Singapore Prime Minister Goh Chok Tong to the Philippines and the threat of breaking off formal diplomatic relations altogether, was dictated by the strength of Philippine public opinion and the political pressure which public opinion put on the government. In non-democracies public opinion is a far less powerful force in political life.

When I first interviewed Ramos he was up to his neck in what was perhaps an even more serious conflict with a neighbour, again brought about by the Philippines' democratic political culture. A private, non-government left-wing group within the Philippines decided to hold a conference on the vexed subject of East Timor, and Indonesia's occupation of East Timor, at the University of the Philippines campus in Manila. This greatly angered Jakarta, which treated the matter as a full-blown government-to-government issue and took a series of deliberately escalating steps to demonstrate its displeasure.

First the Indonesian government, through Foreign Minister Ali Alatas, protested vigorously to Manila. Then they started arresting Filipino fishermen in Indonesian waters. More significantly, the 200 Indonesian businessmen who were to have participated in an important regional business conference in Davao, pulled out. This was a serious blow to the Philippines. The conference was designed to promote what is an ugly acronym but an attractive concept—the BIMP EAGA growth triangle. (This acronym stands for Brunei Indonesia Malaysia Philippines East ASEAN Growth Area.) Then the Indonesian province of East Kalimantan announced that it was pulling out of province-to-province economic cooperation with the Philippines. Most ominously there were suggestions that Indonesia would slacken its hitherto constructive and energetic efforts to mediate in the conflict between the Muslim separatist Moro National Liberation Front in Mindanao and the Philippine government. Indonesia has been critically important in its refusal to assist the Muslim rebels, its refusal ever to allow the MNLF's problems even on to the agenda in the Organisation of Islamic States. It has been by far the Philippines' best friend in the Muslim world.

Ramos was greatly distressed by the dispute. He sent former foreign minister Raul Manglapus to Jakarta to explain. He took the extraordinary step, for which he suffered considerable political cost, of banning foreigners from coming to the Philippines to attend the conference. An ally of Ramos even obtained a court order banning the conference, although this was almost instantly overturned by a higher court. Ramos was in a diabolical bind. He could not possibly ban the conference outright without fatally compromising his democratic credentials. But Indonesia was playing extreme hard ball and much that was important to the Philippines was at stake. In the end the conference went ahead. It may be the shape of conflicts to come within ASEAN.

In any event that day at Malacañang I asked Ramos about the dispute. Despite the pain it was causing him, he smiled with that combination of irony and self-deprecation which is so endearing about Ramos, and claimed to have found 'a Solomonic solution'.

'It was constantly the national interest I upheld,' he said. 'We upheld the basic freedom of Filipinos to freedom of assembly and free expression of their opinions.' But there were broader issues of national interest he had to consider: 'What was at stake here? Some 19 billion pesos ($US948 million) of potential Indonesian investments and joint projects. This represents about 200 000 Philippines jobs, mostly not capital intensive jobs, but not cottage industry either.' As well, Ramos said, there were direct questions of national security: 'There was our peace process, especially in Mindanao, which has been the scene of bloody conflict which we would like to see finished.' Then there was the question of solidarity and cohesiveness within ASEAN:

> ASEAN has been strengthened over the last 25 years. Many
> countries would like to join ASEAN. Indonesia and the
> Philippines are the leading archipelagic nations and their
> stability has contributed to the stability of the region. We
> chose to approach this also from the outlook of ASEAN
> solidarity and we decided we cannot allow the Philippines to
> be used as a propaganda base for attack on one of our
> neighbours. So we are patiently taking our lumps.

The great East Timor conference controversy was a sad and disturbing lesson to both the Indonesians and the Filipinos. It showed the Indonesians that even the Filipinos, traditionally the whipping boys of Southeast Asia, can only be pushed so far and Jakarta's heavy-handed, gratuitous and hostile diplomacy not only damaged bilateral relations but were ineffective in their own terms. Jakarta only succeeded in drawing much greater international attention to the East Timor conference, without getting it cancelled. But the episode, in which Ramos so rightly described his administration as 'patiently taking our lumps', also reinforced a severe lesson for the Philippines. Without economic, and to a lesser extent military, power a nation is apt to be pushed around.

No one in the Philippines wants to achieve national glory through a power-projecting military but getting the economy going again is fundamental to Philippine self-respect. Certainly when I met Ramos he had plenty to be happy about on that score. Ramos confidently predicted to me that his country's annual economic growth rates would reach 6 to 8 per cent by the end of the decade. That may not exactly turn the Philippines into South Korea, but it would transform the Philippines nonetheless. Ramos read out to me a litany of compelling economic statistics. In the week in which we met the Philippines Stock Exchange index had broken through the 3000 barrier. When Ramos came into office the Philippines' per capita income was about $US720 ($A966). After two years in office that had increased substantially, to around the $US800 mark. 'I think our Philippines 2000 goals [which aim at per capita income of $US1000 by the year 2000] are very modest. Confidence and optimism about the Philippines economy has kept climbing up.' Ramos pointed to 1994's economic growth rate of just under 5 per cent. Throughout that year investment was growing at nearly 20 per cent, gross exports by 15 per cent.

Of course these figures don't solve the problem of the terrible gap between rich and poor in the Philippines. But neither does anything else. Ramos's government has addressed social programs towards the poor but nothing is more likely, over time, to alleviate the hardships of the poor than sustained economic growth. Country after country in East Asia demonstrates this. South Korea in the mid-1950s was much poorer than the Philippines is now, so was Taiwan. Both these countries are now better off for everyone, though of course the rich are much richer than the poor even in those societies. Economic growth brings jobs and a tax base. It is facile for leftist western critics to carp at economic development in the Philippines because it does not immediately transform the country into Switzerland. There is no easy road out of poverty. But East Asia has shown there are some fast roads. These involve high rates of economic growth sustained for two decades or more.

Foreign investment has been flooding into the Philippines under Ramos. This recovery has been investment led. As Roberto deOcampo, the finance secretary, told me: 'It is important to have a president like Ramos who will not be distracted from reminding people to focus on the economy in a country that used to put politics before all.' Certainly it has been critically important to the Philippines to move under Ramos's presidency to an essentially post-ideological period.

These were themes Ramos took up in our second lengthy interview during his visit to Australia in August 1995. The economic figures were even better than they had been at the time of our meeting in Malacañang. Economic growth was bumping along at something like 6 per cent, exports the previous year had risen by 18 per cent and investment by a whopping 25 per cent. Once again the encounter was easy and endlessly affable. It took place in the sumptuous surrounds of Melbourne's Grand Hyatt Hotel, a different kind of palace from Malacañang, a palace instead for the new princes of commerce, the corporate high flyers whom Ramos wants to attract to the Philippines, and whom Ramos also wants Filipinos to emulate in ever greater numbers. On the way to the interview I had run into Mike Costello, then head of the Australian Department of Foreign Affairs and Trade, at Melbourne airport. It was late morning and Mike, who is a big guy, was looking plainly tired. He was on his way back to Melbourne after eighteen holes of golf with Ramos and a few others. His tiredness was understandable. Ramos's Australian hosts had asked him what time he would like to tee off and he had replied simply; 'First light.' So they had hit off at 6.20 a.m. I met Ramos in the mid-afternoon after he had had a ferocious day's schedule of appointments. In a six-day visit to Australia he attended functions, and gave a total of 21 speeches, in Sydney, Canberra, Melbourne, Brisbane and Darwin. He exhausted his handlers, his hosts and everyone else. But when I met him that day he was once again as relaxed and apparently cool and unruffled as ever, the ubiquitous and still unlit cigar rotating slowly around his mouth, the posture utterly at ease, only the swarms of surrounding officials nervous.

As I say, I think one of Ramos's most attractive features is his down-to-earth, non-ideological style in a country which has had a surfeit and more of ideological politics, flamboyant leaders, even the poetry of people power. The best kind of people power is exercised at the ballot box, not in the streets, and produces boring, competent, diligent, reliable, effective government. I asked Ramos whether he thought the change in Philippines political culture which he represented, towards pragmatism and results-oriented problem solving, was going to be permanent. He replied:

We have to continue working at it. The only ideology that I preach and practise as president is the ideology that would make Filipinos continue to be proud of themselves because of their performance, because of their accomplishments. There was a time when Filipinos were not held in such high respect around the world, when the Philippines was considered the sick man of Asia. My ideology is to get our country out of that kind of a feeling. But this must be accomplished through real, practical means, not by oratory or drama or hype or sensation. We must just do it.

He identified his five priorities as social cohesion and national stability, economic growth, upgrading infrastructure, protecting the environment and using resources efficiently, and pursuing social reform. So how would he like to be remembered? 'As a peacemaker, as a builder, as a problem solver and as a reformer. It's a big order, but it's doable.'

During this visit to Australia he also devleoped further his thinking on regional issues. In his interview with me he proposed an association of Asian middle powers involving Australia to act as a counter-weight to the influence of the region's major powers. He said that Australia and New Zealand should join with South-east Asia as 'the voice of moderation in the region'. He said: 'Australia and the ASEAN states have shown that the middle powers need not be passive spectators in the interplay among the great powers of the region.' He identified the great powers of the region as the United States, Japan, China and Russia. He also strongly supported Myanmar's entry into ASEAN (which demonstrates yet again how isolated and ineffective is Australia's attempt to isolate Myanmar) as well as Cambodia and Laos, which would give ASEAN a membership of ten nations and 500 million people.

His thinking specifically about Australia had clearly developed somewhat from our earlier encounter at Malacañang. He said that: 'As far as the Philippines is concerned Australia is accepted as a full partner in the Asia–Pacific. But maybe there's room for more positive actions in being there. Just do it, instead of talking about labels and definitions and hemispheres. Just do it.' He cited particularly Australia's dismally low level of investment in the Philippines as an example of our failure to 'just do it'. He also pledged to give strong support to Australia's bid to attend a second Europe–Asia summit planned for 1988. He would not say on the record what was widely known, that he had also supported Australia's inclusion in the first meeting, but that Australia had been blackballed by Malaysia. However, the Philippines foreign secretary, Domingo Siazon, confirmed to me separately that the Philippines had indeed argued for Australia's inclusion in the first meeting. In his official speech at Parliament House, then prime minister Paul Keating, acknowledged that the bilateral relationship had been to some extent neglected. Indeed the Philippines was one of the few Southeast Asian countries which, by the end of his second and last term, as prime minister, he had not visited. This was a serious dereliction on Keating's part. Keating and Ramos got on very well together in private, although 90 per cent of their meeting was concerned with APEC. This is understandable perhaps but Keating probably overdid the grand vision of APEC and tended to neglect other opportunities of a more purely bilateral and prosaic kind with visitors such as Ramos.

During his visit to Australia Ramos did take a very strong line on another highly contentious issue. He gave strong, unprecedented support for Japan's bid for permanent membership of the United Nations Security Council. He said: 'Japan, because of her economic power, must be given a political role commen-

surate with this.' Strikingly, he was very positive about the
apology made on the 50th anniversary of the end of the Second
World War by Japan's then prime minister, Tomiichi Murayama,
for Japan's actions in World War 11. In fact Ramos called on
the nations of the region to put the events of World War 11
definitively behind them. On the apology he said:

> That subject has been so thoroughly debated especially in the
> Philippines. At this stage, without giving up some efforts to get
> private compensation for the comfort women, we think the
> more important thing to do now is move on so we can
> continue to avail ourselves of Japan's fraternal assistance. As
> well there is the need to keep Japan as a key political player in
> our part of the world. I don't think it will be very productive
> to continue keeping Japan at arm's length as though she must
> keep atoning for the sins of 50 years ago.

Ramos stressed the credibility of the Philippines in making
this kind of judgment, pointing out that a million Filipinos died
in World War II, including 100 000 in Manila alone: 'We have
had this year the celebrations of battles of 50 years ago in which
Japan was the enemy. In all of these we invited Japanese to
participate and they did so.'

On APEC he remained optimistic that the Bogor declaration
of free trade among APEC members would be implemented by
the target date of 2020: 'On our own we have taken steps. Just
before coming to Australia I announced tariff reductions on
hundreds of items.'

Ramos is effecting a revolution in the Philippines, and it is a
revolution with significant consequences for the broader region.
Of all the countries in East Asia the Philippines has had the most
rigid relationship between capital and government but Ramos,
through throwing open the economy to international investment,
deregulating it domestically and getting growth going again is
transforming that traditional picture, creating a middle class of
consumers and a smaller but highly dynamic class of native son,
and daughter, entrepreneurs. Of all the countries of East Asia the
Philippines has had the most ambivalent and distended sense of
regional identity, but now Ramos is taking the Philippines back
to the heart of Asian diplomacy, in APEC and ASEAN and the
other regional forums, where it belongs. Of all the countries of

East Asia the Philippines has had the most intimate yet difficult relationship with its former colonial power, the United States. The closure of the American bases in the Philippines, although overall damaging to East Asian security (it is difficult to imagine China being as assertive in the South China Sea if the American navy were still deployed massively in the Philippines) can be seen as a necessary stage in the development of Philippine independence, as clearing away the postcolonial neuralgia of the relationship. Now Ramos, a long and trusted friend of the US, has got the relationship on a better basis than ever before. The security treaty is intact. President Clinton chose to visit the Philippines in conjunction with the Bogor summit. And while America is still a crucial economic and security partner of the Philippines, Filipinos now have a greater mental space, a greater cultural and spiritual sense of themselves in pursuing their destiny in Asia. At the same time Ramos's government has brilliantly transformed the two former American bases, Clark and Subic, into commercial growth centres.

Of all the countries of East Asia, probably the Philippines has had the greatest chasm between its huge capital, Manila, and its far flung countryside. Like many Southeast Asian nations the Philippines is dominated by its capital. In Manila the fabulous wealth of salubrious residential enclaves such as Forbes Park, or the business district, Makati, contrasts with the enduring poverty of most of the country. But increasingly growth centres are emerging around the country which offer investment-friendly alternatives to Manila and spread the benefits of economic growth. This is particularly true of Subic Bay and Clark Field, but cities such as Cebu, General Santos and even Davao are increasingly attracting foreign investment. A multiplicity of growth centres is just what the Philippines needs. Of the two former American bases, Clark suffers from its proximity to the still-active Pinatubo volcano but its overall facilities are so good that it has still managed to attract support. But Subic has positively boomed. Its runway can accommodate the world's biggest aeroplanes. It has a huge, deep-water port, five-star work and service standards, and has attracted a range of foreign investors, especially from Taiwan, Malaysia and the United States itself. This success at Subic and Clark is typical of the Ramos presidency, it is unexpected, commonsensical and turns an apparent negative into a positive.

Of all the countries of East Asia, few suffered more at the hands of Japan in World War 11 than the Philippines, yet Ramos is sensibly telling not only his countrymen but the region to put that behind them and get on with the business of cooperating with each other. Of all the countries of East Asia few have had more florid, ideological, dramatic or confrontational politics than the Philippines yet Ramos's very ordinariness, the plain unaffectedness even of his nickname 'Steady Eddie', is helping his countrymen move on to the arena of pragmatism and results-oriented government which is typical of so much of the region.

In conversation Ramos often talks of the still unfinished business of cleaning up the remains of the mess from the Marcos years. Yet in truth it is not only Marcos that he is rejecting. Everybody loves Cory Aquino, Ramos would never speak ill of her, he would never criticise her. Her achievement, in bringing back democracy and throwing out Marcos, a result of her exceptional moral and physical courage, was of the first order. But she ran an ineffectual regime. The poetry of people power was not a government program. In this she was rather like Argentina's Raul Alfonsin, or El Salvador's Jose Duarte, brave social democrats, and brave democrats, who brought back democracy to their countries but could not either conceptualise or deliver an effective economic program. In tackling his top priority of ending Manila's brown-outs and restoring the reliability of electricity supply Ramos recreated the Energy Department which Aquino had abolished altogether because it was a creation of Marcos.

Ramos is altogether a much more prosaic figure than either Marcos or Aquino. He holds weekly press conferences at which he generally eschews soaring rhetoric. He makes frequent, at times almost weekly, visits to distant provinces and always finds a problem which his government can solve. Like all successful politicians he never stops campaigning but his most important campaign promises are to make the lights work, to deliver the mail, to provide jobs, to get things actually done. He knows his country intimately and he knows the structures of its government intimately. Above all, he knows how to make it happen.

One of his most important remaining tasks will be to influence the choice of his successor. This is widely assumed as likely to be the vice-president, Joseph Estrada, a former film star. This thought turns many Filipinos, and many foreign investors, cold with apprehension. But democratic politics, and especially the politics of direct presidential elections, are inherently unpredictable. If Ramos's standing in his country remains anything like it is at present he may well be able to exercise a decisive influence on the identity of the next president.

In the meantime Ramos, soldier, engineer, perennial cigar fondler and fanatical golfer, remains one of Asia's most engaging leaders. I have seldom met a national leader with less 'side', who seems at the same time both not to take himself too seriously yet to be utterly relaxed with himself. If poets are the unacknowledged legislators of the world, perhaps they should remain unacknowledged. In a nation suffused with political rhetoric and political poetry a combination of modesty and competence, toughness and humour, is no bad combination at all.

3

LEE KUAN YEW AND GOH CHOK TONG: OLD TIGER, YOUNG TIGER

To build a country, you need passion. If you just do your sums—plus, minus, debit, credit—you are a wash-out.

—Lee Kuan Yew, National Day rally, August 20, 1989

Interviewing Singapore's Lee Kuan Yew is a rite of passage, a ceremony of initiation, for regional journalists. He is one of the most interviewed figures in all Asia. A visit to his office is more or less mandatory for anyone seriously interested in covering opinion in Asia. Despite Singapore's tightly controlled nature, or perhaps because of it, security procedures are surprisingly straightforward and easy for a head of government interview. I take a hotel taxi down to the government Istana building, set in a spacious, elegant but discreet park right in the centre of Singapore, show some ID to the guard at the gate and seemingly within seconds am being taken by Lee's press secretary, James Wu, into the senior minister's spacious office. It has been wisely said of Lee that he runs (or ran) Singapore in much the same way he organises his office. It is air-conditioned, with the room temperature precisely controlled, austere, anonymous, neat, comfortable enough, and rather antiseptic.

Interviewing Lee for the first time is a somewhat intimidating experience. There is no small talk, no inquiry as to how you are liking Singapore, no flattering reference to show he's read some of your work (all standard techniques used by other political leaders putting journalists at their ease), only the limpest and most perfunctory of handshakes. It is of course perfectly polite but it's remote, detached: Sit down and listen while I tell you the geostrategic realities, then leave, seems to be the subtext. And the face doesn't change expression in the course of a long interview. The eyes, as everyone has noticed, are intense and bore right through you, but the body is limp, inert. You feel as if you are sitting for an important public examination after a pretty dim performance at school and very soon you will make a mistake and ruin your life.

But Lee's quiet body language does not obscure the passionate intensity of his convictions. Lee has always been a man of passions, of burning, brilliant passions. He has been passionate about the big things: Singapore's independence, communism in Indochina, the benefits of a free-market economy. But he has also at times been amazingly passionate about the amazingly trivial—about the length of young men's hair, about the cleanliness of Singapore's streets. His passionate concerns have ranged from the merely civic—the right height of trees needed to keep his city state green—to what other leaders would regard as distinctly private and non-political issues, such as the alleged dangers to society of large numbers of professional women remaining unmarried. Despite being in effect a lord mayor with sovereign powers, Lee is undoubtedly one of the great men of Southeast Asia, one of that exclusive and rapidly diminishing club of nationalist leaders who took their countries from colonialism to independence.

In November 1990 he retired as prime minister to be replaced by the much softer-edged, more affable and easy-going Goh Chok Tong. But retirement is a misnomer. Lee remains in the Cabinet with the title 'senior minister'. For a couple of years after his retirement he also remained secretary-general of the ruling People's Action Party. In an interview in the middle of 1991 Goh admitted that in Cabinet meetings he frequently handed over the second half of the meeting for Lee to run, almost as of old. And Lee has said that if the ideas which he believes are central to Singapore's success are ever abandoned he will rise up, not only from retirement, but if necessary from the grave, to put his successors straight.

But in recent years Lee has been spending more time away

from Singapore. Although he has always been wont to speak his mind, his new position gives him the freedom to say just exactly what he wants without necessarily having to commit the Singapore government to every detail of his sometimes controversial views. As a result he has become one of the most powerful independent voices in Asia. Governments which once reviled him, such as the Chinese and the Vietnamese, now earnestly seek his advice. Influential Taiwanese proposed him as an informal mediator between Taipei and Beijing. Perhaps only a handful of individuals in the world—Margaret Thatcher, Henry Kissinger (before his death Richard Nixon was in this class)—are more sought after as speakers at international conferences. Yet Thatcher and Kissinger were dominant figures in powerful countries. Lee, in a formal sense, was little more than a mayor of a prosperous, medium-sized Asian city. But four decades of uniquely successful leadership, combined with a penchant for speaking bluntly, combined with the legend of the Lee strategic view, all work now to sustain his celebrity. It is astonishing the respect and influence accorded to his views. When you read the memoirs of the most important figures of American foreign policy, men like George Shultz, Henry Kissinger and Richard Nixon, it is instructive how frequently they refer to Lee's judgments on contentious international issues. This is an intellectual status not routinely accorded to any other Asian statesman. Especially when an American policy maker is arguing that a particular line of policy is hardheaded, pragmatic and effective, he will rhetorically call Lee to his side.

One former senior American official, who was at the very heart of the American national security structure under Ronald Reagan, told me that he and his colleagues were always apprehensive when Lee met Reagan. Lee's mystique, and his record of successful anti-communism, economic development and conservative social engineering, had so enthralled Reagan that the president tended to agree with whatever Lee said, and endorse any proposal he made. 'It was not the broad thrust of what Lee told Reagan that worried us,' my friend said. 'That was always 95 per cent dead on. But there was always something extra that was in the end special pleading for Singapore, always some particular thing that would benefit Singapore but wasn't necessarily good American policy. But undoing an idea in Reagan's mind that had been planted by Lee was always the helluva job.' Even the caning of the American student, Michael Fay, in Singapore, after Fay was convicted of charges of vandalism, apparently did nothing to dim Lee's star in the US and internationally.

It is fair to say no other Asian leader has ever enjoyed influence like that. On the occasion of my first interview with Lee, in mid-1992, he quickly moved into giving a strategic overview of East Asia whose broad outlines remain as relevant today as they were then. Indeed the issues he identified then have come if anything to dominate East Asia even more in the subsequent few years. It was a big picture, drawn in primary colours, and swift, bold brushstrokes. He was that day very concerned with what he saw as a developing American fear of East Asian economic success. He bluntly stated that this fear grew in part out of racism. It is part of Lee's uniqueness that he can read the most severe and unpalatable lessons to the US, as he does to Australia and even neighbours such as the Philippines, and not dent his credibility or his attraction as a guru. His message on racism in American attitudes to East Asia, as I say, could hardly have been more blunt. 'It always goes back to racism in hard times,' he told me. 'For so long the oriental was portrayed as sly and devious and somehow not quite human. Although Americans have made tremendous strides, in troubled times people react in a primitive way.'

Few political leaders can have been more sensitive to issues of race than LKY, as he is often known (Singaporeans seem to have a love for reducing their names to acronyms—Lee's redoubtable son, the Cabinet minister, Brigadier General Lee Hsien Loong, is known as BG Lee). Lee Kuan Yew was born on September 16, 1923, in Singapore. Lee's father worked for the Shell oil company while his mother was a cooking teacher. Lee started his education at Raffles Institution, which was a well-regarded preparatory school. He later attended Raffles College, which was the forerunner of the University of Singapore, studying English literature, economics and mathematics. Lee's grandfather wanted him brought up as a colonial English gentleman, an identity Lee would later reject, seeking to become instead of a second-class Englishman a first-class Singaporean.

As was the case with so many Southeast Asians of his generation, the Second World War was a formative experience, especially the Japanese invasion of 1942. He learned to speak Japanese and survived the Japanese occupation relatively well. On one occasion he saw a Japanese soldier slap a local man across the face. The humiliation of powerlessness seared itself into Lee's consciousness. He determined that eventually he and his countrymen would have self-determination. Japanese occupation had turned him into a nationalist. All of the big formative experiences of Lee's life have had an overlay of race: British colonial rule followed by British humiliation and defeat, brutal Japanese occupation, his university studies in Britain, the anti-colonial struggle and the brief incorporation of Singapore into Malaysia in the early '60s.

After the war Lee went to study at the London School of Economics and Cambridge University, where he was a 'double first' man, led the honours list and won academic honours unprecedented for a Singaporean or Malay. After completing his studies in England he returned to Singapore and set up a law practice with his formidable wife, another brilliant young Singaporean he had met at Cambridge. He was in those days a socialist, as was most everyone of progressive opinion, although he was certainly never a communist. In Singapore he represented labour unions and became a leading left-wing activist, promoting decolonisation, equal rights for women and free speech. Lee is one of those authority-upholding Asian leaders who earlier went through a period of being a rebel wanting to fundamentally reform and restructure an existing political and social order. Moreover, while he has been socially conservative as Singapore's leader the relentless, thrusting economic development he has pushed for his society has in fact wrought enormous social change in Singapore over the decades of Lee's rule.

In 1954 Lee was involved in founding the People's Action Party, which still rules Singapore today. In 1955 he entered the colonial Legislative Assembly, as the member for Tanjong Pagar. In those days Lee was seen as, and by virtue of his constituency was actually, a representative of the poor. It was at this period that Lee learned Mandarin Chinese, and later Malay. He had refused to learn Chinese at school and later would share Nehru's lament: he could not speak his mother tongue as well as he could speak English.

After his election to the Legislative Assembly Lee adopted an increasingly radical position. He consciously collaborated with the communists in the cause of decolonisation. Yet in this Lee was utterly remarkable. He was one of very few cases this century of a basically social democratic force forming a united front with the communists and then outmanoeuvring and defeating the communists. He in effect out-Leninised the Leninists, adopting a tight, highly centralised principle of political organisation. Successive years of declassified Australian Cabinet documents demonstrate that Australian intelligence at the time thought Lee was virtually a communist. The Australian government did not want an independent Singapore under Lee because it thought him too radical, and the Chinese generally too prone to communism. Instead Canberra wanted Singapore to be subsumed into a larger Malay identity under the rule of the reliable Malay nobles.

In 1959 the British finally granted independence to Singapore although London kept control of foreign affairs and defence. Lee was by then leader of the PAP and it won a landslide in the election. On June 5, 1959, Lee Kuan Yew, Harry Lee as he had been known in Cambridge, became independent Singapore's first prime minister. Lee has always been incorruptible financially and has demanded this of his fellow ministers in government. Today Singapore's politicians, and top civil servants, are probably the best paid in all Asia and this is occasionally the subject of extremely foolish comment in the foreign press. For undoubtedly Singapore's government is also the least corrupt in Asia, and the two facts are hardly unconnected. In any event Lee started out as he meant to continue. On becoming prime minister he left the family law firm and ordered that it should be given no special favours from the government.

Lee's first government was the sort of thing the 1950s socialist international, with which the PAP was affiliated, would have liked very much. It was full of intellectuals and academics, and it strove to develop industry and education, the two pillars of modernisation. Those who know only the gleaming, clean Singapore of today cannot imagine what a slum-filled, often squalid and certainly poor place Singapore was then. Again foreigners who lament the loss of the atmosphere of the 'old Singapore' are both patronising and missing the point. Singapore, and Singaporeans, do not exist as a quaint location of exotic Eastern colour for western travellers. They exist as an independent society in which people crave the good life as much as people do in the west. Perhaps Singapore's government has gone too far in tearing down old buildings and redeveloping old neighbourhoods, but Singaporeans certainly prefer today's affluence to their parents' struggle and squalor. Lee's first government, as well as pushing development, announced a 'clean-up' campaign, cracking down on pornography, the grosser public disorders and generally trying to give Singapore a better tone. Lee would later recall: 'As prime minister of Singapore my first task was to lift my country out of the degradation that poverty, ignorance and disease had wrought. Since it was dire poverty that made for such a low priority given to human life, all other things became secondary.'

In 1963 Singapore joined the federation of Malaysia. This was a disastrous experiment which could easily have had even worse results than it did. What were Lee's motives? Defence and security were certainly considerations. These were the bad days of the Cold War. North Vietnam was threatening its neighbours. China was promoting insurgent movements around the region. The erratic Sukarno in Indonesia was coexisting distressingly with one of the largest communist parties anywhere in the world. Obviously one day the British would leave the region. In any event the Second World War had cruelly demonstrated their incapacity to provide for the security of Singapore. What were the chances for a tiny, impoverished Chinese enclave like Singapore in this turbulent and troubled region?

Moreover Malaysia was, like Singapore, composed predominantly of Malays and Chinese, with a sizeable Indian minority. But the position of the races was reversed: in Malaysia, Malays were in the majority, in Singapore, Chinese were the majority. The time of actual merger was one of great instability for both countries. During their two-year cohabitation Singapore and Kuala Lumpur fought over everything, from race relations to legislation to fiscal arrangements. Race riots broke out between Malays and Chinese. With Singapore as part of the federation the Malay majority in Malaysia overall was reduced to something like parity between the Malays and the Chinese. Lee's PAP started to organise politically on the Malay peninsula, especially in areas like Penang and Kuala Lumpur, themselves both with Chinese majorities. Eventually Singapore was virtually booted out of the federation and Lee broke into tears on television at this rupture.

It may be that Lee thought he could rule a united Malaysia, a country which would have had several times the overall population and physical resources of Singapore alone. But it was not to be, although it took the Singapore elite some years to come finally to that conclusion.

In 1968 London announced that it was withdrawing its military forces from Singapore. This was not only a blow to Singapore's always fragile sense of military security but also a huge blow to its economy. This development contributed to one of Lee's most important decisions, to consciously seek to attract as much foreign investment to Singapore as possible. This has been a hugely successful strategy. In many ways it has been the multinational corporations, plus the government-linked corporations, which have built the dynamo of Singapore's modern economy. And Lee's legitimacy grew and grew with Singapore's economic success. By 1978 per capita income in Singapore had risen to $US3000, an increase of 500 per cent on the level in 1960. In the 1970s the economy grew consistently by better than 9 per cent a year, and in the 1980s by better than 8 per cent a year, apart from the blip of the recession in the middle of the decade. By the end of the 1980s Singapore's per capita income had risen to $US10 500, making Singaporeans the richest people in Asia after the Japanese (not counting the rather peculiar, oil-drenched per capita statistics of Brunei).

As is well known, Lee also oversaw a tightly controlled society. In 1971, two newspapers which voiced opposition views were closed down. Opposition politicians were heavily harassed and often enough ended up spending periods in jail. Singapore was such a small place it was difficult in any event for Opposition forces to feel they had the civic space to develop. The Singapore government also enforced all kinds of social regulations. You were fined for littering; the result is that Singapore is a clean place. You were fined for smoking in public restaurants; the result is

Singapore is a healthy place. If you were a man you couldn't wear your hair long. There was even a fine for not flushing a public toilet after you used it. You would be fined for spitting. It was, as the joke went, a 'fine' society. In recent years a ban on chewing gum got derisory attention around the world. Yet as Kishore Mabubhani, the head of Singapore's Foreign Affairs Department, has argued, this is a peculiar overreaction. In most American cities, he caustically points out, you can buy crack cocaine easily, in Singapore you can't buy chewing gum. Which of these two social realities ought to excite the moral indignation of world opinion? This is no trivial argument by Mabubhani, and Singapore's western critics do themselves no good by ignoring the positive elements in East Asian social conservatism, for which a ban on chewing gum seems to me a very small price to pay.

Lee was always ready to offer a defence for his government's strong social intervention, observing during a speech in 1986: 'I say without any remorse that we would not have made the economic progress if we had not intervened on very personal matters—who your neighbour is, how you live, the noise you make, how you spit, or where you spit, or what language you use. It was fundamental social and cultural changes that brought us here.'

Similarly his government was strongly redistributionist, and still is. Singapore has certainly avoided creating a welfare state and it operates with a broad free market paradigm. It is certainly a competitive place. But there is no doubt that the government sets the directions of the economy and intervenes to promote an egalitarian social order. Its Central Provident Fund provides for retirement incomes. Its Housing Development Board has built thousands upon thousands of good quality home units, and the vast majority of Singaporeans are home owners. It also uses the intersection of economic and social policy to promote conservative social values, to give these values real economic consequence. It is easier for a married couple than a single person to get housing finance in Singapore. Health benefits are emphasised for families. The family is not only the centre of Chinese social life, it is the centre of Singapore's economic life. The society is ordered on the assumption that people will and should live in families.

You are not therefore forced to live in an intact family, but financial incentives encourage you to do so.

Some of Singapore's social engineering has had strange echoes of eugenics, in particular the Social Development Unit, a kind of government-run singles service which is designed to get more university-educated women to marry. Lee's ideas on these issues, his desire not to 'waste' good genes, have echoes of his neighbour Dr Mahathir's early ideas on human genetics.

In 1982 Lee made another critical decision, to reintroduce into schools and reinforce throughout society Confucianism. In his early years as leader Lee had said that he was no more Chinese than the American politician, Tip O'Neill, was Irish. But in the 1980s this attitude changed and Lee's, and Singapore's, Chineseness came to the fore. It may be that this was necessary in order to justify maintaining the broad status quo of Singapore, as well as useful in a region in which interpreting and dealing with China was becoming ever more crucial, and in which the Southeast Asian networks of 'overseas Chinese' businessmen were a critical economic force. But above all emphasising Singapore's Chineseness gives a cultural and social justification for Singapore being the way it is, and a broader sense of identity and pride for Singaporean Chinese, many of whom could easily take their excellent educations and migrate to more liberal, less intense societies.

I asked Lee how important Chinese values had been to Singapore's success. His response was unequivocal: 'Without them we could not have done it. No amount of exhortation, laws or coercion could have done it. there has to be those cultural underpinnings in the people: a desire to be educated, to acquire knowledge, to be useful.'

Despite his criticisms of modern America Lee remains the most unambiguous and trenchant defender in all Asia of the necessity of the American strategic presence in the region. Again, this may reflect Singapore's peculiar position, the fragility of all Chinese in the vast Malay sea of Southeast Asia. Oddly, it means that Singapore's view of strategic and even trade issues is often very sympathetic to Australia's view. Singapore's reflex is to multilateralise issues and thus avoid a direct Chinese–Malay ethnic split. Multilateralising means bringing in outsiders, of which the most important is the United States, but also important in this context is Australia. Thus Singapore is often arguing for Australia's inclusion. When Australian diplomats were trying to sell the idea of APEC to the region in 1989 Singapore was decisive in convincing the rest of Southeast Asia to go along. Indeed Singapore's diplomatic role often mirrors its trade role, as the entrepot of ideas, the broker of goods traded by bigger players, the lubricant of communication. I asked Lee how important he thought the American military presence was in the region: 'It's absolutely pivotal,' he replied. 'The US has been the balancer and the moderator since 1945. Before America it was a colonial balance between Japan, the French, the British and the Dutch. Over the next 30 to 40 years it will be an American and an indigenous balance as China, Korea, India, Russia and others build up. I hope there will always be an American factor in that balance. American withdrawal would be inviting problems.'

That is a fairly orthodox East Asian view, though at odds with his neighbour Dr Mahathir, but no one expresses it as forcefully, or as much without reservation, as does Lee. Like other East Asian leaders he was profoundly concerned about the continuing trade battles between the US and East Asia. He said:

> It's a problem which only to a limited extent can be resolved by Japan and other East Asian countries, by opening up our economies to buy more from America. The basic remedy is in American hands. First there is a problem of the [US] Budget. It has to be balanced and then the trade deficit will diminish. Then comes the longer term problem of competitiveness which goes back to training, education and productivity. The loss of discipline in the public schools must reduce the standards of the new recruits into the work force. For several decades since the war in Vietnam the American people have been used to living as an affluent people. They are not willing to accept that they are not as affluent as before and that some belt-tightening is necessary. If the Americans do not regain their self-confidence, which they will do only when they begin to put their own house in order, then this will be a problem. It's not that East Asia has suddenly become so dynamic and productive. It's simply that they have caught up from a very low base and the Americans have allowed themselves to slip behind.

Over recent years, his belief in the absolute necessity of a strategic American presence in the region notwithstanding, his highly critical views of western and in particular American decadence have conflated with a view as to the defects of full-scale democracy such that he has seemed at times to bundle them up as a kind of single disease. He caused some pain to his Philippines hosts on a 1992 visit when he told them:

> I do not believe that democracy necessarily leads to development. I believe that what a country needs to develop is discipline more than democracy. The exuberance of democracy leads to indiscipline and disorderly conduct which are inimical to development.

In a justly famous interview with *Foreign Affairs* magazine in 1994 he gave a considered judgment on the social system of the United States. He admired the ease of American social relations and the openness of policy debate but also said:

> As a total system I find parts of it totally unacceptable: guns, drugs, violent crime, vagrancy, unbecoming behaviour in public—in sum the breakdown of civil society . . . the liberal, intellectual tradition that developed after World War II claimed that human beings had arrived at this perfect state where everybody would be better off if they were allowed to do their own thing and flourish. It has not worked out and I doubt if it will.

That is a pretty definitive Lee view. But America is not the only western country to which Lee regularly reads lessons. He has been providing the same service for Australia for 30 years. In the last couple of years his attitude to Australia seems to have warmed slightly, although he is still critical of many things. On that day in 1992 I asked him about Australia's recent increased engagement with the region. He replied:

> Diplomatically you are part of the region. You have been active all these years. But economically you are not fully engaged. Your gears have not meshed in to engage those of the region because yours was a protected economy. You led a sort of separate economic existence. It will be a few years more before you pull down all the barriers. Ten or twelve years ago Singapore opened a consulate in Sydney, hoping to build up

economic links with Australia. After a few years we shut it down. Trade wasn't growing. You were living in a capsule industrially. It was comfortable because it was protected. You were not going at the same speed as the rest of East Asia. As we were upgrading our economies you were carrying on with your old ways. Now you have the painful process of catching up. It's the price for having led a quiet, comfortable life since the end of World War II. Within five to seven years you can bring all the barriers down and begin to mesh in. But it will be painful at the beginning because you will import more than you will export. Koreans can import your iron and your coal and make steel. Now Korean wages have gone up. It should not be impossible for Australians to export different kinds of steel instead of just exporting iron ore and coal. It does mean your unions have got to change their philosophy of life and management has got to get trim.

I asked Lee whether Australia's economic failings reflected weaknesses in our national culture.

Culture here means a comfortable, protected way of life that has bred a certain complacency. Australians, sitting on all these riches, believe the world owes them a living, as indeed it does because it buys those resources. But it is no longer a good living now. Similar resources are available from Canada, Latin America and elsewhere.

These were themes which he would basically repeat at a Sydney luncheon I attended in April 1994. Australia's decade of economic reform in the 1980s had not been enough to make us a competitive partner in Asia–Pacific dynamism, he told the luncheon, and we still suffered from a 'lucky country' mentality that made us complacent and uncompetitive. We were an 'unintense society' already suffering from 'reform fatigue'. 'More reform is unavoidable to complete the restructuring of the economy or the ordeal already endured may be wasted,' he said. Then, referring to a recent waterfront dispute, he commented:

For a handful of dock workers in 1994 who have been made redundant because of restructuring to bring the export trade to a standstill is unbelievable. Union leaders and members seem to be out of touch with reality. When people are still beating the system by accepting lower than union award wages in the informal sector and then claiming the dole, and the government still takes nearly half of every dollar earned by individuals in the top tax bracket, then more changes are needed if Australians are to become competitive.

Australians, he said, still suffered from a 'resource rich syndrome', that resulted in a 'relaxed, not an intense society'. He characterised Australians as having high consumption, low savings, low competitiveness, high current account deficits and high debt, with the majority of our merchandise exports still coming from agricultural and mineral commodities:

> Australians must be weaned from welfare dependency and become self-reliant and competitive. This is not painless. Deep-seated problems of work ethic, productivity, enterprise, bloody-minded unions protecting unproductive work practices, feather-bedding and inflexibility in wages are neither quickly nor easily cured.

East Asian societies were the opposite, characterised by 'a resource-poor syndrome' that led to low consumption, high savings, high competitiveness, current account surpluses and low debt: 'They have had to gear themselves culturally for a very hard, driving way of life.' Among countries with a 'resource-poor syndrome' he included Singapore, Japan, Korea, Taiwan, China and Vietnam.

He did not see Australia as a total wash-out, however. On the same trip he was urging Australian business to form partnerships with Singapore to go together into third countries. He also urged Australia to see Singapore and Malaysia as our 'old friends' in the region and praised changes in our regional diplomacy, especially on issues like human rights. He also seemed to be at one with Canberra over APEC. In his interview with me he was wholly positive about APEC, describing it as 'an organisation of immense potential'. Like the former Australian prime minister, Paul Keating, he saw its main roles as being to keep an open and friendly trading system across the Asia–Pacific, and ultimately to persuade the Europeans to join in such a system.

In our interview Lee was optimistic about the reform programs in both China and Vietnam. He did not fear a reversal of the economic reform programs in either country: 'Reversal means going back to squalor, misery, poverty and real rebellion. Both these peoples now have seen life get a little better, with the prospect of it getting even better. If they reverse policies they will kill off any hope of a normal life.' Like many Asian leaders, Lee does not believe that democracy in China is workable, and he argued that the demonstrations in Tiananmen Square had been widely misinterpreted in the west:

> The pre-conditions for representative government are not there, in China. There is no history, no tradition, nor do I think there is a demand for it. The demonstrations in Tiananmen were not a demand for democracy or representative government. It was a demand for honest government that would knock out nepotism and corruption. They were not asking for democracy in the sense of one man, one vote.

Now, he said, China was back on the path of economic growth and this was entirely a good thing, for 'a hungry China unable to solve its own problems must export troubles across her borders.'

Taking over from Lee was no easy task for Goh Chok Tong, who is as easy, affable, friendly, solicitous as Lee is dry, precise and forbidding. Over the years I've had a series of interviews with Goh, whose career has been much more conventional. Lee is one of the extraordinary figures of Southeast Asian history and it is unfair to compare Goh with him. Lee represented the independence generation. Goh's task is not to fight the British for independence, oust the communists, come to grips with the huge Malay population around him and establish a modern economy. It is rather the far more mundane task of running an already affluent, already functioning modern society. Yet in some ways Goh's task is no less delicate than was Lee's. For one thing, managing a highly successful economy is in some ways more complex than getting one going and the stakes can be even higher. There's less room for error. For another thing, while the Chinese–Malay racial situation is much less intense than it was in the 1960s it is hardly less delicate.

I once asked Goh what it felt like to be Lee's successor, to have that enormous weight of expectation on his shoulders. 'He is one of the giants of history,' Goh said. 'I make it clear to people that I cannot fill his shoes. I fill my own shoes instead. They're smaller but more comfortable.'

In a 1992 interview I asked Goh whether he would liberalise social policy in Singapore. He replied: 'I have trouble with the word liberalising.' But, I reminded him, when he first became prime minister he argued that there should be fewer regulations:

> Correct. But I don't know whether that means liberalising because that tends to have a political meaning. What I thought Singapore should have at this stage is a change in the style of government. Instead of government being overwhelming, dominant in every area, I try to involve the people in programs, in projects and even in major decision making. It's a more participatory style of government. I want to see which rules stifle people's creativity and see whether we can remove them entirely, or if we can't, modify them. We would, of course, want Singaporeans to have more social room. But at the same time we are cautious. If I may borrow a metaphor from a colleague—he used golfing terms—we are at the stage where we want to widen the fairway, put the out-of-bounds markers further apart so it's easier for the golfers. You can have a wide swing but you don't get into the rough.
>
> But we're in transition so we don't know quite where to put the out-of-bounds markers. So we do it by trial and error. Film censorship is a good example. We thought we could put the marker wide and allow Singaporeans who enjoy adult films to go because it's by choice, it's at the cinema, not like on tele-vision. But there was a reaction from the public. Our society is more conservative than we thought. So we brought the marker back a little, not to the original position, but back a little.

So did he think Singaporeans were at heart a very conservative people?

> Yes, I would think so. You may be just talking to the English-educated, you may get a different sense. But the bulk of the population would not be fluent in English and their thought processes are still not influenced by the west. It's very much an Asian society. This ability to work together as a team has been critical to Singapore's success. That's part of the hierarchical structure of a Confucianist society, also the emphasis on thrift and hard work, that the government does

not owe you a living. If you are in trouble you look first towards your immediate family, or members of your clan.

Goh outlined his thinking on the vexed questions (and they would become much more vexed in the subsequent two or three years) of international reporting on Singapore, and international magazines and newspapers which circulate inside Singapore. He said:

> You can write about Singapore, you can write critical articles and so on, but if they're written in a way which is meant for a foreign audience that's all right with us. If you write a critical article on Singapore based on what you have seen, and you are addressing Australians, we would not object to that. But if you are writing with a view to influencing Singaporeans, that's different. We can be relaxed about objective articles but we are still very much an Asian society and we believe that the members of parliament and ministers who have earned their respect must not be ridiculed. We run a very different system from the west, where political leaders are caricatured, ridiculed.
>
> The basis is this. If politicians have low public standing the authority to govern diminishes. In the US, according to a recent survey, the least well regarded profession is used car sales-man. Politician is one above that. In the UK a survey I saw some years ago put politicians right at the bottom, except for journalists. So if politicians were to be right at the bottom, where would the moral standing be to govern? Ministers and MPs are well regarded in Singapore. We've earned it and we make sure that none of us abuses that position so as to attract disrespect, ridicule or derision from the public. So we would not allow the press to diminish our position through biased, inaccurate, disrespectful reporting.

Goh's views if anything became more conservative over the next couple of years. When he delivered his National Day speech on August 21, 1994, if you closed your eyes and just listened, it was possible to imagine that Goh's predecessor was giving the speech, so redolent was it of talk of Asian values, rejecting corrupt western ways and the need for strong government. It was an emphatic return to core Singapore values. His speech was inter-preted at the time in three aspects: first, as a political call to arms to his countrymen; second, as a self-confident reassertion of core Singapore values by a government buoyed by continued extraordinary good economic figures. It was also seen as a response to western criticism of Singapore following the caning of Michael Fay.

The speech was fairly strong even by Singapore standards. It began with well-earned praise for Singapore's continued amazing economic performance. Singapore is disproving the common economic notion that at a certain level of affluence very high rates of economic growth become impossible to sustain. In 1994 Singapore's per capita income was ahead of New Zealand's and Hong Kong's and just behind Australia's, yet its growth rate for the year was in the vicinity of 9 per cent.

Goh then went on to talk at length about family and moral values. What was remarkable was not just the extolling of traditional 'Asian' values for Singapore but the bluntness of the criticisms of western societies, notably the US and Britain. Goh said:

> Singaporeans today enjoy full employment and high economic growth, and low divorce, illegitimacy and crime rates. You may think decline is unimaginable. But societies can go wrong quickly. US and British societies have changed profoundly in the last 30 years. Up to the 1960s they were disciplined, with the family very much the pillar of their societies. Since then both the US and Britain have seen a sharp rise in broken families, teenage mothers, illegitimate children, juvenile delinquency, vandalism and violent crime. In Britain one in three children is born to unmarried mothers. The same is true for the US.

Rather surprisingly, Goh criticised the spread of obesity in Singaporean children as a sign that their parents were indulging them and went on to say:

> In Confucian society a child who does wrong knows he has brought shame upon his whole family. In America, he may win instant stardom, like Tonya Harding, the ice skater who tried to fix her rival. The difference is stark between what traditional Asians demand of their children and what many Americans now allow theirs to become.

Goh continued for page after page on his government's deter-mination to support the family by thorough and at times tough action. Medical insurance would continue to be channelled through the male head of the family to reinforce the structure of the family. To discourage sole parenthood the children of unmarried mothers would not be entitled to civil service medical benefits. Similarly unmarried mothers would not be allowed to buy Housing Development Board units direct from the HDB, but only on the resale market. Allowing them to buy units directly from the HDB would be to imply acceptance of unmarried mothers. The government would also provide legal redress so that impoverished elderly parents could sue their adult children to force them to provide financial assistance to their parents in their parents' old age. Similarly, favoured financial treatment would be provided for adult children who want to buy home units near to their parents, thus preserving the extended-family link.

Some of the things that upset the prime minister seemed rather trivial, including one newspaper advertisement:

> Recently the *Straits Times* [Singapore's main newspaper] carried an advertisement showing a boy saying 'Come on, Dad, if you can play golf five times a week I can have Sustagen once a day.' I found the language, the way the boy speaks, most objectionable. Why put an American boy's way of speaking into a Singaporean boy's mouth? Do your children really speak to you like that these days? These advertisements will encourage children to be insolent to their parents. Many American children call their fathers by their first names and treat them with casual familiarity. We must not unthinkingly drift into attitudes and manners which undermine the traditional politeness and deference Asian children have for their parents and elders. It will destroy the way our children have grown up, respectful and polite to their elders.

Importantly, Goh finished his speech with a section in which he explicitly rejected the western liberal model as the future for Singapore:

> Western liberals, foreign media and human rights groups also want Singapore to be like their societies and some Singaporeans mindlessly dance to their tune. See what happened to President Gorbachev because he was beguiled by their praise. Deng Xiaoping received their condemnation. But look at China today and see what has happened to the Soviet Union. It's gone,

imploded! We must think for ourselves and decide what is good for Singapore, what will make Singapore stable and successful. Above all else, stay away from policies which have brought a plague of social and economic problems to the US and Britain.

Goh's speech was important because it was so forceful a restatement of the core Singapore beliefs. It is no criticism of Goh to say that his words, and his leadership, lie very much in the benign shadow of Lee Kuan Yew. This is also true of his strategic outlook. In a conversation in 1993, he gave the most enthusiastic endorsement I've ever heard from a Southeast Asian leader of what might be termed the maximalist, Australian vision for APEC, and specifically for Australia's APEC diplomacy. He strongly distanced himself from Malaysian reservations about APEC and said he would like APEC to move at the pace which Australia has been proposing for it. Southeast Asians who felt their concerns were being overlooked in APEC should come up with their own initiatives for APEC. At that stage he did not believe ASEAN was being overshadowed by APEC, but said:

Certainly if ASEAN doesn't come up with initiatives and ideas on how APEC should move and leaves it to Australia and the US, then of course ASEAN's role would diminish within APEC. Essentially, Singapore supports Australia's position. We think APEC is good for all of us and we should aim at the maximum over a number of years.

He said he hoped APEC would be the main vehicle for North American–East Asian trade negotiations. He also signalled Singapore's willingness to join any extended version of the North American Free Trade Agreement. The possibility of extending NAFTA across the Pacific is controversial in Asia because it would allow the US to develop a hub-and-spokes system of preferred Asian trade partners and less-preferred nations. Some American policy makers have even referred to this as a method for encircling Japan in a trade sense. However, Washington's efforts at implementing NAFTA itself, and trying to extend it even into Latin America, have run into so many problems that expansion across the Pacific is probably not on.

Goh's views about Australia, however, kept getting warmer as the years rolled by and the then Keating government's drive to engage Australia in the region took effect. At a dinner I attended in Sydney in September 1994, Goh proposed a regional partnership between Australia and Singapore to push for greater trade liberalisation and to take advantage of the region's investment opportunities. 'Australia and Singapore share a warm and close partnership,' he said.

> We have no bilateral problems. We share a commitment to freer global trade and open markets. We both want Asia to be integrated into the world economy and APEC to grow in strength. As Australia reaches out for a greater role in Southeast Asia it will have a friend and partner in Singapore. Singapore's drive to go regional is inclusive, not exclusive. We need partners and Australia is a suitable one.

Most fascinatingly, he also described Australia as 'the most Asianised country of western origin', and even promoted the idea of Australia as something of an east–west bridge, words Canberra loves to hear but which Asian leaders rarely utter. He said: 'Australia's location and evolving cultural mix place it in a good position to link up Asia and the west. After years of identifying itself economically and socially with the west, Australia is increasingly aware of its Asian neighbours and interests.'

The Singapore government is very well qualified academically and intellectually, although it tends to be dominated by a few stars and has had some difficulty recruiting the brightest people in its society to politics. Goh is the leader of the so-called second generation of Singaporean politicians. His change of style after the all-dominant Lee seems to have gone down well, although there are no real differences of substance between them.

The undeniable leader of the third generation of Singaporean politicians is George Yeo, who is extremely close to the Lee family. Yeo, in 1996 just 41, has held a variety of portfolios in the government. He was a 'double first' man at Cambridge and has a Harvard MBA (with high distinction). He is talked of as a future prime minister and is a close friend of Lee Kuan Yew's son, Lee Hsien Loong. Yeo is reported as having helped the younger Lee cope with the tragedy of his first wife's death. He travels extensively with Lee Kuan Yew, who is still certainly a decisive influence in Singapore politics. Some have even described Yeo as LKY's alter ego. In numerous interviews and speeches Yeo has often projected Singapore's big-picture strategic view. In a long conversation in his spacious 39th-floor office in the Port of Singapore Authority building he outlined an inclusive and benign vision of increasing East Asian economic dominance.

He said: 'In my mind there is little doubt that within twenty years East Asia will be the integrator of the world economy. And to be the integrator of the world economy you need all kinds of pan-Pacific institutions.' Would this lead to a reaction against East Asia in Europe and America?

> Some of this is inevitable. Whenever power shifts from one group to another there is bound to be a reaction. No one concedes a transfer of power away from himself without a struggle of some kind. When power shifts it is very uncomfortable for those giving the power. The challenge for politics is keeping those conflicts within reasonable bounds.

Like many in East Asia Yeo was greatly vexed by the famous article in the journal, *Foreign Affairs*, by the American adacemic, Sam Huntington, on a supposed impending clash of cultures. Huntington's bizarre and preposterous thesis was that the world is divided into nine main civilisations, and that, with the end of the Cold War, the conflicts of the future will be dominated by the inevitable clash of cultures—a case of the west versus the rest. Yeo said:

> I thought Sam Huntington's prescription [that the countries of the west should club together against the others] was quite mischievous. In the US and Canada and Australia there is already a strong Asian component so these societies have already absorbed some eastern ideas, just as East Asia has already absorbed many ideas of western civilisation. It's not that we have ceased to be eastern, but in the process there will be a certain closing of the gap. That should be the prescription of the future.

Huntington's thesis, if true, would of course be disastrous for Australia because it would mean that we were surrounded by countries preordained by their cultural heritage to be our enemies. Yeo, while acknowledging the importance and persistence of culture, does not believe this to be the case. He said:

> In Australia I often hear the saying that Australia's future will

be determined by its geography rather than its history. But no society can deny its history. The past rests on the present. Perhaps it would be truer to say that Australia's present was determined by its history, but that the future will be increasingly influenced by its geography.

The other point of view that you often hear from the Japanese is that Australia must be included in the region because of its importance as a supplier of resources. But I'm not sure that's altogether satisfactory from an Australian point of view. What you want to do is bring your strengths into play and be an active player. There has to be a realistic appreciation of your strengths and weaknesses. Given your small population, you're not going to be a major power. In present-day GNP terms you do carry more strength than many countries in Southeast Asia. But this is a temporary situation and you want a position for the future.

On many issues it would be in Australia's interests to tack more closely to Southeast Asia. It's already happening. I've been watching closely the relationship between Australia and Indonesia. Australia has close links with former British colonies in Southeast Asia [Singapore and Malaysia] and these are precious attachments.

Yeo graciously acknowledged that Australians were gradually learning to deal with the ambiguity which is such an important part of regional diplomacy in Southeast Asia. ASEAN, he said, uses ambiguity as a positive tool in diplomacy. The ASEAN culture has facilitated the US, Japan, China and Russia coming together in a regional security dialogue body, the ASEAN Regional Forum. He said:

This new security forum is one which goes beyond ASEAN but is started by ASEAN. It is curious why this should be so. The reason is the cultural nature of Southeast Asia. This puts heavy emphasis on gradualism, consensus and consultation. This is an emphasis you don't find in Northeast Asia. The ambiguity which some westerners find so confusing is part of the magic of ASEAN. In ASEAN communiques you often find great emphasis on getting the process right. In Southeast Asia ambiguity provides room for people to save face and find accommodations.

Both Goh Chok Tong and George Yeo have been intellectually

formed in no small measure by Lee Kuan Yew and echoes of his voice are readily discernible in the words of the younger men, although each has his different tone and nuance. But for most foreigners LKY himself remains the embodiment of Singapore. He is certainly one of the most extraordinary leaders Asia has produced. As James Minchin wrote in his biography of the long-time Singapore leader, Lee's view is always singular. Although a resolute anti-communist throughout the Cold War, he was on Vietnam neither a hawk nor a dove, 'but an owl glaring balefully at all sides'. There have been human rights abuses in Singapore, but compared to most countries in the region they have been very minor. Overwhelmingly the achievement is positive, and it is huge.

This doesn't mean that one has to endorse every aspect of Lee's sometimes rebarbative opinions. His neo-Confucianism seems just a little too convenient. His view of the superiority of Chinese civilisation just a little too smug. His recent embrace of China and his occasional criticism of Taiwan is perhaps also a little too convenient. But to assess the man is to look at the wider canvas of history.

The real monument to Lee's extraordinary career is modern Singapore itself, its gleaming skyscrapers, its green and pleasant streets, its safe and peaceful ambience, its astonishing affluence, the industry and sparkle of its people—this is the substance of Lee's achievement. And the truth is that no society other than Singapore could possibly have produced a Lee Kuan Yew. He is not a traditional Chinese mandarin of the type that rules in Taipei, nor does he remotely resemble the dusty Stalinist bureaucrats who still comprise so much of the Beijing elite. He is nothing like the avaricious, amoral Hong Kong businessman of legend. The late Chinese leader, Chou En Lai, once said of him that he was like a banana—yellow on the outside, white on the inside. Yet he is utterly unlike any western democratic leader. Nor has there ever been a hint of financial corruption about Lee, something that cannot be said about all Asian leaders.

Richard Nixon once said: 'The fact that a leader of Lee's breadth of vision was not able to act on a broader stage represents an incalculable loss to the world.' One can see what Nixon was driving at but perhaps he underestimated how Singapore, and only Singapore, could have shaped a Lee Kuan Yew. Singapore's complex interplay of British, Japanese, Chinese, Malay and Indian influences all moulded Lee. And Singapore was perhaps uniquely suited to the type of leadership Lee could offer—was even, because of its unthreatening size, a perfect perch for him to exercise the regional leadership and global influence which he undoubtedly accumulated, and which have not entirely dissipated, even in his semifictional semiretirement.

4

SUHARTO: THE
JAVANESE KING

 It was one of those scorching Jakarta days, with the sun fierce and inescapable, when only the mosquitoes seem energetic. The leaden sky of the previous few days had cleared, as if out of respect for Indonesia's 47th Independence Day anniversary celebrations. Hundreds of local dignitaries, diplomats, military and political figures, foreign and local businessmen, bureaucrats and civic leaders had gathered, by invitation only, at the Istana, the gleaming white palace of Indonesia's President Suharto, for 1992's version of the annual flag-raising ceremony. Some hundreds of soldiers, smartly turned out in formations, variously in crisp white, brown or blue uniforms, stood to attention on the fringes of the expansive palace lawn. Rivulets of sweat trickled down the backs of the onlookers when, seemingly from far away, a low, tortured moaning filled the air. The moaning slowly gathered in volume. The crowd was disconcerted. Then a wild-looking, half-naked young man, wearing only a multicoloured pair of loose-fitting shorts, his dark hair thickly matted, raced onto the lawn, wailing like a banshee.

In about three seconds a group of security men had run out after him, grabbed the intruder and whisked him away. Ripples of excited conversation spread through the crowd. The young man was unlikely to have had a happy evening ahead of him but neither, I thought, would the head of security, which had generally been pretty tight. Not only were you not allowed in without an invitation, this was one of the few Indonesian occasions I've attended where you weren't allowed in without a coat and tie, such that an Australian camera crew had caused hilarity by turning up in the usual TV designer casuals. They raced back to their hotel and rented from the Avis Rent-A-Car desk staff their red jackets, came back to the Istana and were admitted after all, looking bizarre and striking another small blow against the idea that Australians can fit in in Asia.

During the kerfuffle caused by the uninvited wailing banshee I was standing in the audience just below and to the side of where President Suharto was standing on the speakers' platform. Throughout the whole performance his face did not register the slightest flicker that anything was remotely amiss. His massive Javanese urbanity was undisturbed. A mere screaming madman was not enough to upset the formidable serenity of the man regarded by many as a modern Javanese king, and perhaps the greatest of all the Javanese kings. It was the perfect metaphor for modern Indonesian politics where the *bapak*, the 'father of development', dominates utterly, without the apparent exercise of effort.

Suharto has been running Indonesia since 1965 when he took over from the highly erratic Sukarno, after a short but gruesome civil conflict. He became acting president in 1967 and full president in 1968. At the start of the 1990s the speculation was over whether he would seek a sixth successive five-year term in 1993. Gradually it became clear he would and after 1993, when he was of course re-elected without demur, the assumption was that he would at least go quietly in 1998, that this surely would be his last presidential term. This assumption, plus Suharto's age, made his choice of vice-president critical. And in General Try Sutrisno, the former head of the Indonesian Armed Forces (ABRI), Suharto apparently picked a vice-president acceptable to himself but acceptable also to the army, someone who would restore the army's influence in national life. Sutrisno was regarded therefore as a certainty to eventually succeed Suharto as president, either in the event of his death or incapacity during his sixth five-year term, or as president in his own right after Suharto stood down in 1998. But as usual nothing was quite what it seemed in the Byzantine world of Jakarta elite politics and it now looks as though the extraordinary Suharto could seek a seventh term in 1998. This will be very tricky for Sutrisno, for no vice-president has ever had more than one term in office and for many reasons Suharto may be thinking of another ultimate successor. Then again, he may not. No one is privy to Suharto's real intentions. With his Javanese flexibility it is likely that Suharto himself is consciously keeping his options open.

Traditional Javanese theatre is known as *wayang*, and has become a central element in Indonesian cultural life. It is a theatre of puppets and shadows. The *dalang* is the pre-eminent puppet master. And that is Suharto today in Indonesia, the pre-eminent *dalang*, the puppet master still content effortlessly to keep all the players dancing on a string while he enjoys the performance.

In the early 1990s I was a frequent visitor to Indonesia. One of the most intriguing, yet in its way at a profound level disappointing, visits I made was in March 1993, to cover the Indonesian presidential election and the subsequent appointment of a new Cabinet. As usual, Jakarta was a city of splendid rumours and insider political jokes. Because it is not really a democracy, Indonesian politics is best considered as a kind of court politics. There are independent interest groups, there are diverse centres of power, there is a civic society of sorts growing up, but the power of the palace is enormous. The power concentrated in the person of Suharto does not make Indonesia a dictatorship but it is overwhelming nonetheless. The Cabinet, for example, hardly ever meets. Suharto prefers to deal with his ministers on a one-on-one basis and prevent even the hint of any real collegiality, any suggestion of a dilution of the president's absolute power, from taking place. Similarly Suharto now personally oversees all military appointments right down to the middle ranks. There is really no other political system quite like Indonesia's. In some ways it has the forms of a democracy—elections, political parties and the rest. And these are not the totally empty charade they are in Middle East dictatorships, for example, yet real power does not reside in them.

Nor is Indonesia in any conventional sense a military regime. Indeed, one of the most striking elements of recent Indonesian politcs has been the episodic and partial estrangement of Suharto from sections, at times from much, of the leadership, of the

Indonesian military. In any event the whole process of Suharto's nomination and re-election in 1993 was disturbing to those hoping for a democratic evolution in Indonesia. Under the Indonesian Constitution 400 seats in the House of Representatives are elected by universal adult franchise (except that ABRI personnel can't vote). One hundred are chosen by ABRI directly (which is why they don't vote in the general election). Another 500 governors, regional leaders, politicians and other worthies are chosen by the president. This group of 1000 constitutes the People's Consultative Assembly and it in turn picks the president. I saw this group in action in 1993 and a more sombre, serious, formal meeting you could hardly imagine. Yet it was ultimately meaningless. The process was circular. The president selects the assembly which selects the president.

Thus in 1993 Suharto was once again elected unanimously as president. But there is something inherently unsettling about unanimous elections. They suggest the election process itself is meaningless, irrelevant. They suggest that anybody wanting real change is going to have to accomplish it outside the electoral process, outside the formal institutions of politics, and that is inherently dangerous. In 1988 there had at least been a challenge to Suharto's choice of vice-president, Sudharmono, who was deeply unpopular with ABRI. But in 1993 not even a flicker of protest or contest was allowed into the deliberations, which bore—and it's an unpleasant reflection—a certain resemblance to old-style Soviet parliamentary gatherings.

After the ritual re-election of Suharto the rumour mill really began to work hard as everyone speculated on the likely shape of the new Cabinet. It was a marvellous and revealing time to be a foreign reporter in Jakarta. Much was revealed by the way things were done. On Monday, March 15, two days before the Cabinet was named, a list of its likely members circulated around Jakarta. It was feverishly updated throughout the day. If you didn't have that list, you certainly were a long way out of the loop in Jakarta that day. The list available by mid-afternoon turned out to be 90 per cent accurate, which was no bad thing because a lot of stocks were bought and sold on the basis of that list. I got my copy in an Indonesian newspaper office. The editor said to me good naturedly that he was pretty sure the list was accurate but he was not allowed to publish it in his newspaper. If I could publish it in my newspaper, however, he would then be able to report my report. In the end there weren't enough days left for this complex stratagem of getting information into the Indonesian public square to work but I could see what a complicated and challenging business being a journalist in Indonesia must be.

It was alleged in Jakarta at that time that every prominent citizen, especially those with teenage daughters, was having second telephone lines installed. This came from the story from 1988, perhaps apocryphal, that when Suharto and his advisers were allocating some of the minor portfolios, if they could not get their first choice on the line straight away they moved on to their second choice. Happily for Indonesia's widely respected foreign minister, Ali Alatas, at 4 a.m. on the morning of Sunday, 14 March, his telephone rang. It was just before time for the only meal of the day until sunset, as March is the Muslim holy month of Ramadan, and fasting is compulsory for good Muslims. But Alatas was happy to hear the phone ring that morning. It was the president, ringing to tell him he would be reappointed as foreign minister the following Wednesday when the whole Cabinet would be announced.

Alatas was relieved. He had overcome the Jakarta elite's version of the AIDS virus: *'aku igin ditelpon Suharto'*, which in Bahasa Indonesia means 'I want to be telephoned by Suharto'. The Cabinet which Suharto eventually announced constituted a sweeping shake-up. Its most dramatic feature was the dropping altogether of the former defence minister, Benny Murdani, the only figure in Indonesia of comparable stature to Suharto himself, and the eclipse of the so-called 'Berkeley mafia' of technocrats who had run the economy along orthodox and highly successful lines for much of the period of Suharto's New Order government. The other notable feature of the new Cabinet was the new prominence given to Islam as a political force.

In some ways, though, 1993 was the beginning of a retreat from the process of increased liberalisation and democratisation within Indonesia, a retreat which if anything has gathered pace in the subsequent few years. The sheer unanimity of Suharto's election, and the process leading up to it, indicated a stalling in what had looked an immensely promising process of democratisation, or at least political evolution. In the previous two years virtually every significant group in Indonesian society had called for Suharto's re-election. In a society of nearly 200 million people, the world's fourth most populous nation, this represented an extraordinary degree of orchestrated, choir-like, one-note-chanting political mobilisation.

The previous few years had nonetheless looked highly promising for Indonesians, and friends of Indonesia, who valued the development of democracy. Even the appalling tragedy of the Dili massacre in November 1991, in which Indonesian troops shot and killed a still unknown number of East Timorese demonstrators, had been handled in a way which took account of public outrage, with the president apologising for the massacre, denouncing it, and sacking and punishing some of the soldiers involved. More generally there had been a great opening up of the political scene. Although in Indonesia the executive totally dominates the legislature, the legislature had been becoming more important. Andrew McIntyre, in his extremely useful study, *Business and Politics in Indonesia*, identifies a series of incidents and trends since 1988 which had demonstrated and encouraged the push for greater liberalisation. One was the unprecedented challenge to Suharto's nominee for vice-president in 1988. Another was the radically increased policy activism of members of parliament. A third was a rash of student demonstrations calling for fairer and more open government. And the fourth, and perhaps the most important, was the far more open discussion of politics in the Indonesian press. The influential *Jakarta Post* had, for example, editorialised in early 1992 that: 'After more than twenty years of political stability and with a greater demand for democratisation in the air, we believe the government should open an even wider corridor of freedom.'

But from 1993 onwards Suharto seems to have grown tired of this liberalisation and reversed it. A partial explanation for this sad trend may be that a central part of the liberal agenda involved two aspects of the president and his family. The first was that he should step aside, or at least make the process of succession clear. The succession question sits on Indonesian politics like an alpine snow mass, huge and apparently immovable, vastly solid from a distance, but in fact likely to crumble and fall in a terrifying avalanche at any moment. Succession dominates all political and even economic and social discussion in Indonesia. In its 50 years of independence Indonesia has had just two presidents—Sukarno and Suharto. It has never had a peaceful transition from one president to another.

The second demand of the liberals was for the business activities of Suharto's children to be reined in. No one knows how this demand would play out if Suharto were not in power. That is why it has been assumed that in choosing a successor Suharto would expect some guarantees about protection for the core interests of the family. But the succession question, at the time of writing, remains utterly unresolved. Suharto's failure to resolve it must be reckoned a significant failure of his leadership and one which has effectively erected a road block to the political evolution which Indonesia must surely make eventually. It appears to lie behind other moves against the previous liberalising trend, of which one of the most tragic was the closure, in 1994, of the three independent magazines, *Tempo*, *Editor* and *DeTik*. This was followed by the sad spectacle of the government manoeuvring to deprive Megawati Sukarnoputri, Sukarno's daughter, from the leadership of the opposition party, the PDI. This, and heavy-handed treatment of pro-Megawati demonstrations, seemed to indicate an unreasonable paranoia on the government's part.

However, these criticisms of Suharto need to be weighed against his overall positive record, and the historic magnitude of his achievements. Suharto is an authentic giant of South-East Asian politics, not only in the history of his own country but of the region more generally. He came to power during a time of chaos and bloody conflict, when the conflicting ambitions of communists, nationalists and the unstable Sukarno were in violent collision. Indonesian friends have described to me what the last years of Sukarno were like, when Sukarno told Jakarta's residents that they could solve two problems, hunger and filth, by eating the city's huge and ravenous population of rats. In 1965 inflation in Indonesia was more than 500 per cent. Indonesians never want to endure a period like that again and Suharto's delivery to them of basic economic security has meant they are prepared to cut the New Order regime a lot of slack.

It is important, assessing Suharto's contribution to his nation, to stress the sheer scale of his achievements. He took over one of the poorest countries in the world, on the brink of famine, with a huge section of the society living below the meanest poverty line. By the mid-1980s Indonesia was self-sufficient in rice, an enormous step forward. Tens of millions of people were lifted out of poverty, which fell dramatically in relative and absolute terms. Suharto took over one of the poorest countries and transformed it by the mid-1990s into a country confidently expected to join the ranks of the NICs (Newly Industrialising Countries) in the coming decade, and with a per capita GNP approaching $US1000. Above all he restored order and coherence to government. He quickly cut inflation back to manageable proportions, which was essential to gaining international aid and international investment, both of which were vital in the country's later economic expansion.

He almost immediately abandoned Sukarno's adventurist and dangerous foreign policy, ending the lurch to the Chinese at a time of Cold War tension, ending the nearly insane confrontation with Malaysia, reassuring his Southeast Asian neighbours of Indonesia's stability and peaceful intent. He was critical in the formation of the Association of South East Asian Nations in 1967, and Indonesia has been the driving force in ASEAN, which has become one of the most constructive and consequential regional groupings in the world. At the same time he kept Indonesia out of military entanglements beyond its shores and he maintained, for Indonesia, the extremely useful double act throughout the Cold War of being formally non-aligned but effectively pro-western, thus gaining aid and political support from the United States without attracting much serious opposition from radical centres in the third world. Suharto also took Indonesia back into the United Nations, which Sukarno had left, and to a respected place in the international community.

Unlike most OPEC countries Indonesia managed its windfall oil wealth relatively sensibly, investing in infrastructure and industries which would give it a secure future. The economy was transformed from one totally dependent on agriculture and oil to a manufacturing powerhouse with an infinitely more diverse array of industries.

After the appalling blood letting which followed the attempted coup in 1965, race relations have been managed surprisingly well. There are spasmodic outbursts of anti-Chinese sentiment but on the whole the army clamps down on these very quickly, and Chinese Indonesians do not live with the kind of personal insecurity they did in the 1960s. More generally, Suharto has overseen a process of extraordinary national unification. Indonesia is the world's biggest archipelagic state, its island chain stretches for 5000 km. It is extremely diverse ethnically and culturally. A Balkans scenario, or much worse, was by no means impossible for Indonesia, in fact it still isn't. Establishing a sense of Indonesianness, a sense and a reality of national identity, has been a huge task, and a huge achievement of the Suharto years.

Generally, he has followed pragmatic economic and social policies, whatever may have been the state of intra-elite feuding and factionalism. He has successfully promoted family planning, as well as greatly expanding tertiary education. He has at all times kept a lid on Islamic fundamentalism so that in many ways Indonesia is, socially and religiously, one of the most liberal of the states which are overwhelmingly Islamic. The economy has averaged growth of better than 5 per cent a year under Suharto. It is no exaggeration to say that this has led to the birth of a new Indonesia, a native entrepreurial class, and a substantial middle class, numbering tens of millions. You only have to visit cities like the hustling, bustling Surabaya, awash with gleaming new buildings and gleaming new cars, to see the Indonesian middle class taking form virtually in front of your eyes.

These are not small achievements. They rank in the first order of any country's history. And the world is full of negative models which Indonesia might have followed—the Philippines under Marcos, Cuba under Castro, Myanmar under the SLORC. There was nothing pre-ordained about Indonesia's relative economic, social and international success since the mid-1960s. Suharto deserves full credit for these achievements.

Of course there is also a downside. The main downside of the Suharto years has been their consistently poor human rights performance, especially but not exclusively in East Timor. It is unclear even today exactly how deep a role the Indonesian Army played in the mass killings after the coup attempt in 1965 but it is clear that some hundreds of thousands of people, mostly Chinese, died. Similarly Jakarta's policies towards East Timor have been little short of disastrous. There was some justification for its initial moves against a Fretilin-led radical regime emerging in Dili, within the Indonesian archipelago, but its heavy-handed military rule since then has been both incompetent and brutal. It is true that Jakarta has allocated disproportionately large development funds to East Timor but these have not resulted in building a sense of legitimacy for its rule there. Worst of all was the massacre of large numbers of demonstrators in November 1991, an incident which the government acknowledges as a terrible tragedy and says was in no way representative of policy. The government's response to the massacre was better than its response to any previous incident. The president appointed the Djaelani Commission which rejected the military's initial claim that only nineteen people had been killed. It acknowledged instead that 50 had died and many more were missing and unaccounted for. Reliable sources in Jakarta at the time told me the true figure was nearer to 280 dead. Some soldiers were punished for their part in the massacre. This was hardly a satisfactory response but did indicate at least that the regime understood it had made a grave mistake in East Timor. But from that realisation little constructive policy has flowed.

More generally, however, Indonesia's human rights performance is poor. Some thousands of people were summarily killed in an anti-crime campaign in the early 1980s. Pancasila, the official state ideology, has been forced onto all groups, even religious groups, as their guiding idea. Political life has completely withered. The strict control of the press has surely gone beyond anything reasonably necessary to maintain order, or even the unchallenged rule of the present government. Corruption is so pervasive that the rule of law in even commercial settings, as well as more generally civic contexts, is extremely tenuous.

There is a great paradox about modern Indonesia. As it has grown more affluent it has become a far more sophisticated, diverse, outward-looking, well-informed, cosmopolitan society. You don't feel routinely under the thumb of the government in Jakarta, or Surabaya, or Bandung or Jogjakarta. More and more Indonesians travel overseas, for business or pleasure or education.

Jakarta has long run one of the region's most liberal 'open skies' policies on receiving foreign broadcasts. A new civic society is struggling, yearning to be born. Yet at every point the logical political expression of this new diversity is cut off. The state remains in a formal sense all-powerful, and power within the state, for such a vast state, is centred in the hands of very few people.

This was all brought home to me once when I was travelling for a few days in East Java as a guest of the information minister, Harmoko. Indonesian official tours have something of the flavour of old-style Chinese indoctrination tours. You seem to spend an awful lot of time in factories hearing more than you ever wanted to know about aeroplane manufacture, or local small goods distribution or whatever it is that the factory does. But at one particular factory visit on that tour we got more than anyone surely had bargained for. I won't identify the business involved, because that would seem to be tempting fate. We were visiting a medium-sized, local, family-owned factory. We were in the company of a group of Information Ministry officials. The factory manager was giving us the routine spiel about production techniques, distribution patterns and the rest. However, he said, his greatest difficulty was that one of his competitors is partly owned by the Family, and it's almost impossible to compete with the Family. What Family was he talking about? I naively asked. The president's family, of course. What astonished me about this tiny episode was how freely the factory manager spoke about this problem in front of government officials. The incident taught me that the business reach of the president's family is indeed vast and constitutes a massive problem which erodes the popular respect for the Suharto government. At the same time the mere fact that the factory manager would speak so freely about this problem to foreign journalists in the company of Information Ministry officials was a startling example of how free, in many ways, Indonesians feel themselves to be.

As I have noted earlier, no political or even commercial discussion in Indonesia goes for very long without the president, or his family, figuring in it. Yet despite the seeming ubiquity of the president in his nation's media, especially in the nightly news broadcasts, few leaders in Southeast Asia, and certainly no other leading figures in partly democratic societies, have remained so elusive, so little known in any intimate or personal sense as has Suharto. The Indonesian media is very delicate indeed in what it says about him and on the whole he just doesn't give interviews to foreign journalists.

But Suharto's personal journey is as remarkable as any in the world. He was born into absolute dirt poverty in Kemusuk village, near Jogjakarta, in Java, on June 8, 1921. He was the second of eleven children and his family was Muslim, and observantly so. Rather in the American fashion he has become fond of celebrating the poverty of his home and upbringing, evoking an Indonesian version of the Abraham Lincoln log-cabin-to-White-House legend. Suharto has always claimed, too, a special affinity with the poor peasant. In his autobiography he says he developed a great love of the soil during his childhood and in his mature years his cattle ranch has been one of his most loved possessions. Indonesian television often features scenes of Suharto giving kindly advice to a village farmer, a part, too, of the *bapak* father image he strives to cultivate. Similarly, a la Bill Clinton, his family life was troubled, and he has spoken and written freely of his childhood traumas. His parents separated and each remarried and the Suharto childhood was in many ways not only poor but unstable. It is an obvious and not unreasonable psychological leap to link this insecure childhood to the extraordinary indulgence and protectiveness which Suharto has shown his own children.

Suharto attended local schools. He lacks the formal education of many of his Cabinet colleagues and many of the senior people in the Indonesian bureaucracy. He went later to a military training establishment run by the Dutch and intended to make his career soldiering. For Suharto, as for many Southeast Asians, the Japanese occupation was a complex and mixed event. Many Southeast Asians at first welcomed the declared Japanese intention of liberating their lands from European colonialism. However, by the later stages of the war Suharto was active in the anti-Japanese resistance.

Suharto was a prominent military man in the campaign to oust the Dutch. His most singular action was in leading a successful assault on the Dutch forces in Jogjakarta in March 1949. He flung the Dutch out of the ancient cultural capital of

Indonesia and established a great cachet for himself in the process. Indonesians felt with complete justification that it was both a betrayal and a gross hypocrisy for the Dutch to attempt to reassert colonial rule after World War II. At this stage Australia, under Ben Chifley, supported Indonesian independence. Under Robert Menzies, sadly, we would revert to supporting European colonial rule and lose much of the goodwill we established in the early days, especially with Indonesia.

By 1950 Suharto was a colonel. In the early days of Indonesian independence there were often insufficient funds for soldiers. Military commanders more or less ran their own shows and Suharto had to generate funds to provide for his troops. It was this pattern of behaviour in the army, entirely understandable in the historical circumstances, which has partly lingered as corruption and partly lingered as the army having an often decisive involvement in local development and business affairs.

In the 1950s Suharto became friendly with two Chinese–Indonesian businessmen, Bob Hasan and Liem Sioe Liong, who were to become fantastically wealthy business leaders under Suharto's presidency, and to stay close to the president as part of his coterie of informal advisers and corporate associates. According to some reports, in the early days they helped him find the wherewithal to supply his troops.

Suharto's military career in the 1950s was successful but essentially routine until he was put in charge of the operation to take West Irian, the western half of the island of New Guinea, away from the Dutch. There were military engagements in this campaign but ultimately the Dutch went peacefully and Indonesia took control. The most dramatic and fateful moment in Suharto's career came in October 1965 when a coup attempt resulted in the assasination of some of the most senior officers in the army. It is still unclear, and will probably never be known exactly, what happened that night of October 1. Later, Suharto's New Order government would paint the coup as a straightforward bid for power by the Indonesian Communist Party, the PKI. In truth the full extent of the PKI's involvement is unclear although there is no doubt the PKI supported the coup attempt. It is also not absolutely plain what the coup plotters intended to do with Sukarno, whether in the end they intended to instal him as their figurehead or destroy him. In any event Suharto, the commander of the Army Strategic Command, swiftly destroyed the coup and took control.

It was a masterful performance by Suharto who gradually took power from Sukarno. Sukarno endured a state not too far distant from house arrest, over the next two years, with Suharto finally becoming president in 1968. In the aftermath of the coup attempt a terrible purge of PKI members and sympathisers took place. Most of these were Chinese, and the violence descended into gross anti-Chinese pogroms in parts of Indonesia. Muslim forces were heavily involved in the violence against the PKI, which had been one of the biggest communist parties in the world, and against Chinese more indiscriminately. Many local scores were settled which had little to do with ideology. This remains the blackest episode in Indonesian history and one Indonesians are determined never to repeat. It hovers like a shadow over much discussion of succession issues.

Suharto then had several years of consolidation in which his own power was uncertain, and of course entirely dependent on his control of the army. During these early years of the New Order, political debate, apart from the banished Left, was brisk. As Patrick Walters, the *Australian*'s correspondent in Jakarta, has pointed out, perhaps Suharto's most important single decision was handing the running of the economy over to the 'Berkeley mafia', a group of western-educated, mostly Christian technocrats who adopted orthodox and hard economic restructuring policies. The period of 1965 to 1968 in Indonesia is commonly cited as one of the great episodes in getting runaway inflation under control which the world has seen. And Indonesia's general economic turn around after the absolute despair of the pre-1965 period was nothing short of miraculous.

In December 1975 Suharto made the decision to invade and annex East Timor. Indonesia's subsequent policies on East Timor have been very poorly executed. The invasion itself was an extreme mess. But in truth Suharto's options were limited. In 1974 the Portuguese colonial government in East Timor had cut and run. The isolated and utterly undeveloped province descended quickly into civil war. The Marxist group, Fretilin, which consciously modelled itself on the murderous African Frelimo group (which had terrorised Angola), declared a People's Republic of East Timor, fully conscious of all the appalling connotations of such a name. Fretilin gained the upper hand in the bloody civil war that followed. This was at the height of the Cold War, with communist insurgencies active throughout Southeast Asia, in the year of the fall of Saigon, the fall of Phnom Penh, the fall of Vientiane. Suharto decided that he could not have a Cuba on his doorstep, inside the Indonesian archipelago, and invaded, and East Timor has been a problem for Indonesia with the international community ever since.

Throughout the 1970s Suharto consolidated political power. The Opposition parties were forced to merge into two small parties which were subsequently forced to adopt Pancasila (which stresses religious tolerance, belief in one God, social justice, humanitarianism, nationalism and democracy) as their guiding ideology. The army, and the vastly empowered bureaucracy, became instruments of political power. Civil servants were subsumed into a subgrouping of Golkar, the ruling regime's political vehicle. The army had 100 seats of its own in the parliament. Islamic groups were effectively prevented from seeking any strong political expression. By the early 1980s Suharto's position was unchallengeable.

The increasing wealth of Indonesia, and the increasing power of the state, meant that Suharto's government acquired vast powers of patronage, and that is really how it ruled. The late 1980s saw Indonesia's increased affluence lead apparently to increased liberalisation. But Arief Budiman, a leading Indonesian sociologist and critic of the government, argued in the early 1990s that liberalisation could take three forms. It could be licensed liberalisation, in which the regime feels so secure that it doesn't mind a bit of tame criticism. It could be liberalisation resulting from conflicts within the elite, as on occasion between Suharto and the army. Or it could be real democratisation. It now seems in hindsight that a lot of what was encouraging in the late '80s and early '90s was an expression of the first two kinds of liberalisation.

I have never been granted a one-on-one interview with Suharto. These are very rare. But beyond Suharto the Indonesian government is very accessible at Cabinet level to foreign journalists and I have had long conversations with numerous ministers and past ministers—Ali Alatas, Benny Murdani, B.J. Habibie, Hartoto, Harmoko, all figures very familiar and very accessible around the region. None is more accessible than Indonesia's long-serving foreign minister, Ali Alatas, the longest serving foreign minister in Southeast Asia, and by far the most influential.

A career diplomat who served as his nation's ambassador at the UN immediately prior to becoming foreign minister, Alatas, with his classical education and his linguistic fluency, is the perfect foreign minister for Indonesia. He is clearly a liberal within the regime and is, during the bad times, as in the aftermath of the Dili massacre, able to put the best and most credible face on Indonesia's government, while in the good times he can convert Indonesia's vast size into effective diplomatic influence. In the past few years Suharto has taken up the mantle of international statesman, chairing the Non-Aligned Movement (NAM) and seeking to address the summit of the Group of Seven (G7). NAM is lucky to have leadership like that provided by Indonesia though I am not so sure that Indonesia really benefits much from its association with NAM, with its backward-looking agenda of debt forgiveness and whingeing about the developed world. But the developing world does have a case that its concerns are being marginalised in the post–Cold War world and Indonesia has put this case strongly at international forums. The G7's refusal to allow Suharto to address it, while allowing Boris Yeltsin a permanent, burlesque gate-crashing role, is a sign of contempt and disregard for the third world. In all of these activities Alatas has grown close to Suharto, generally travelling with the president, and certainly serving as his chief source of advice, when they do travel together. In this Alatas has been able to leverage his good international name into significant domestic influence, even though as an arm of the bureaucracy, the Foreign Ministry is not particularly well regarded in comparison with some of the economic ministries.

The first time I met Alatas for a long, private interview was at the ASEAN summit in Singapore in early 1992. I had written, completely wrongly as it turned out, that Alatas had been gravely damaged at home, and may not even have long to go as foreign minister, because of the Dili massacre in November 1991. This was because Alatas had sponsored the proposed visit of a

Portuguese delegation which had been blamed for increasing the tension in the lead-up to the massacre. Alatas began our interview by saying that he read my articles on Indonesia with interest and agreed with most of what I had written.

Like a fool I asked him which parts he disagreed with. 'The part where you say who was up and who was down in Indonesian politics,' he replied with just that small, dry smile he sometimes gives. I couldn't imagine an Australian politician reacting quite so gracefully, in quite so measured and restrained a fashion, to a journalist who had virtually said his career was finished. But that was Alatas all over—urbanity, charm, and generally great patience with the journalistic community.

At that time Australia and Indonesia were still caught up in the aftermath of the Dili massacre and Alatas and I discussed at some length the Indonesian–Australian relationship. Although in every sense a moderate, Alatas certainly had some complaints about the Australian media. His response to the Australian media is instructive of Indonesia's response to the west generally. Indeed some Indonesians argue that Australia, as a part of the west which is small enough to be non-threatening but close enough to be interested, is a useful partner for Indonesia, as it learns to cope with the wider western agenda emerging from North America and Western Europe. In recent years this view has become even more important to Indonesians, who have seen an Australian prime minister (Paul Keating) argue Indonesia's case effectively in Washington. Similarly, it was this thinking in part which lay behind Indonesia's decision to break with all its own strategic doctrine and enter into its first mutual security treaty with Australia in late 1995.

That day in Singapore Alatas was remarkably frank in acknowledging the dangers posed by hardliners within Jakarta's government. Exaggerated Australian criticism of Indonesia, he claimed, strengthened the hand of those hardliners. He said the Indonesian government fully accepted that the killings in Dili were tragic and must never be repeated. He acknowledged that the killings were totally unacceptable and that something had gone terribly wrong. He said: 'We accept that [Indonesian soldiers] did something wrong.' However, he claimed that in Australian media reporting of the incident there had been insufficient reporting of

the views of the Indonesian government. There had been little
weight given to the Djaelani judicial inquiry. Moreover, he said,
'our president has publicly apologised three times. If you continue
to criticise us even when we do the right thing, you only
strengthen those who say, "Look, even if you do the right thing
they still criticise you. Let them go fish."'

Alatas emphasised that he was not critical of all the Australian
media. But he believed some parts of it were neither balanced
nor fair:

> Our [the government's] views were not given the same weight.
> It's as if they did not exist. This is not an apologia for what
> happened [in Timor] but there is a need to provide balance.
> There was provocation, the demonstration became rather wild,
> it strained the restraint of young, inexperienced soldiers . . .
> there was some involvement of foreigners. All we ask is
> balance. We know what to expect from journalists, from a free
> press, but there should still be balance . . . we are reasonable
> people, don't portray us as wild things.

He also expressed concerns about demonstrations against
Indonesian diplomatic missions in Australia and industrial action
taken against them, something that has been a recurring sore in
Australian–Indonesian relations:

> I must frankly admit that we were deeply worried by the
> pickets and by the erection of East Timorese structures that
> were put in front of the embassy for weeks on end.
> Demonstrations we understand. These happen in all countries.
> We do understand your democracy and how it works. But
> pickets are something else.

He had finally told his Australian counterpart, Senator Gareth
Evans, that pickets and industrial actions preventing the delivery
of mail and other services to the embassy were in breach of the
Geneva Agreement on Diplomatic Missions, which also provided
that the dignity of diplomatic missions be protected.

For all that, Alatas remained, correctly as it turned out, an
optimist on Indonesia–Australia relations. He was at the time
involved in negotiating Prime Minister Keating's first visit to
Indonesia. He had collaborated with Gareth Evans on the Timor
Gap Treaty, which allowed for the joint development of mineral

resources lying between Australia and Indonesia, and on the Cambodian peace settlement, in which both foreign ministers were critical players. I asked him about his friendship with Evans and he recalled that they were both appointed foreign ministers at about the same time:

> He made a visit to Indonesia and I made one to Australia and we clicked. The first thing he said to me was: 'Why don't we stop making a fuss about the relationship—always taking the pulse all the time? We should just get on with it, and build up the positive side, build the pillars of the relationship.' I said, 'I'm game. You do it on your side and I'll do it on mine.'

His final words on the bilateral relationship were encouraging: 'We are neighbours, we are very close geographically, let's make the best of it.'

Alatas's views on the Australia–Indonesia relationship were representative of what became common ground in the Jakarta elite, a view both friendly and at times critical, but seeing Australia as a natural partner in the region if political differences could be overcome. The ASEAN summit in 1992 was an important meeting at which it was decided to embark on the ASEAN free trade area and to develop ASEAN as the vehicle for a new region-wide security dialogue body. Alatas stressed to me that day the need for security solutions to be generated within the region rather than being imposed from the outside. Within ASEAN he was very much the elder statesman. At times he would slap down those he thought were getting a bit uppity. He grew very impatient with the way Malaysia pushed its East Asia Economic Caucus concept, which Indonesia was quite ambivalent about. He had to carry Jakarta's completely unreasonable argument that the Philippines should ban a conference on East Timor. But mostly he was the voice of sweet reason, the best face Indonesia could present to the outside world and a voice for moderation within the highest councils of the Indonesian government.

In another contentious episode with Australia he was a key interlocutor. When the redoubtable Indonesian ambassador and former journalist, Sabam Siagian left Canberra to go back to Indonesia, Jakarta nominated Lieutenant-General Herman Mantiri to replace him. It turned out that Mantiri had made some extreme and highly distasteful remarks on the Dili massacre and an uproar broke out in Australia about his appointment. Although the Australian government had given formal agreement to Mantiri's appointment Evans in effect began a public campaign to persuade the Indonesians to withdraw the appointment. Very frequently during that period he was on the phone to Alatas, who bore it all stoically enough. Alatas was eventually instrumental in getting Jakarta to withdraw Mantiri and send a senior career diplomat instead.

Alatas a few years later would suffer serious heart trouble and choose to undergo surgery in Australia. He had been a good friend of Evans's but the evidence is their relationship soured somewhat in the last years of the Keating government in Australia. But Alatas remained a good friend of Australia's and was delighted with the relationship President Suharto developed with then Prime Minister Keating. Alatas also became a foreign recipient of the Order of Australia. He seemed however to be sidelined on one of Suharto's grandest initiatives, the free trade declaration at the APEC Bogor summit in 1994, and he became a fraction more irascible after his heart surgery but he remained hugely influential, both within Indonesia and throughout the region.

His role as a moderate within Indonesia's government is insufficiently recognised. One private incident illustrates the point. In early 1992 Alatas had a meeting with the top brass of the Indonesian navy. A protest vessel was due to sail from Darwin to East Timor to dramatise Indonesia's occupation of East Timor. 'How are you going to handle it?' Alatas asked the navy. 'Don't worry, we'll handle it,' the navy replied. 'That's not good enough. I need to know exactly what you are going to do,' Alatas said, perhaps not in those exact words but in words to that effect. The navy eventually surrounded, and peacefully warned off, the protest boat as it neared Indonesia's waters. There was no drama, no injury, no damage to Indonesia's international reputation. This is just one of literally hundreds of occasions when Alatas has had not only to represent Indonesia to the world but to mediate the international community's expectations back to the military-dominated elite in Jakarta.

My personal introduction to a man who has been at the very centre of that military elite, Benny Murdani, was much more prickly. It was the very end of 1991. I was in Indonesia to cover

a three-day visit by Gareth Evans. His trip was a consequence of
an Australian Labor Party caucus resolution demanding tough
action by Canberra in response to the Dili massacre. It was a
tense and forlorn trip. Evans was treated politely but coldly, being
denied appointments with President Suharto, and with the then
commander of the armed forces, Try Sutrisno, and the defence
minister, Benny Murdani. On the day Evans arrived in Jakarta
Paul Keating deposed Bob Hawke as prime minister. At the
beginning of the day Evans did not know who his prime minister
would be, nor even who Australia's foreign minister would be, at
the end of the day. We Australian journalists accompanying Evans
were all given just three-day visas and required to go into Jakarta
on the same plane as the foreign minister. The tension in the
trip was everywhere apparent—in Evans's truncated schedule, in
the long lecture he was delivered by Moerdiono, one of Suharto's
closest Cabinet colleagues, in the criticism of Australian meddling
in Indonesian politics. Even we travelling hacks were caught up
in the tension. Evans left Jakarta early on the morning of the
third day of the visit. Because access by Australian journalists to
Indonesia was so limited in those days I decided to go out on
an afternoon flight, and spend the day talking to people. When
I got to the airport, however, the soldier who checked my passport
decided that although I had spent three nights in Jakarta I had
actually spent four days there and had thus breached the terms
of my visa. As he cradled his rifle he led me away to a small
detention room where I was told to sit and wait. I had a letter
from the Australian embassy stating that in its opinion I had
complied with the terms of the visa and this was taken away as
my immediate fate was considered. I was only detained for about
40 minutes or so and allowed to board my scheduled plane. But
I found the experience unnerving. It further demonstrated to me
something I have long known about myself, I tend to do as I'm
told pretty meekly when the person telling me is carrying a gun.

For all the tension of the visit Evans did manage to get the
human rights dimension of the Dili tragedy back on every
Indonesian front page, and at or near the lead of every Indonesian news broadcast, for the duration of his stay. He was received
by three Cabinet ministers, among them his good friend Alatas,

but was clearly snubbed by being denied access to Suharto, Sutrisno and Murdani.

In terms of access to Murdani I was a bit luckier than Evans on that trip, owing entirely to the remarkable personality and friendship of Indonesia's then ambassador to Australia, Sabam Siagian. Siagian, a former editor of the *Jakarta Post*, was a phenomenon in Australian diplomatic history. He was the most successful ambassador Indonesia has ever sent to Australia, energetic, engaging and utterly at ease dealing with the robust Australian press. He always acknowledged Indonesia's problems but put the best case possible for his country. He was also determined to create personal linkages between Indonesia and Australia. On the last night of my stay in Jakarta on that visit I was rather desultorily watching television in my hotel room. The air-conditioning was arctic and I was suffering the beginnings of what was to become an epic episode of tummy trouble familiar to western travellers in Indonesia.

While the air-conditioning in my room was freezing, the Jakarta night outside was dense, humid and tropical, oppressively hot and full of possibility. The phone rang. It was an Indonesian journalist friend to tell me that Sabam would like me to join him for dinner. Would I meet him at the Jakarta Hilton at 7 p.m.? Of course I readily agreed. The ambassador and I were joined by a couple of other Indonesians. We crowded into a car and drove out to a spacious villa on the edge of town, for a small dinner party of about a dozen or fifteen people, most of whom were associated vaguely with the Centre for Strategic and International Studies, as well as some from the now-banned *Tempo* magazine and one or two businessmen. The CSIS was traditionally the most important think tank in Indonesia. In fact it was much more than a think tank. As is the way in numerous Southeast Asian countries it was really a semi-government body, with some of the best strategic and economic thinkers in the nation attached to it. Because of its think-tank status it could be intellectually far more adventurous than any government department, but it had direct and powerful access to the decision makers. It conducted a great deal of what is known as 'second-track' diplomacy, that is, semi-official negotiations and consultations, on behalf of the government. It lobbied for Indonesia with important foreigners. It also reported their views back to Jakarta. Its bosses were powerful figures in Indonesia. But the CSIS was very closely associated with Murdani. As his eventual eclipse was engineered by Suharto, so the CSIS lost some of its influence, although the sheer quality of its work, and its panoply of foreign and domestic connections, meant it remained important.

The guest of honour that night was General Benny Murdani. My Indonesian journalist friend told me as we walked up to the front door that Murdani's people had not wanted a foreigner, certainly not an Australian journalist, at that dinner. They had in fact refused permission for my attendance. Stay near the ambassador and don't ask any questions, was my friend's advice. When he first saw me Murdani glowered with displeasure. This man was a military legend in Indonesia. He had planned the invasion of East Timor. He had reportedly challenged Suharto about his family's business practices. He was revered within ABRI. As a Catholic within a Muslim country he could never be president himself but he was enormously influential. It was said that after Sutrisno became vice-president he had to force himself to resist an urge to salute Murdani. Should Sutrisno ever become president it was assumed that Murdani would have immense influence. Should there be a crisis over the succession it was expected that Murdani would play a key role. All of which made the look of rock-hard hostility which came into his face when he saw me that night somewhat disconcerting.

'Is this man from the *Sydney Morning Herald*?' Murdani asked. (The *Herald* had a few years earlier run a piece on the first family's business activities which had enraged the Jakarta government.) On being assured that I was not from that publication Murdani was gradually placated. To my astonishment the evening developed into one of lengthy, relaxed and intimate conversation about the political situation Jakarta was facing. The group thus informally gathered seemed to have one overriding message for Murdani, whom they referred to respectfully as *Pak* Benny: there had to be a credible and broadly humane response to the massacre. Indonesia's international reputation was on the line. The Japanese, one of the dinner guests said, had told him that if the Europeans withdrew their aid from Indonesia in protest at the killings, the Japanese could probably continue to give

Indonesia the level of assistance it traditionally gave. But if the Americans withdrew aid the Japanese would probably be left in an unsustainable situation and would have to withdraw, or at the least greatly curtail, aid to Jakarta. And there was likely to be heavy pressure against Indonesia in the American Congress. I could see the purpose of the evening. One liberal part of the Jakarta elite was telling the government at the highest level that it must handle its response to the Dili massacre decently. I suspect that a lot of political consultation, a lot of what might be termed informal democratic process, occurs at occasions much like that which I attended that night in Jakarta.

Murdani is a phenomenon in Indonesian politics. He is known as a military tough guy who also has an appreciation of the complexities of domestic and international politics. He is also known as one of the few men to have challenged Suharto and maintained his influence. Suharto has moved against Murdani twice. In the late 1980s Suharto moved Murdani out of the post of commander of the armed forces and into the Defence Ministry. In fact this was a demotion because the defence minister's job is essentially ceremonial—the real power lies with the commander of the armed forces. Some analysts have speculated that Suharto did not want Murdani directly in control of troops. But Murdani was a hero and father figure to many in ABRI, he fully maintained his influence as defence minister. Moreover, although a military tough guy Murdani was often seen as the protector of minorities within Indonesia, perhaps because he was a Catholic. Suharto's move against Murdani in 1993 was more decisive, removing him from the Cabinet altogether and putting ABRI through a process of 'de-Bennification', getting rid of many of 'Benny's boys' from the most senior positions. But Murdani retains enormous informal influence. Should Sutrisno one day become president, which is still probably at least an even-money bet, Murdani's influence would rise dramatically again.

He is not without a certain droll sense of humour, either. When Keating made his first visit to Indonesia as prime minister he was a neophyte in international relations, but he knew that Murdani was a political sex symbol and he wanted a meeting with him. In this meeting Keating, who masters a brief well, sketched a strategic overview for Murdani, who said little. At the end of Keating's strategic outline Murdani lent forward and said words to the effect, well, Prime Minister, I can see you and I have something in common. Keating's interest quickened. Had he once more exercised his powerful charm, made another convert to the cause? Was Murdani enchanted by the clarity and brilliance of Keating's strategic overview? We both, said Murdani, married airline hostesses! Not exactly what Keating had had in mind perhaps, but Keating was equal to the situation, coming back with his own droll remark that they also had in common the fact that they were both Catholics in non-Catholic countries.

However, while Murdani polishes his golf game, dotes on his daughter, travels widely and remains a potentially decisive force in a crisis, he is now more sidelined than ever before in Indonesian politics and once more Suharto has removed from the national stage a figure whose strength of personality offered at least some implicit challenge.

But removing alternative leaders of quality is not the way to prepare your society for succession and transition. Failing to address the succession question remains a significant failure of Suharto's recent years and a growing challenge for the future.

Covering his bets after his troubles with sections of the ABRI leadership, Suharto has in recent years cultivated a more self-consciously Muslim identity. In 1991 he made his first pilgrimage to Mecca. He favours and indulges his eccentric technology minister, B.J. Habibie, who heads the Organisation of Islamic Intellectuals, ICMI, while the state apparatus has put the far more independent Abdurrahman Wahid, of the Nahdlathul Ulama, under some pressure. Some liberal Indonesians worry about Suharto turning Islam on and off like a tap. It has always been a central tenet of the New Order that Islam was to be subordinated as a political force in the interests of national unity. ICMI figures did well in the Cabinet reshuffle of 1993, although they were mostly moderate ICMI figures, not radicals.

Much of Suharto's efforts in recent years have been involved in international issues—chairing the Non-Aligned Movement, trying to interest the G7 in third world issues, cutting a figure at the UN. One of his most remarkable efforts, however, was his leadership of the Asia Pacific Economic Cooperation summit in 1994 at Bogor. Substantially because of his leadership the leaders of the eighteen APEC economies agreed to commit themselves 'to complete the achievement of the goal of free and open trade and investment in the Asia Pacific no later than the year 2020, with the pace of implementation to take into account differing levels of economic development among APEC economies, with the industrialised economies to achieve the goal no later than 2010 and developing economies no later than 2020.'

It is unclear in the long march of history how much this declaration will achieve. But if the region does go down the free trade route it is likely that the Bogor meeting will be regarded as pivotal. Moreover, simply getting such a diverse group of such powerful leaders from such major economies (the United States, Japan, China, Korea, Canada, Australia etc.) to sign up to such a goal was a significant achievement. It was certainly at the very least a huge political boost to the momentum of regional trade liberalisation. And really it was all a consequence of Suharto's leadership. He massaged Malaysia's prime minister, Dr Mahathir into attending Bogor after Mahathir had boycotted the first APEC summit the previous year in Seattle. Suharto was perhaps the only Southeast Asian leader who would have had the stature to do this. Similarly he overrode Mahathir's late objections to the wording of the leaders' declaration and an attempt by Mahathir to add a qualifying statement. Suharto smoothed the way for the declaration with all the other Southeast Asian leaders who were naturally a bit cautious and shaky about making such a vast commitment with such huge partners as the US, Japan and China. But Suharto also handled the US well, enticing an increased investment from American leaders, especially Clinton, in the APEC process. And he overcame the hesitation, if not downright opposition, of members of his own Cabinet and the Indonesian bureaucracy, among both of whom were to be found plenty of old-fashioned protectionists and other more agnostic types who were still extremely cautious about such a bold free trade declaration. The whole performance was a triumph for Suharto and for the personalised diplomacy with which he went about securing the Bogor outcome.

Those who know him well say Suharto is essentially a shy, private person, with a strong streak of traditional Javanese mysticism tempering his Islamic identity. He likes to play golf, speaks

Dutch well and English moderately, as well as Javanese and Bahasa Indonesian. He is in good health for a Javanese of his age although associates say, naturally, that he is slower than before. He is the quintessential Javanese, avoiding confrontation and achieving his ends indirectly where possible. Arief Budiman was quoted in a press interview in 1995 as describing him thus: 'He knows his enemies. He never attacks frontally. He moves slowly and surely and then strikes, suddenly and abruptly.' In his autobiography Suharto characteristically refers to the guiding lights of his life as 'three don'ts': 'Don't be easily surprised, don't be overwhelmed by anything and don't overestimate your position.'

Suharto must eventually deal with succession, and with the place of his family in national and business life. Some analysts believe his daughter, Siti Hardiyanti Rukmana, is destined for big things politically, but certainly Indonesia does not need a dynasty.

Despite the abuses and the excesses Suharto's careeer can be reckoned a mighty success. He is a leader who has truly done great things for his nation and his people. But how he now plays the endgame, whether Indonesia can get through a presidential succession without bloodshed or social division, with its sensible economic and social policies intact, and surely with a more representative political system, will have a huge bearing on how history ultimately judges him.

5

PAUL KEATING AND JOHN HOWARD: AUSTRALIA INTO ASIA WITH THE DYNAMIC DUO

PAUL KEATING AND THE AUSTRALIAN CULTURAL REVOLUTION

In 1993 Paul Keating introduced Bill Clinton to Indonesia, in an episode that explains much of Keating's success in Asia and his vision for Australia, and the region. In the run-up to the Seattle summit of the Asia Pacific Economic Cooperation forum in 1993 Australia's prime minister, Paul Keating, had a scheduled meeting with the new US president, Bill Clinton. After the meeting one of the first things Clinton said at their joint press conference was that it would be foolish to ignore Indonesia and that the two men had discussed Indonesia at some length. On the same visit Keating said publicly that the US should moderate its human rights pressure on Indonesia and see human rights as one strand among many in its relationship with Jakarta, a remark which one Indonesian Cabinet minister described as 'music to our ears'.

But these public manifestations were only a small part of the high-powered regional diplomacy that Keating engaged in on that visit. Keating had in 1992 himself first proposed that APEC national leaders should meet (at that stage APEC was a very loose grouping of Asian, Australasian and North American economic and foreign ministers meeting for the purpose of economic dialogue). This, in Keating's own elegant language, would give APEC more 'horsepower'. When Clinton took up the proposal as his own Keating was absolutely delighted. But the initial response to the Clinton initiative in Southeast Asia was lukewarm at best. The then Thai prime minister, Chuan Leekpai, made a very equivocal statement, Malaysia was outright hostile, other Southeast Asians were very quiet and there was a worry, throughout ASEAN capitals, that they may be swamped by developments in APEC, the influence of ASEAN diluted and the agenda of the big powers, particularly America, become dominant.

At the same time, the new US administration of President Bill Clinton had Asians thoroughly spooked. It was engaged in rancorous trade disputes with China and Japan and in a range of disputes with Southeast Asian nations. It was putting pressure on Indonesia over East Timor, labour rights and a range of other, lesser issues which it was threatening to link to trade. Keating used his meeting with Clinton to press ahead with the APEC agenda. Indonesia's President Suharto, Keating told Clinton, was such a 'big figure' in Southeast Asia that APEC could not succeed without his active and willing participation. In the words of one impeccably placed source: 'Keating told Clinton, you've got to look after Suharto.' Keating argued to Clinton that he should try to engage Suharto and his giant country constructively, not allow various arms of his administration to put pressure on Jakarta in an uncoordinated and counterproductive way. In any event, if Clinton wanted Seattle to succeed he would have to take care of Suharto.

Keating was so engrossed by what he saw as an APEC window of opportunity that he made an unscheduled stop in Jakarta, where he saw President Suharto on the briefest of working visits. He had two crucial messages for the Indonesian president. First, he wanted Suharto to know exactly what he had said to Clinton. So Keating brought with him and gave to Suharto copies of the official diplomatic transcript of his conversation with President Clinton. Second, he wanted to sell Suharto on the benefits of APEC and the proposed APEC leaders' meeting. American pressure over issues such as human rights, labour rights and the environment was unavoidable, Keating told Suharto. The end of the Cold War and the new dynamics in American and international politics made this inevitable. But APEC offered Indonesia a framework in which to moderate and absorb this pressure, to multilateralise it, make it more civil. An American president simply cannot go Asia-bashing in quite the same way he otherwise might if he is preparing to meet the Asian heads of government.

It was a masterful and effective performance by Keating and must be one of the few occasions in Australian diplomatic history when an Australian prime minister has engaged in effective shuttle diplomacy with the leaders of the world's largest and fourth largest nations. (Keating had adopted the coalition building strategy from his earliest days in office. When he first publicly raised the idea of having APEC meet at a heads-of-government level he had privately canvassed the matter in advance with President Bush, President Suharto and Prime Minister Miyazawa of Japan, the leaders of the three countries he saw as critical to the idea being translated into reality.) The 1993 episode with Suharto and Clinton tells us a lot about Keating's prime ministership, in both substance and style. In substance it shows us that he thought the Indonesian relationship was central for Australia, that he thought the American relationship was also still critical and an asset for Australia in East Asia, and that he accorded the highest priority to APEC. In style it reveals Keating as the quintessential political manipulator, always trying to build a coalition behind his position, always seeking a common interest, a point of leverage he could work on. It reveals too the essentially holistic cast of Keating's mind, a mind which always sees what Henry Kissinger would call 'the linkages'. Of course Keating made plenty of mistakes in his conduct of Australian foreign policy, but no Australian prime minister has been more ambitious in his foreign policy. No Australian prime minister has ever put Asia, specifically East Asia, so much at the heart of Australian life.

Like many Australian political journalists, I feel as though I know Keating fairly well. Certainly I've had plenty of conversations with him. But this is a feeling shared by many Australians from various walks of life who have never even met Keating face to face. Keating's personality is so striking, and his role in Australian politics has taken place over so many years, that he is a familiar psychological presence to Australians, whether they like him or not.

In one of my first conversations with Keating at an Australian Labor Party national conference in the early 1980s, I was introducing myself and explaining who I was when Keating cut in and said: 'Oh, don't worry, I know all about you, I've had a swab done on you.' It was typical Keating—the automatic assumption of intimacy, in this case in a moderately friendly if fairly crude way, the striking metaphor, the automatic placement of his interlocutor in an inferior psychological position. These have been formidable traits of Keating throughout his career, a key to his success. Keating certainly has a remarkable love of and ability to use language, to fashion it into a devastating political weapon. For example, for a time when he was treasurer (the post known in most countries as finance minister), Keating was confronted by an opposite number who blushed easily. As a result Keating took to referring to him in the parliament as 'old Rosy', words which always provoked the blush to which they referred. On another occasion he famously asked of Andrew Peacock, renowned more as a flashy playboy than a leader of real substance, in his second stint as Opposition leader: 'Can a soufflé rise twice?' Such Keating sayings are endless. He once described another Opposition leader, John Hewson, as 'a shiver looking for a spine to wriggle up'.

Commenting once on a television interview that the leader of the National Party, Tim Fischer, had given, Keating said: 'It reminded me of Muhammad Ali's phrase when he had someone on the ropes: "rope a dope" he called it.' He frequently characterised Hewson's successor as Opposition leader (and now prime minister), John Howard, as a relic from the 1950s. Speaking of Howard and Hewson together once, and linking them to the proposal to turn Canberra's old Parliament House into a museum, he said: 'We thought we could basically put some of the cultural icons of the 1950s down there: the Morphy Richards toaster, the Qualcast mower, a pair of heavily protected slippers, the Astor TV, the AWA radiogram and, of course, the honourable member for Wentworth [Hewson] and the honourable member for Bennelong [Howard] could go there as well. When the kids come and look at them they will say, "Gee, Mum, is that what it was like then?" and the two Johns can say, "No, kids. This is the future."'

Because Hewson was Opposition leader when Keating became prime minister he drew many of Keating's most memorable lines. Keating once said of him: 'This is only zealotry. This is the feral abacus at his best. So listen to me, brother: You will be sorry you ever heard the word tax when I have finished with you.'

That was very much another aspect of Keating's use of language, the sheer psychological intensity of it, the often raw, often enough ugly, note of intimidation. Asked once by Hewson why he would not call an early election Keating said: 'The answer is, mate, because I want to do you slowly. There has to be a bit of sport in this for all of us.' Perhaps most savage of all was when John Howard was Opposition leader and one of his front-benchers made an attack, wholly unjustified, on Keating's personal life. Keating's response was to tell Howard that from that day forward he would 'wear his leadership like a crown of thorns'.

Keating's use of language has also been utterly Australian. He has used his gift of metaphor not only to create striking and memorable images—which often dominate the headlines the next day and sometimes, as in the soufflé rising twice, characterise their subject forever more. He has also used these metaphors to make his opponents the subject of ridicule and derision. But he also uses them to subject his opponents to a debilitatingly intense psychological exchange. Keating has been perhaps the most intense politician Australia has seen.

His time as prime minister was a revelation. There had been little really in his previous career to prepare observers for what became the major themes of that prime ministership—Australia's engagement with Asia, reconciliation with its Aboriginal community on the basis of recognising native title to land, the promotion of Australia severing its links with the British monarch and becoming a republic, the promotion of a distinctive Australian identity, the further internationalisation of both the economy and the society more generally, a greater recognition of the role of the arts in national life and the traditional social democratic aim of maintaining a social safety net under the disadvantaged.

Keating was born in 1944 and grew up in the Bankstown area of Sydney, a working-class to middle-class area regarded as neither inner city nor a distant suburb. He was born into an orthodox Labor-supporting family, though not one that was particularly active. He was born and has always remained a Catholic. For such a public person Keating is private about some things. Certainly his spiritual life, and his family life, fall into that category. But his Catholic identity has been important to him. It was the basis of the social network of the Sydney right wing of the Labor Party to which he automatically gravitated, it seems to have fuelled his republicanism, and it has perhaps helped give him a slight chip on his shoulder about the Anglo-Australian establishment. He attended the De LaSalle Brothers School at Bankstown, but did not complete high school until later, while at work, when he did the final requisite subjects. He never attended university but became active in Young Labor in his teens. He was ruthlessly ambitious and effective, forming alliances that would remain intact for his entire life, quickly reaching elective office in Young Labor and entering parliament by his mid-twenties.

He was briefly appointed a junior minister in the last days of the Whitlam government in 1975. Labor was then in Opposition from the end of 1975 to 1983. Keating played several roles for the Labor Party in that period. He was the chief attack dog for Labor in parliament and as spokesman for minerals and energy he helped rebuild Labor's links to the business community. He was also elected president of the New South Wales state branch of the ALP. The Labor power brokers did this mainly to have a high profile and successful national politician in the job, and so stop the Left from taking over, at a time of uncharacteristic weakness for the Right.

Before he became prime minister, Keating made his chief impression on the country as treasurer. He was regarded as effective but somewhat narrow, a misjudgment which can now be seen as a function of Keating's extraordinary intensity in any job that he does. As treasurer, Keating dominated the government and always came across as supremely self-confident. It wasn't always so. Keating was appointed shadow treasurer in January 1983, when Labor was still in Opposition, in a fruitless attempt by the then leader, Bill Hayden, to shore up his leadership by revitalising his front bench. Keating was at first reluctant to take on the job and uncertain in his first months as treasurer, after Bob Hawke, having replaced Hayden, defeated Malcolm Fraser in the 1983 election. At first as treasurer Keating was cautious and worked hard just learning. But soon the flaming inferno of Keating's ego, combined with, it must be said, brilliant parliamentary and other public performance, cast all shyness and reticence aside. It was a very similar sequence to his development as a foreign policy–oriented prime minister.

Keating was certainly dynamic as treasurer. In a policy sense he came to dominate the Hawke government. Keating was treasurer from 1983 to 1991 and in that time he really established himself in the Australian psyche in three distinct roles. First, and perhaps most important, was the traditional politician, completely in love with the business of politics, happy in the company of journalists, switched on intellectually by policy, switched on emotionally by combat, (both conflict between the parties and within his own party), above all in love with power and the use that could be made of power, convinced of the futility of not using power if you had it. Keating once remarked that it made pretty good sense, when you were establishing who was boss, to go out in the middle of the road, find some appropriate target passing by and give him a bloody good belting. It solved a lot of problems later.

Second, he was a powerful economic reformer, one of the greatest agents of change the federal treasury has ever seen. He reversed 100 years of Australian economic policy, and he did it from a party which was rarely in power and therefore unused to its pressures and opportunities, a party which owed its birth and previous *raison d'être* to the maintenance of much of the old economic order and which had in fact traditionally campaigned against the direction of reform Keating was championing. This was no mean feat.

And third Keating established himself as something of a unique cultural icon, originally the essential 1950s man from a working-class, Catholic background, with hardly any formal education who somehow or other remained true to all that while completely updating himself to be the embodiment of contemporary policy attitudes.

Keating can be credited as treasurer with nothing less than internationalising the Australian economy. In December 1983 he floated the Australian dollar, initially against some strong advice from senior echelons of the treasury department. In June the next year he convinced the national conference of the ALP to allow the entry of foreign banks. In February 1985, he announced the entry of fifteen foreign banks into Australia. These were momentous changes for the ALP, reversing the direction of its economic policies which had prevailed virtually unchanged since federation in 1901.

In the early years of his stint as treasurer he was anything but unpopular. In September 1984, the magazine *Euromoney* named him finance minister of the year, a title which would lead to his being hailed as 'the world's greatest treasurer', a title that would become ironic only in the later years, in the depth of recession. Keating's first two budgets as treasurer were expansionary, traditional Labor budgets. But the growing level of foreign debt convinced him of the need to increase national savings and the main instrument for government to achieve this was fiscal policy. So he turned around the situation of a growing federal deficit and produced four successive budget surpluses.

Keating suffered a defeat at the 1985 tax summit when he was unable to construct a consensus in favour of a consumption tax. Australia continues to rely too heavily on taxing income and savings and too little on taxing consumption. But he did broaden the tax base substantially by introducing, against great opposition, a capital gains tax and a fringe benefits tax. Most importantly, under Keating tariff protection fell continuously. Labor governments of the 1980s also moved to target welfare payments more precisely to the poor, whereas many other OECD countries effectively churn income through the transfer payments system and give it back to the middle class. Under Keating, Australia could claim to have one of the better targeted welfare systems. His other great achievement as treasurer was the introduction of compulsory occupational superannuation, a move designed to increase national savings and make a serious contribution to retirement incomes for the baby boomers. It was in its way the most Asian of all his policies.

Keating's failures as treasurer were threefold. There was a massive blow-out in Australia's foreign debt, which has continued through to today; a too-late and too-tight approach to monetary policy produced a too-severe recession at the beginning of the 1990s (and one of Keating's worst-ever public lines: 'this is the recession we had to have'); and as a result unemployment climbed to unacceptable levels.

Keating was always determined to be prime minister and grew increasingly impatient with his predecessor, Hawke, for holding up the baton change and reneging on a previous agreement the two had as to when the change-over would come. After one unsuccessful challenge Keating retired temporarily to the back benches and the Hawke government floundered without him. Then, at the end of 1991, in a bitter and tight party room ballot, Hawke was deposed, Keating was prime minister.

After such bloody internal conflict Labor's electoral prospects looked extremely bleak in the first months of the Keating prime ministership. Keating had never had a very detailed or sweeping view of foreign policy beyond its impact on his job as treasurer. Keating threw himself into the task of trying to revive Labor's fortunes electorally. He recognised foreign policy both as an area of danger and of opportunity. His foreign minister, Gareth Evans, had backed Hawke in the leadership challenge, which had led to some bad blood between the two men, but foreign policy had been seen as a successful policy area for Hawke and Evans and for Labor generally so Keating kept Evans in the job. At the same time Keating was determined that at no function, during no overseas trip, during no prime ministerial engagement in foreign policy issues, would he ever allow himself to be overshadowed by Evans. There would never be seen to be an occasion on which Keating appeared to be learning foreign policy from Evans. This consideration was important in Keating not taking Evans with him on his first overseas trip as prime minister. Keating deliberately made this trip to Indonesia and to Papua New Guinea to demonstrate his regional priorities.

As a foreign-policy prime minister, Keating had one stroke of good fortune early in his prime ministership. Dr Ashton Calvert, the head of the foreign affairs department's Asia division, was seconded to Keating's office as his foreign policy adviser. In the chaos of transition, Calvert for a time acted as Keating's general press secretary. The two men became close. Keating often develops close relations with his personal staff. He places an absolute premium on personal loyalty and, unlike some leaders, he gives loyalty as well as receiving it. Calvert was one of the best brains in Australia's foreign policy establishment. Oxford educated, but very phlegmatically Australian, he was a fluent Japanese speaker (with a Japanese wife).

Hawke had loved to play the international statesman, especially on east–west issues where his American connections from his days as Australia's trade union boss stood him in good stead, and on African issues, where Australian prime ministers have an entrée through the Commonwealth. But with the end of the Cold War, east–west issues were of receding importance. African and Middle Eastern issues, although they had greatly preoccupied Hawke, were almost entirely marginal to Australia's national interests. They were also Hawke's strong suit. Keating would have looked ridiculous had he tried to pretend a knowledge of the Arab–Israeli peace process. Instead he and Calvert worked out that he could be most effective by concentrating on a few issues of relevance to Australia's core interests.

This was, remarkably, a new approach for an Australian leader. But a prime minister's time is a precious commodity. It should be rationed carefully. Keating and Calvert decided to concentrate Keating's foreign policy time on those areas where prime ministerial involvement could really 'add value'. Thus, in those days, Keating did not express views about the Middle East, made only pro forma statements about the Balkans, did not personally seek to save the Brazilian rainforests, look after the Antarctic penguins or bring democracy to central America. That's what foreign ministers are for. Keating instead decided to concentrate on Australia's region of primary interests, Southeast Asia and Northeast Asia, and to institutionalising APEC. To be effective in regional endeavours he realised that he would have to say no to lots of other commitments.

In the days when he was still fairly modest about foreign policy Keating did not generally do extended interviews with the press on the subject. He didn't want to get tripped up on details about the far-flung corners of the world. But eventually he chose to set out his foreign policy priorities in a lengthy newspaper interview. Keating decided to do his first ever extended interview about foreign policy with me in April 1992. What is remarkable, looking back on that interview, was how thoroughly and consistently, at even that early stage, he had thought through the themes that were to dominate his prime ministership. It was in the lead-up to Keating's first visit to Indonesia as prime minister. During this trip, remarkably, Keating was able to strike up an extremely productive relationship with Suharto. This was a result of several factors. First being a novice and knowing he was a novice at international affairs, Keating was deferential and sought Suharto's advice. Keating is generally deferential for about five minutes a decade. It was a striking piece of good fortune for Australia that these five minutes should coincide with his first visit to Suharto.

After the combination of general indifference punctuated by periodic brash moralising which the Indonesians felt they had received from Hawke this style was highly effective. Further, as everyone with direct experience of him knows, Keating can be exceptionally charming in private. Moreover Keating had an old-fashioned Catholic boy's respect for people much older than him. His career has seen a number of friendships with much older men. Suharto had all the qualities in a leader which Keating admires—age, longevity in power, the ruthless and effective use of power. It was a match made in heaven, and was to prove important in all of Keating's subsequent regional diplomacy.

The other notable aspect of that first foreign policy interview was the bluntness of the language Keating used to underscore what he saw as Australia's move away from Europe towards Asia. Australia, he said, should not be content with sharing in Europe's '1 or 2 per cent growth a year', or with trying to knock down trade barriers with the US, but should go where the 'growth is greatest', namely the Asia–Pacific.

By then he had already proposed that APEC should meet regularly at heads of government level. In a private codicil to our formal interview, he was absolutely blunt about the power dimension of what he wanted APEC, and especially the APEC leaders' meetings, to achieve:

> Think of the message that would send to the world. A meeting with the president of America, with the prime minister of Japan, the president of China, the president of Indonesia, the president of Korea, the prime ministers of Australia and Canada, all sitting at the same table—and not a European in the room. Think what that would say to the world about where the new centre of power lies.

But, naturally, it was what APEC and regionalism more generally offered Australia that excited him most: 'It's about saying
the Asia–Pacific's where the future is. Europe's the old order, this
is the new order.' And, even then, he certainly saw the US as a
key: 'The more we can involve the greatest of our liberal democracies, the US, and the more the US can leave its imprint on
the institutions of the Pacific, the better off we'll be.' And APEC
offered a great deal to the US as well:

> US policy in the Pacific has been the policy of the US navy,
> basically. Most of US trade is in the Pacific but all of the
> institutions are in the Atlantic. APEC's got everything going for
> it. Having the US and Japan work their problems out in the
> APEC context can be very important. US policy revolves
> around the bare bones of the treaties it has with Japan, Korea,
> Australia. What it needs is another overlay to that. I said that
> to President Bush when he was here. The Americans call it the
> fan, coming from California out to a spoke to Korea, Japan and
> Australia, and what I was saying is we've got to put some
> fabric on the spokes. The fabric's got to be a greater
> institutional and economic presence, and bilateral relations by
> the countries of the Pacific occurring independently of the US.

He was also prepared to be quite critical of both the US and
Japan. He said the US administration (then the administration
of President Bush) understood the importance of the US–Japan
relationship, and that there 'had been no closer bilateral cooperation than that between Japan and the US in the second half of
the 1980s'. Of course, the Bush administration in hindsight looks
a model of regional lucidity compared with the incoherence of
the Clinton years. But even then, Keating thought, America was
blaming Japan for its own economic failures:

> The US indebtedness has been effectively funded by the
> Japanese in a clear government policy of purposefully making
> financial arrangements to fund the current account and the
> budget deficit of the US. The US has let itself become a
> debtor country. It's dropped its guard on its economy, its
> efficiency, its product innovation, its entrepreneurs like its
> motor car makers have let themselves fall into second place.
> Instead of paying a very high price, that is with interest rates
> that would render the US a recession-prone economy, they've

been able to live and grow, and indeed take the rest of us along, by virtue of a very enlightened policy by Japan. There's this great dichotomy between the [US] administration, which knows the truth of the relationship and the causes of the problem, and the people in Congress who represent manufacturing centres in America.

It is a sad reflection on what has happened since then that the dichotomy Keating spoke of has now substantially disappeared— now the (Clinton) administration is just as foolish as the Congress.

Keating said that Americans were failing to recognise their own problems, and that the solutions to these problems lay essentially in their own hands:

The problems the US have are basically one of a savings imbalance the same as we [Australians] have. They've become a debtor country to maintain their standard of living using someone else's savings. Their savings problem is basically a consequence of the Reagan years, that is, providing big tax cuts at the same time as lifting defence expenditure, producing very large budget deficits which have in fact denuded the US of savings to the point where they can't afford their investment programs without relying on someone else's savings. That's a US problem, it's not a Japan problem. That's not to say that the Japanese haven't exploited the problem. They've exploited it almost wilfully in trade terms, particularly when the US dollar went up in value in the '80s. They flooded imports into the US.

But Japan came in for plenty of free advice as well:

The problem is that the US has not properly balanced its economy and its savings. And that the US has failed in making Japan play a proper international role, a role commensurate with the opportunities given to it and its size. It's not good enough for Japan to say it can't play a role in international trade liberalisation or develop strategies for trade liberalisation when it's capable of developing the most sophisticated strategy for the motor vehicle industry or for any other competition.

Of the changes even then under way in Japan's political culture he said they were:

Slowly, too slowly. Japan requires of people to understand its hesitancy, its inexperience in international affairs while it can quite ruthlessly pursue commercial strategies in computers, cars and other commodities. Japan should play the role given to it by the rest of the world and not rely on the US as the body which will be arguing for trade liberalisation, which is trying to accommodate adjustment pressures in the countries of the South, giving them access to the countries of the North.

Perhaps because his mind was never cluttered up with the too early or excessive categorising process of university education, perhaps because of his lifelong immersion in politics, perhaps because there is about him much of the autodidact, or perhaps just because that's the way God made him, Keating's cast of mind is very holistic. He always looks for the big picture, and connects everything to everything else. Certainly he believes that his attempt to redefine aspects of Australian national identity, essentially by moving us to a republic, is intimately linked with the nation's push into Asia. It is not that he seeks the republic in order to win favour from Australia's neighbours, but rather he sees the republic, and the engagement with Asia, as aspects of Australia's modernisation.

He told me:

Much that I was about in the 1980s was getting us ready to really be a competitive, international country. And part of that was to take our place in this part of the world. But you can't go here [Asia] if you don't want to go here. In recent times we continue to hear the echoes of the past, the sort of people Manning Clark called the Austral-Britons, who want to keep going home, home in inverted commas being Europe. I just thought it was time to make it clear that home is here, that we are Australians and no one else. If we approach the Asia–Pacific as we are, stripped down to do business with them culturally, psychologically, economically stripped down to do business with them, life will be better.

I think it's worth saying these things. There's been a big cultural change inside Australia. This is not the pre-war Aus-tralia. The view that we could separate our interests from that of Britain or its empire is a pretty late development. This sepa-ration of view has only occurred from the 1970s. It was never a part of the Menzies [Australia's pro-British prime minister from 1949 to 1966] scene. He [Menzies] is the cause of it. He

and all the people around him, like Casey and Bruce, they left
us in a sort of torpor. Menzies governed the place so long, by
default. He's still regarded by the Liberals as the icon, something to look up to, whereas in fact he subjugated this country's interests to Britain, in World War II and in the peace. Mr
Howard [the Liberals' leader] was talking of going back to the
era of Menzies and tranquillity. It just has to be finished.

Keating claimed that he had received strongly positive reaction
from the region to his attempts to redefine Australian national
identity and pursue a republic:

I didn't make these remarks anticipating that reaction but it's
not a surprising reaction. Basically, I think Australia is well
liked around here. People do want to live with us and get on
with us. The barriers have been set by us, not them, and I
think they see it that way.

It's the attitude [of Australians] that matters most. While I
think it's inevitable that the others [constitutional reform,
change of the flag] will follow, the attitude matters now. It is
because the region is growing so rapidly, and growing politically
as well, growing in its own independence. You've seen the development of the Association of South-East Asian Nations, the
emergence of China, of Guangdong province as a new tiger, the
general shift in the attitudes of the people in the region so that
now is the time for us to be there. To be missing this epoch on
the basis that we have some kind of notional barrier, that we're
still European, paying some lip-service to the region, is too
transparent. They see right through that and they won't deal
with you honestly, openly.

Keating also claimed in that interview that Australia's racially
non-discriminatory immigration policy was a source of credibility
for it in the region:

I think that while you had any basis of racial selection [in the
immigration program] you couldn't hope to be accepted as part
of the region. There are a few countries in the region that have
a racial base of selection themselves. That's not to be admired
and that doesn't mean we should adopt that standard. I think
the multicultural feature of our country plays very well in the
Asia–Pacific. How can anyone say there is any discrimination
here when the pace of the program and its settlement
characteristics are such that we pretty well outstrip any of our

near neighbours in such a policy? It's the old thing, if they look at what we actually do, they will approve of us.

There is a lot of snide comment in Australia about Keating's conversion to the cause of Asia, comment to the effect that in his long time as treasurer he had to be prodded into going to Japan and rarely went to other parts of Asia. Keating rejects this criticism, although it is largely accurate. Nonetheless, it has always seemed to me a criticism without a point. If he was a late convert to the importance of Asia so much the better, all the more credit to him for having the intellectual flexibility to take on board a fundamental new theme in the second half of his life. In any event Keating responded vigorously to this criticism during our interview:

> I just reject those notions. When I was treasurer I did all I could to open this country up, all the things my critics never had the courage to do, like removing exchange controls, pulling down the tariff barriers and wearing the adjustment pressures as a result—on the exchange rate wearing the big 25 per cent fall in the dollar in 1986 and the attendant inflation that came with it and the wage reductions that came with that. They're the things which have mattered most and that was not to be doing trade with Europe principally, or even with North America, but with this part of the world where the trade is to be done.
>
> That was the first thing. The second thing was relaxing foreign investment policy. Most of the investment has come from the Asia–Pacific. I've been happy to facilitate that. As to my contact with the area, I've always gone out of my way to see people from the area who visit Australia. My own contacts have been principally with Japan, where I've been on quite a number of occasions. But when I was treasurer I was not the foreign minister. I wasn't roaming around. But if you take the Asia Development Bank, I was always a very strong supporter of the ADB, lifting its capital, doing more with it. This was for the same reason—trying to give us a role in the Asia–Pacific that on a bilateral basis we couldn't afford or effectively do. With a multilateral institution we can effectively do more. That's why we play a very large executive role in the Asia Development Bank. Next to Japan, we play the next major role. That might be contested by the US, but I doubt it.

I spoke to Keating just before he left for his first trip to Indonesia. Already he was developing his main lines of argument: that Indonesia was fundamentally important to us, that Suharto was a senior statesman of the region, that the Indonesian government had overall performed well and that this was hugely to Australia's benefit, and that he would pursue a dialogue on human rights with Indonesia but that this was only one strand of Australia's relationship with its giant northern neighbour. As he said:

> We don't see enough of the president. This is an opportunity for Australia to do that, for me to get to know him for a start. Personal relations matter a great deal in the way in which they do business. I don't think we can do business without having a personal relationship. And I think we have achieved a lot together recently—Cambodia for example—and Dili [by which Keating meant the Dili massacre] notwithstanding there's a lot happening now in commercial ties. They have come a long way in economic reform. Now is the time to be drawing the threads of all of that together.

And would he raise East Timor with his Indonesian hosts?

> I don't have to. It raises itself. The important thing about Dili is that even though the underlying problems can be put at the door of the management of the province, it [the Dili killings] was not express state policy. I think the response made by President Suharto and the government has been by all measure of past episodes a very credible one.

Keating also chose to visit Papua New Guinea on his first visit overseas as prime minister. This was partly to claim an ownership in the PNG–Australia relationship, an ownership which subsequently faded as the relationship soured, PNG's intractable internal problems became more severe and more dramatic and its government took to harsh public criticism of Canberra. However, Keating had another motive in visiting PNG. One of his chief functions there was to attend an ANZAC Day ceremony, to celebrate the wartime courage of Australians who fought the Japanese in PNG. This has been a big theme of Keating's, his attempt to use Australia's participation in the Pacific war, in which we were clearly defending our own national interests, to

refocus the Australian identity in a nationalist way which he sees
as more relevant to Australia's contemporary and regional interests than the distant battles of empire which were so prominent
a part of Australia's pre–Second World War history.

He explained:

> I think the history of World War II, our involvement in it, has
> not been told, or where necessary glorified, in the way in
> which the history of our original ANZAC involvement [in
> Turkey, at Gallipoli] has been told. It was only in World War II
> that this country came under threat of invasion. This was not
> true in World War I. And the invasion force was being
> assembled and was thwarted only really at Coral Sea. And it
> was attempted from the north coast of New Guinea through to
> Port Moresby, where we thwarted that advance. That was an
> exclusively Australian thing and it was there that Australia was
> saved, in turning that back. I think that's important to
> highlight. That's one of the reasons why I think the 50th
> anniversary of the actions at Milne Bay and Kokoda are
> significant and symbolic.
>
> Milne Bay was the first Japanese defeat in the Pacific,
> entirely by Australians. And the Kokoda campaign was the key
> campaign which pushed the Japanese back to Buna and to
> Gona and thwarted their attempts to occupy Port Moresby. I
> think it's important that we know that from that time on, 50
> years ago, we were on our own, and were supported materially
> only by the US. Commonsense tells you that from then on we
> were in essence on our own and had to make our own way.
> The notion of looking for someone to look after us is not the
> way to behave.

Keating said that it had taken us a long time to reach that
point

> particularly in respect of Britain, because it's all about imperial
> defence and the nostrums of imperial defence were key to the
> Menzies view of World War II. Menzies could not separate the
> interests of Australia from the interests of Britain and the
> empire. It was only when Britain had made clear its
> determination to preserve itself in 1940, and then to preserve
> the Middle East and India, that the Far East became
> expendable. And it became obvious only to Curtin [Labor's
> wartime prime minister]. It was never obvious to Menzies. He

[Menzies] then went back there after the war, looking for the baubles of imperial approval, like the Cinque Ports and the knighthoods and the rest. In terms of nationhood, which goes beyond constitutional things, which goes to attitudes, Menzies cost us twenty years, from 1950 to 1972. Gorton and McMahon were only the remnants of him. Between them that nest of them nearly cost us our liberty.

Even then Keating's views on the British royal family were clear: 'It has no social relevance here.'

I interviewed Keating again at the end of that year in his Parliament House office. The Australian Parliament House is a weird confection of modern design ideas. Built into a hill, from the front it looks like a high-class bomb bunker while from the back it has a more conventional appearance, but with all the distinction and style of a pre-war German munitions factory. One of the oddities of its design is that it is built as a glorified rectangle encompassing various open and closed spaces in the middle. The best offices, naturally, are on the top storey (although at only three stories high this is not terribly elevated) and facing outwards to the surrounding hills. Alas, the threat of terrorist attack means that the prime minister's office must be on the interior of the building, facing onto an utterly soulless concrete prime minister's courtyard, and otherwise devoid of outside contact. It seems the perfect metaphor for the dangers of isolation inherent in the modern post of prime minister.

On the day I see him, however, Keating's energy is barely containable. This is not the way he looks at first. I am ushered into his room and find him slumped behind his desk, reading glasses slipped down his long nose, seemingly completely engrossed in a book. The interview takes place not across a desk but in a couple of comfortable armchairs. As the interview wears on Keating becomes not tired but ever more animated, excited by the ideas he is discussing. Eventually the armchair cannot contain him. He starts to pace up and down as he talks. The interview goes way over time. He wants to tell me about what he has achieved, what he will achieve, for Australia in Asia. The book he is reading when I arrive turns out to be a collection of Churchill's speeches. Keating is reading one, that he particularly loves, attacking the House of Lords. 'Listen to this,' Keating says.

'A useless relic of feudal times' [or words to that effect]. 'That's Churchill in 1909 on the House of Lords.' Keating is a lifelong admirer of Churchill's, although he once told me he thought Churchill lacked 'killer rhetoric', which seems a pretty tough judgment on one of the great masters of rhetoric of all time. But Keating's argument was that Churchill's rhetoric of the 1930s was not sufficient to turn around either his party or his country in the period of appeasement of the Nazis.

When I met Keating that day he had just returned from Japan, where he had made an historic commitment. He had promised Japan Australia would never join a trade agreement designed to discriminate against Japan. This was at a time when the Americans were talking of extending the North American Free Trade Agreement across the Pacific and getting certain favoured Asian countries, though certainly not Japan, to join NAFTA as a way, in the words of one American policy maker, of encircling Japan. Keating consciously saw his statement as a landmark declaration of Australia's interests. It was not designed to annoy Washington but it was certainly designed to appeal to the Japanese, and to enhance a process Keating was then, and remains, very keen on, producing a special diplomatic partnership between Canberra and Tokyo. And it was meant to indicate a certain Australian displeasure with the deepening anti-Japanese tilt of so much American rhetoric and policy. If anything Keating's remarks were over-interpreted in the region, where they earned him a lot of goodwill, and in Washington, where the reaction was sour.

Keating told me that day his had not been a one-sided declaration:

> In return Mr Watanabe [then Japan's minister for international trade and industry] gave me a clear assurance that we wouldn't be disadvantaged by any trading arrangements Japan made with other countries. I do think we have fundamental interests with Japan.

It is a measure of Keating's brazenness as a propagandist, his ability to take more or less any set of facts and fashion a convenient argument out of them, that he claimed to see cultural similarities between Japan and Australia, particularly in the area of community and egalitarianism:

There's a sense of sharing and community which does make Japan have a sense of equality through it. So when they come to Australia, they don't find, as they would in Britain, that everyone is listening to the first ten syllables to determine what part of the country one is from or whether one is noble born and if not then one is to be ignored. They come here and find a very open, tolerant country and I think that plays well with them.

This is at best a highly tendentious interpretation of Japan's hierarchical social structures, as well as a very self-serving use of anti-British prejudice. But not to worry. It is one of the functions of national leaders to reinterpret, if necessary re-create, bits of national mythology in ways which serve the nation's interests. Japan and Australia have got on remarkably well with each other diplomatically. Perhaps there is something in Keating's at-first-glance-bizarre theory of cultural affinity.

In any event, he was full of the Japan–Australia relationship that day. He had taken the mildly controversial position that should Emperor Akihito accept an invitation to visit Australia he need not necessarily apologise once more for Japan's actions in the Second World War. Keating has laboured over the symbols and mythology of the Second World War, and the uses these symbols can be put to in contemporary Australia. But he is also conscious of not wanting to offend the Japanese by taking his often enough given advice to them, that they should acknowledge more fully the events of the Pacific war, to the emperor. He explained:

> The invitation [to the emperor] was given without condition and I think we should leave it to the Japanese side to decide what sort of reference they want to make to the past. It's important to note that former Prime Minister Kiishi when he visited Australia in 1957 expressed his 'heartfelt sorrow for what occurred in the war' and at the time that visit was accepted as a point of reconciliation. I said in Darwin that Japan's emerging leadership role would be strengthened if the Japanese public and particularly the young people had a better awareness of Japan's actions in the region earlier this century. But what the emperor may say is entirely a matter for him and the Japanese government. I don't think we should ever forget the sacrifice of those who fought to protect our interests but nor should we be obsessive about the past. It's now half a

century since those events and I don't think it does us any
good to be obsessive about it.

As to the developing intimacy between Tokyo and Canberra,
Keating thought that it went far beyond Australia's having a
usefully activist foreign policy apparatus (and in Gareth Evans a
hyperactive foreign minister) and Japan being somewhat con-
strained because of the legacy of the past in its regional diplomacy. Keating said:

> It's more than just that we have a foreign policy infrastructure
> with depth to it and one which is more free ranging. The
> complementarity of the two economies is quite unique. We've
> got space and they don't. We've got most of their young
> honeymooners coming here. In a survey that was taken recently
> in Japan the great majority said that if they had to choose any
> country to live in outside Japan they would choose Australia.
> The other thing is now we've got more than 100 000
> Australian students learning Japanese as a second language.
> There is a higher percentage of children studying Japanese than
> in any other part of the world except China and Korea. This
> relationship travels quite far. It goes down into the industrial
> culture. And I think by so many Japanese tourists coming to
> Australia it goes to the wider culture.

I asked Keating whether he thought Australians were really
ready for the type of intimate relationship with Japan that he
was proposing. His answer, as usual, was blunt: 'Not entirely. But
they do take a lead from their governments who have to think
these things through for the long term.'

In the months and years to come Keating was to be disappointed, as he expressed to me in our first interview, with the
slowness of political reform in Japan. It became a theme of his,
at least in private conversation, that before Japan could assume
its rightful place either of leadership, or even unambiguous equal
membership, in the region it would need a lot of reform and
modernisation of its politcial system. He was disappointed with
the fall of the Hosokowa government although he worked surprisingly well with Prime Minister Tomiichi Murayama, especially
on APEC issues. In May 1995 he paid a formal state visit to
Japan, unlike his numerous, previous working visits, and obtained
a remarkably fulsome joint declaration between the two prime

ministers, in which Japan described Australia as 'an indispensable partner on regional affairs'. This may be the stuff of international diplomatic platitude but it does confirm the intimacy with which Tokyo and Canberra have worked on international issues.

On that day late in 1992 Keating was also greatly taken up, as usual, with APEC. His ambitions for the Australian creation had grown rapidly. Always most at home with the language and concepts of power, Keating boldly predicted to me that APEC would become more important than the Group of Seven leading industrial nations, and that APEC summits, for which he was then campaigning vigorously, would become more influential than G7 summits. 'The G7 is a European club,' Keating said.

> It's got the North American foot in the door and the Japanese have got a sort of visitor status, but there's Italy, France, Germany and Britain. APEC can put a check on European economic and financial power but that's not its principal objective. The thing I see as being most attractive about it [APEC] is that you can engage the United States more in the region. The thing to do is engage the US and make them more institutionally and commercially involved in the region.

In the years that followed, Keating would add the objective of socialising China as one of the great ambitions of APEC, making China feel it was part of the regional community, greatly extending its avenues of consultation with the region, socialising it into productive and acceptable behaviour within the region. Indeed in some ways APEC became for Keating the magic pudding, undertaking all tasks and solving all problems.

Keating also argued strongly in a later interview that tariffs on the Australian automobile industry should not come down below 15 per cent, the end point in the government's tariff reduction program. Keating made this a strong point of his astonishingly successful 1993 election campaign. This, as with so many Keating positions, is full of irony. As a result of the 1994 Bogor APEC declaration Keating committed the Australian economy to complete free trade by 2010. But at the time of the 1993 election in Australia, Keating successfully demonised Hewson as a free market zealot and used the commitment by Labor to keep motor tariffs at 15 per cent, as against the Opposition's commitment to reach zero protection, as a key case in point. Keating was assisted in this by some motor vehicle manufacturers' saying they doubted whether they could survive in Australia if tariffs went to zero.

Keating made the point:

> I went to the Toyota plant in Japan. It's got a run of 300 000 vehicles a year. We have reduced since 1988 the number of models in Australia from fourteen models to six but the best run we've had is 38 000. You can't get the economies of scale out of a 38 000 run that they're able to secure out of 300 000. So why would Toyota spend $800 million locating in Australia to produce cars in a run of maybe 30 000 to 50 000 at suboptimal cost when they could do it in Japan? It can't be done at zero [tariffs], in my view.

These arguments are all well and good in their way but of course they are exactly the same kind of argument that could be made against any decrease in protectionism at any stage in any industry. In his attempt, wholly successful, to portray Hewson as an ideological extremist, Keating was prepared to embrace, albeit for a relative nanosecond, the arguments of protection. In the same interview, however, he also reclaimed his more usual mantle of free marketeer and destroyer of protectionist barriers. He said, 'I say we've knocked the tariff wall over and we have, but we haven't knocked it over absolutely. But compared to 250 per cent of effective protection for motor cars [in the past] we have knocked it over.'

This whole elaborate double argument—I am the courageous economic reformer but don't go near my opponents because they, in embracing policies similar to mine, are lunatic extremists driven by a hateful ideology and would destroy the social fabric of the country—was the formula for Keating's extraordinary success in the 1993 election. Very few pundits thought Keating had any chance of winning in 1993. Labor had been in office too long, Keating was too unpopular, the divisions of the leadership contest had been too great. It was the election Labor had to lose. I was lucky that I was foreign editor at the time of the '93 campaign, and therefore didn't have to comment on domestic Australian politics, or otherwise I would have embarrassed myself with false prophecy. Like most analysts I thought Labor would lose heavily.

Luckily, on election day I was in Indonesia covering the Indonesian presidential election, a very much easier contest to pick.

Of course we all knew Keating had guts and would go down fighting. No one realised just what a fight he would put up. He focused with extreme vigour on the Opposition's plan to introduce a goods and services tax. Most economists thought this a good idea, to transfer tax from savings and income to consumption. Keating himself had strongly backed the proposal in 1985. But with the thinnest imaginable intellectual justification—that between 1985 and 1993 he had broadened the tax base and therefore a goods and services tax was no longer needed—Keating set out to demonise the GST and the Hewson Opposition. And he succeeded. To almost universal amazement Keating was fairly comfortably returned to office in the '93 election.

The election victory had many perverse consequences. Keating got in a sulk with Australian newspapers which he believed had wrongly written him off and been too generous to his opponents. Thus there were no more extended foreign policy interviews. Indeed hardly any newspaper interviews of any kind. He hailed his triumph as a victory for the 'true believers' and if anything, was more confirmed than ever in the infallibility of his own judgment. In regional policy and in his attempts to redefine and to some extent remake Australian national identity he was stronger than ever.

His closeness to Indonesia's President Suharto grew, especially in the period leading up to the Bogor APEC summit and its sweeping free-trade declaration. Both before and after the summit he was fulsome in his praise of Suharto. He also tried to get Australians to realise the importance of Indonesia to them. In March 1994, he declared that no country was more important to Australia than Indonesia. This was another historic Keating declaration, and one he was to repeat frequently. Keating was the first Australian prime minister ever to elevate Indonesia's importance to Australia to the same rank as that of Japan and the US.

Before the Second World War, if Australians had been asked to nominate the foreign country most important to them they would have answered overwhelmingly 'Britain'. After the war it would have been the US, with Japan, after many years as our number one trading partner and by a huge margin our number

one export market, eventually coming to occupy a roughly equal
status. But Keating unambiguously added Indonesia to those two.
He frequently said that Suharto's establishing stability and growing prosperity in Indonesia since 1965 has been the most benign
strategic development for Australia in 50 years.

The Australia–Indonesia relationship remains vexed in many
ways. The two are unlikely and vastly different neighbours. But
Keating and Suharto have overseen an extraordinary change in
the nature of the relationship. Whether this can survive the
passing of the two strong men from their respective national
leaderships remains to be seen.

But Keating's engagement with Indonesia was just part of his
broader push to have Australia see itself as fully a nation of its
own region. There is no doubt that this was a consequence of
Keating's deepest thinking about Australia's strategic, economic
and cultural future. But it may also be that Keating realised that
while no Australian prime minister could play a credible role as
a world statesman, he could make some contribution as a regional
leader, and use the leverage of regional institutions, such as APEC,
to have a global impact. It could be that Keating's ambition, and
his deep sense always of where the real lines of power lay,
impelled him towards Asia.

His ambitions for Australia in this respect also involved
fundamental developments in Australia's own identity. In a sem-
inal speech to the Asia–Australia Institute at the end of 1994
Keating adumbrated his vision.

He said:

By the turn of the century, by the centenary of our
nationhood, I hope this will be a country:

- in which more and more Australians speak the languages of
  our neighbours,
- in which our business people are a familiar and valued part of
  the commercial landscape of the Asia–Pacific,
- in which we are making full use of the great resource of the
  growing number of Australians of Asian background,
- in which our defence and strategic links with the countries
  around us are deeper than ever,
- in which our national identity is clearer to us and our

neighbours through the appointment of an Australian as our head of state,
- in which our national culture is shaped by, and helps to shape, the cultures around us.

The one part of Asia about which Keating has had the deepest reservations is China. Again the complementarities of Keating's domestic political evolution and his world view are startling. China was just about the only part of Asia about which Keating's predecessor, Bob Hawke, was unreservedly enthusiastic. On one occasion Hawke fatuously declared that no country on Earth was closer to China than Australia. It all ended in tears, of course, with the Tiananmen massacre.

Keating gave a rare glimpse of his deepest thinking about China in a short newspaper interview in 1994, in which he claimed a natural linkage of interests between Australia, Indonesia and Vietnam. He said:

> What are the defining elements of Indonesia and Vietnam's foreign policy? Answer: suspicions of China, China's maritime capacity in the South China Sea etc. The other thing is Vietnam wants to be part of a trading system which gives them some opportunities, where it hasn't got to scratch and claw for everything. So they've now got full observer status in ASEAN. It's a possibility they'll become a full member of ASEAN. [Vietnam formally joined ASEAN in 1995.] If they do, ASEAN gets a lot of weight added to it, doesn't it? You would then have, in the trading entities, the bigger weight coming from Indonesia, Vietnam and Australia.

Asked then how important this was in terms of setting up a non-China bloc of interests, Keating replied: 'It's not a primary objective of Australian foreign policy because we have nothing to fear from China. But do we want to be in the Chinese orbit—in other words, the pull of gravity from China? No, of course we don't, and this sort of resists that, doesn't it?'

This was an extremely clumsy and inelegant verbal formulation. And it preposterously overstates any role Vietnam might have in an emerging anti-Chinese axis. But Keating's view of China as the chief threat to regional stability, and especially to Southeast Asia, finds some resonance throughout the region, although most leaders would not be prepared to say it publicly.

Indeed Keating was not prepared to say it publicly most of the time.

The remark also discloses the constant linkage in Keating's mind between the economic and the strategic. Keating's efforts to bring Australia and New Zealand into a formal association with the ASEAN Free Trade Area can be seen in the light of these comments as having a clear, strategic dimension, to be an attempt, in terms ASEAN might use, to forge a resilient region, to forge some strength out of solidarity in the non-Chinese East Asian region. Keating's foreign minister, Gareth Evans, even on occasion suggested a more formal strategic association between Australia, ASEAN and Indochina. Similarly, Australia's Strategic Review and Defence White Paper identified China as the greatest source of uncertainty in the region. Governments do not generally go very far in identifying potential enemies, for to do so can have the effect of a self-fulfilling prophecy, but clearly the Australian government under Keating viewed China as the most likely threat, even as it identified the need to engage China positively. And this very much reflected Keating's own thinking.

Keating has been by a very long distance the most dominant and formidable Australian politician of his generation. He is an Australian original. Whether the Asian orientation he has sought to give his country will be a permanent thing, taken deeply to the heart of Australians, it is still perhaps too early to say, although the signs are overwhelmingly positive. Not the least of these positive signs is that the present prime minister, John Howard, basically accepts Keating's Asian agenda. The main exceptions are that he defends the Liberal Party's historical record on engagement with Asia and that he claims the issue of whether Australia becomes a republic will not affect the country's standing in Asia.

Certainly Keating had big dreams for Australia. He wants it to stand for something, and to count for something. It is ironic that the Asianisation of Australia, by which I mean the emergence of a crucial Asian dimension to almost every aspect of national life and policy and the ever-deepening engagement with East Asia, should take place under, be driven by, not a university-trained intellectual with a fascination for Asian culture or language, but a Bankstown boy with a love of French clocks and Empire furniture.

One key to Keating has always been his sense of power, his comfort with power, his desire for power. Australia, it seems to him, can only find its destiny, maximise its potential, safeguard its interests, in the context of its own region. He has been by Australian standards an extraordinarily tough politician, at times cruel and certainly ruthless. Yet he is also the most charming of interlocutors, especially when he's convincing you to join him on a great crusade. He is devoted to his family, whose privacy he guards jealously. He is a publicly passionate figure who nonetheless generally seems finally in control of his sometimes florid emotions. Language has been a great weapon, even if sometimes it has run out of his control, as for example when he so foolishly labelled Malaysia's prime minister, Dr Mahathir, 'recalcitrant' for failing to attend the 1993 APEC summit. This led to a nasty diplomatic incident in which Mahathir completely outplayed Keating. The other notable time his language got away from him was when he talked of 'the recession we had to have'.

Just a couple of months before he lost office in the 1996 election Keating pulled off perhaps his most dramatic diplomatic coup. On Thursday December 14, 1995, Keating announced that Australia and Indonesia had negotiated a mutual security treaty. It was the only such treaty Indonesia had ever negotiated with anybody. As a bilateral treaty it was the only one of its kind Australia had with any Southeast Asian nation. It was the first security treaty of any kind that Australia had negotiated in 25 years, since the Five Power Defence Arrangements, which brought together Australia, New Zealand, Britain, Malaysia and Singapore for the defence of the Malay peninsula and Singapore. It was also the first such treaty Australia had ever signed with a nation whose troops had seen combat action against Australian troops, as happened in Borneo during the *konfrontasi* between Sukarno's Indonesia and Malaysia.

There was a deeply idealistic element to the treaty. No two countries so close together could be so unalike. That two such different neighbours, Muslim and Christian, poor and rich, numerous and few, should decide to work so intimately together was a resounding rejection of the notion that there must inevitably be a 'clash of cultures' between western democracies and Islamic societies.

The treaty's gestation was a classic Keating operation, involving great secrecy, shuttle diplomacy, extensive leader-to-leader negotiation and patient, subtle work by Keating on his Indonesian counterpart. Keating first raised the idea of such a treaty in a Cabinet security committee meeting in early 1994. A few years earlier Jakarta and Canberra had been working on a Joint Declaration of Principles, but the idea was dropped after the Dili massacre at the end of 1991. It would also have been more difficult to sustain, and less use, than a security treaty because it would have implied general shared values, whereas Australia and Indonesia have some shared values and some divergent values. The security treaty captures the more tangible reality of shared interests.

The 1993 Australian defence department's strategic review identified defence cooperation with Indonesia as of the highest importance to Australia and it was from thinking in that document that Keating developed the idea for the treaty. Keating first raised it with Suharto in June 1994, when Keating was in Indonesia for an Australian trade promotion. Suharto's reaction was classicly Javanese—interested but cautious, noncommittal. Keating had the sense not to push it too hard, too early. He chose General Peter Gration, a former head of the Australian Defence Force, as his special envoy. Gration was accompanied by Keating's personal foreign policy adviser, Alan Gyngell, who, like Ashton Calvert before him, had become close to Keating. On their numerous trips to Indonesia to negotiate the treaty they dealt with Indonesia's Cabinet secretary, Moerdiono, Suharto's closest Cabinet colleague.

In both countries secrecy was maintained. The Australian ambassador in Jakarta at the time, Alan Taylor, knew what was happening but the matter did not figure in normal diplomatic cables, which are prone to leak. Keating and Suharto met again in Indonesia in September 1994, and then at the APEC heads of government meeting in Osaka, Japan, in November, when the final touches were put to the deal. No other countries, and no other diplomats, knew of the treaty's negotiation. On Wednesday night, the night before the treaty was to be announced, the

American ambassador to Australia, Ed Perkins, was called in and briefed on the treaty. No one else knew in advance.

In its way this is a history-making treaty. Crucially, it was supported in principle by the then Opposition leader, John Howard, who criticised only the secrecy of its negotiation. If it works, the treaty can form the basis for a new partnership between Australia and Indonesia, who are bound to be neighbours for a very long time. The treaty does not automatically commit either side to the defence of the other—very few security treaties do—but it does provide that the two nations will

> consult each other in the case of adverse challenges to either party or to their common security interests and, if appropriate, consider measures which might be taken by them individually or jointly and in accordance with the processes of each government.

This is pretty much the straightforward treaty language of collective security, telling other countries that they cannot rely on knocking off either country individually without a joint response. As security treaties go, it is a substantial commitment.

I interviewed Keating a few weeks later, in mid-January, at Kirribilli House, which serves as the Australian prime minister's Sydney residence. At one point in the interview he asked me to turn the tape recorder off and put down the notebook. Do you want to know why I really negotiated the treaty now? he asked. The answer was in case Labor lost the forthcoming election (which it did). Keating felt there was hardly likely to be another Australian prime minister willing to take the step, with the strength to take the step, and with the right relationship with Suharto. Similarly there was no guarantee that a future Indonesian president would have Suharto's interest in Australia and command over the Indonesian political scene.

What Keating had effectively done was secure a long-term institutional result for Australia from his personal relationship with Suharto. Although there was some criticism of Keating over the treaty what was remarkable was how quickly, and with comparatively how little fuss, the treaty was accepted in Australia. This may reflect a new maturity in Australian public appreciation of its strategic environment and it may also reflect that even at his politically weakest, just before a disastrous election loss,

Keating was a strong and decisive leader and people accepted bold actions from him that may have got a weaker leader into much more trouble.

The interview overall that day was a slightly odd experience. Keating was at his most relaxed and charming. He showed me over the grounds of Kirribilli House, which nestles right by the water on Sydney Harbour. He complained good-naturedly about the tourists on the ferries that sail by and wave and gesticulate at the prime minister's residence—'they all expect me to do a little handstand for them'—he pointed out which were the ugly and which the beautiful buildings on the city's skyline across the water and discussed at length one of his great passions, urban aesthetics.

What surprised me about the meeting, just days before he announced the election date, was how relaxed, even serene, he was, and how generous with his time. He was clearly more interested in governing than campaigning. He reminded me a little of the impression the American president George Bush gave during the 1992 presidential election, as a man who couldn't believe in his heart that he could lose, but couldn't see in his head how he could win. Thus came a certain detachment.

In any event he didn't talk about grubby politics that day but about high foreign policy. He spoke with great warmth about Suharto:

> The fact that President Suharto and I were able to work together on APEC . . . there's been a sort of relationship of work and value between the two of us. During this time of course our defence links have grown more and more. The time was there to say well, look, we do share a strategic outlook, we do have common interests, we don't have territorial designs on one another, we are by geography bound to live together so let's clear the decks and declare that we are friends. Let's declare our mutual interests in the region and by so doing solidify also the attitude in Southeast Asia.

I asked him whether the treaty would have been possible without his personal relationship with Suharto. He replied:

> I don't think so . . . Generally if you start out wanting to be cooperative with a person you can see good in they'll mostly see it in you. I think that happened with President Suharto

and me. To carry on one's back for 30 years executive authority and managing your country from poverty to where it is now is one hell of a commitment which must draw admiration from anybody. The other thing is that the event of greatest positive strategic significance to Australia in the postwar years was the advent of the New Order government [in Indonesia] and that deserved to be recognised. I just don't think it was really honest for Australian strategic advisers to make the point privately but the point never be acknowledged publicly. I think that was the acknowledgment President Suharto deserved, he thought he was entitled to and was pleased that we'd made it.

He was optimistic about Indonesia's ultimately being able to handle peacefully a succession from Suharto to a new president:

I think that the Indonesian management group, what are called in the think pieces the elites, are determined that the progress their country has made won't be diminished by an unseemly, unorganised transition whenever the president decides to retire, and that may be some time off, of course. I think they know that the world will be watching them and they know for that reason, and for the drum beat of their own development, the pace of their own development, that it is important for there to be a managed transition.

Within the bounds of normal politeness he was critical of American mismanagement in the region. Although he didn't say so in this interview he had been very disappointed at President Clinton's failure to attend the APEC summit in Osaka and had conveyed this disappointment in a sharp conversation with US Vice President Al Gore (although he praised Clinton's earlier attendance at the Bogor summit in 1993). But he did say to me that day at Kirribilli House that he did not think that 'institutionally' the Americans really understood what APEC offered them, 'how neatly it fits US commercial and strategic interests in the area'. He pointed out that US exports to East Asia were rising at three times the rate of East Asian exports to America.

We were speaking before the outbreak of tension across the Taiwan Straits in 1996. Keating was critical of America's China policy:

I don't believe the US has the weights right in the China

relationship—the focus on Taiwan, and human rights. In respect of human rights laudable as that is, it doesn't substitute for a policy of looking at China as a whole. China's the biggest emerging economy of the world. One of the principal reasons for APEC is to establish the framework in which to proceed into the world and to see that growth continues to be fuelled in East Asia, including and especially in China. One of the big tasks of the post–Cold War period I think is engaging China, putting our arm around it, helping it into the world successfully, seeing that the income growth there is as even as it can possibly be and disagreeing with them on issues as we must do from time to time.

Keating never saw Australia's traditional close alliance and relationship with the US as being in competition with the engagement with Asia he always pushed as prime minister. Rather he saw the two as reinforcing one another:

We carry much more regard in the United States because we are not simply seen as another mendicant, as someone who will ask you for strategic protection. They [the US] want us to make a way for ourselves. I think they would applaud it [the security treaty with Indonesia]. I'm sure they applauded the fact that we are doing our part in building durable structures here where we live. Yes that residual strategic support [from the US for Australia] is there but in what circumstances could only be answered at the time when they arise. Therefore we are better assuming that we will have to secure ourselves.

Nonetheless he thought the people-to-people relationship between Australians and Americans, as well as the government-to-government relationship, would ensure that the military alliance between the two countries would endure.

Keating was also effusive about the relationship between Australia and Japan, saying it had 'come of age', and pointing to support from then trade minister (and later prime minister) Ryutaro Hashimoto for Australia's presence in regional bodies.

But there was only ever going to be one answer to the question of what Keating saw as his greatest foreign policy achievement:

I think the most important thing in foreign policy terms has been building the architecture of APEC. Because I think we have created a new institution there. The feeling we had at

Osaka [APEC summit 1995] was much more eager than the feeling at Bogor [1994], though there was rejoicing about the clarity and strength of the declaration of Bogor. But the fact that people signed up to an action agenda at Osaka gave a kind of inner satisfaction and quiet rejoicing. They knew they were in a new institution. I do think that each leader's commitment to it and to each other will strategically change the character of the region. When people from countries are meeting when they've never met before and they are meeting now with regularity and with common interests, it changes their view. So it is that piece of overall structure which matters to the region, its peace, its prosperity.

But perhaps Keating is wrong there. Perhaps his greatest contribution, his greatest single achievement, has simply been to change the way virtually all Australians now think about foreign policy. His larger vision of total engagement with Asia may still be in the balance, although as I've said the signs are positive, but his foreign policy structure and priorities have been accorded the greatest accolade of all—they have been embraced by his opponents.

Keating lost the 1996 election and lost it quite badly. Thirteen years in office was just too long for Labor. But his overall contribution to Australian history is immense. Through it all there has been Keating's passionate belief in Australia as a nation of the new world, confronting momentous decisions of identity, security, economics, on the edge of Southeast Asia, a determined player with a not unreasonable hand.

Above all Keating wanted it to happen. And the power of his will alone was a mighty force in the creation of his vision. For a democratic politician, that's no mean achievement.

* * *

BACK TO THE FUTURE: THE REINVENTION
OF JOHN HOWARD

I arrived at my office one morning in 1992 to find a message
to ring John Howard urgently. As we hadn't had any personal
contact for a couple of years I was surprised by this and rang
back as quickly as I could. Howard, now Australia's prime
minister, was then a senior front-bencher with the Liberal Party
in Opposition. He was furious with a column I'd written that
morning accusing him of making periodic anti-Asian statements.
He intended to tip a bucket of abuse on me in the parliament
that afternoon and wanted to let me know in advance.

It was a fairly typical Howard performance, blunt and aggressive, straightforward, aggrieved, though not scatological like his
opponent Keating in similar phone calls (the only time Keating
as prime minister personally tried to ring me to complain about
a column I was happily between home and office and missed the
call). It was also the end point of a long feeling of injustice that
Howard had that I gave him too much grief over Asian issues.

But in truth, and remarkably, Asia has been decisive in
Howard's career, at its highest point and its lowest point. Howard,
a totally traditional middle-Australia man with no discernible
special affinity for anything Asian, is in his way a classic example
of how Asia has become an inescapable feature of the political
universe of all Australian politicians. It was a speech on Asian
immigration in 1984 which was pivotal in propelling Howard to
the leadership of the Liberal Party and it was an interview about
the same subject in 1988 which was pivotal in having him thrown
out of the leadership. And it was perceptions of him on the Asian
issue, more than any other, which he had to correct before he
could resume the leadership of the Liberal Party in 1995.

I had greatly admired Howard's 1984 speech and written
about him in a complimentary way as a consequence. Howard
was in those days a social conservative, but by no means social
reactionary, liberal on issues of race and championing liberal
economic reform. Howard twice in that period asked me to come
and work for him, as a general political adviser and speech writer.
I had a lot of sympathy with Howard in those days, at the height
of the Cold War when anti-communism, which Howard

embraced, was more important than it is today, and when his plain-man image contrasted appealingly with the perpetual psycho-drama and politics as personal therapy practised by the then prime minister, Bob Hawke. But I felt no particular affinity for the Liberal Party and no desire to leave journalism so I declined both times, which was just as well.

Howard was born in 1939 and had grown up in Earlwood, a suburb in Sydney's inner southwest. His father owned a service station in nearby working-class Dulwich Hill, just one suburb from where I grew up, and a strong Labor area. In Sydney the most affluent areas are in the eastern suburbs and on the north shore. These, and the countryside, are the conservative heartland and it is from these areas that most prominent Liberals come. The suburbs around where Howard was brought up normally vote Labor (indeed they are only a few kilometres from Keating's home territory of Bankstown). To grow up in these areas is generally to grow into a Labor milieu, at least for the politically inclined. So Howard's background was not really that of the traditional Liberal. Nonetheless it would not be quite right either to paint Howard as a 'working-class triumph'. Earlwood, as the historian of the Liberal Party and former Howard staffer, Gerard Henderson, has pointed out, was a small island of rather greater affluence than its surrounding suburbs. This happens frequently in Sydney's vast western suburbs: one suburb, be it Earlwood or Strathfield or Ashfield, manages to flourish as a distinctly more affluent and exclusive neighbourhood than its surrounding areas. Howard really grew up in a *petit bourgeois* environment which often produces highly conservative individuals. Indeed he was even named after Churchill. His full name is John Winston Howard. Given that he was born in 1939 this shows a considerable degree of political awareness on his parents' part.

In the first long, set-piece interview I ever did with Howard, way back in 1984, when he was deputy leader of the Liberal Party in Opposition, in his tiny cramped office in the old Parliament House, he told me he was brought up in a Methodist family in which 'religion was a part of the environment'. He and his family by then belonged to the local Anglican Church (Methodist to Anglican being a fairly normal progression for Liberals) near his Sydney home on the north shore. And he was, on church-going, he said, 'about halfway between an every-Sunday man and a twice-a-year man'.

His father's values as a small businessman influenced Howard as a child. In postwar Australia the Chifley Labor government had become unpopular by continuing petrol rationing long into peacetime. Howard, aged ten or eleven, first became conscious of politics as Menzies stormed the Labor barricades, and the Howard family particularly identified with the Liberals' policies of 'emptying out the Chifley socialists and filling up the [petrol] bowsers'. Of course, that his family shaped Howard one way does not mean that they would not have influenced him differently if he had made different decisions. One of Howard's brothers, Bob, an academic, became an influential member of the Labor left.

Young John Howard went to Canterbury Boys High School and to Sydney University, where he studied law. Canterbury Boys High School was a government school whereas many Liberals attended private schools, but it was a selective school and catered to bright, competitive boys. Sydney University Law School was located off campus and functioned almost as a separate institution but in any event Howard went to university long before the radical influences of the late 1960s and early '70s. Much like many of his later Labor Party political opponents, Howard was extremely active in party machine politics from an early age. By 24 he was leader of the NSW Young Liberals. He became a successful city solicitor. But a safe seat in parliament was a relatively long time coming. In 1974, after an exhaustive nine preselection ballots, he won the seat of Bennelong, on Sydney's lower north shore.

The Liberals under Malcolm Fraser won government in 1975 and Howard was quickly promoted to the outer ministry, becoming in 1975 the minister for business. He was later, briefly, minister for trade negotiations. But his big break came in late 1977 when the treasurer, Philip Lynch, was forced to stand down from his position and Howard got the key economics portfolio in any Australian government, the Treasury. Howard was treasurer for nearly seven years, from late 1977 to the election in March 1983.

This was both Howard's big break and his big test. It was a long time to be treasurer and in the end the judgment must be that Howard did fairly little with this opportunity. This is certainly a taunt Keating frequently made to Howard, that it was Keating, a Labor treasurer, who was able to bring about financial deregulation, budget surpluses, tariff reductions and the rest that Howard, as a supposedly free-market treasurer, was never able to convince his supposedly free-market party to embrace while in government.

I asked Howard about this line of criticism in our interview in 1984. His reply was instructive:

> Within the [Fraser] government there were two streams of
> thought about how far you should allow market forces to run.
> There were those, in both parties, who had been influenced by
> the Menzies–McEwan years, who believed in the benign hand
> of government. And there were those of us whose economic
> influences came from a later period. There were two
> fundamentally different views. There were people who believed
> in regulation and there were people who didn't.

Malcolm Fraser, Howard said, believed in regulation. And that was the problem.

'In saying that [Fraser believed in regulation] I don't think I'm telling any tales out of school. He would be the first to agree. Like all of us he was a mixture. His instincts on things like foreign policy and defence were first class, and he's perhaps not given as much credit for that as he should.' Nonetheless, Howard said, he and Fraser differed on economic policy. Howard said he regretted that the Fraser government had not gone much further down the road of financial deregulation:

> I would have liked to have done a lot more. The opposition of
> the Labor Party to any change strengthened the hand of those
> within my own party who opposed it. They would say: 'John, if
> you do that the Labor Party will exploit it, it will be politically
> difficult.' The Labor Party opposed everything we tried to do in
> that area tooth and nail in Opposition. They've changed
> completely in government. I've made it easy for Keating to
> deregulate.

This defence for a timid effort at reform is reasonable so far as it goes, but it is extremely feeble if Howard is considered in comparison with other right-wing reformers of the 1980s, whether it be Thatcher in Britain, Reagan in America, Roger Douglas in New Zealand, the so-called socialists in Spain or Paul Keating in Australia. That the Opposition opposed it and the *zeitgeist* wasn't wholly favourable seems a lame excuse for delaying the task Howard himself believed essential, internationalising, modernising, deregulating and reforming the Australian economy. Different people will question whether the whole thrust of 1980s reform was right or not, but the damning criticism of Howard is that he knew what he wanted to do but wasn't effective enough to do it. Then there was the last Fraser budget, which was an irresponsible fiscal blow-out.

But Howard certainly looked good as treasurer. Australian treasurers generally do look good, as do Australian foreign ministers, for the simple reason that they have one of the giant, elite public service departments behind them. Moreover they are always in the news, talking about the important subject of the economy. Their words affect markets and are thus given great attention and value. They inevitably develop a familiarity with the jargon, and the latest information, sufficient to impress at least the layman. Opposition spokesmen on treasury matters also look good because they too appear on TV almost every day, cautiously welcoming any good news but expressing sober concern over interest rates, unemployment, investment levels, whatever, and thoroughly bashing the government for any bad news. Thus the treasury portfolio, in government and Opposition, (and Howard has had it in both), has become one of the great stepping-stones of Australian political life.

In any event on that day in 1984 Howard would certainly not accept a totally negative view of the Fraser years. He pointed out that in seven years under Fraser the coalition increased federal expenditure only by about 2 per cent a year in real terms, a better effort at fiscal restraint than any previous postwar government. Other achievements of the Fraser years that Howard nominated included the introduction of the dependent spouse rebate, which made a small (very small) contribution to offering married couples a measure of choice about whether the wife went out to work, energy conservation through oil parity pricing (pricing Australian-produced oil at the global market price), the beginnings of financial deregulation and the acceptance of large numbers of Indochinese refugees into Australia.

During that interview Howard described himself as 'an unregenerate free marketeer on economics', a position he would certainly modify for the 1996 election campaign. But it was Indochinese refugees, and Asian immigration generally, which gave Howard his big break in Opposition in 1984. In March 1984 the historian Geoffrey Blainey had made a nasty speech saying too many Asians were coming into Australia. As the months went by Blainey's position became increasingly extreme. He seems to have greatly misled the Liberals of the time about what they could get from the Asian immigration issue politically. The Liberals' then immigration spokesman, Michael Hodgman, made a series of offensive interventions in which he basically backed Blainey's position and said he thought the Opposition would win a dozen seats from Labor on the immigration issue. Andrew Peacock, the Liberals' then leader, devised a cynical, superficial and ultimately ridiculous formula of saying that the immigration program was unbalanced because too many Asians were coming in but the solution was not to cut the number of Asians but increase the number of Europeans, so the proportion of Asians would fall.

In fact Asians had entered Australia in large numbers for the first time under Malcolm Fraser when Australia had decided to accept substantial numbers of Indochinese refugees. The Hawke government in its early years cut the overall size of the immigration program and the proportion of the program who were Asian had risen by less than 10 per cent. So the whole episode, as well as being ethically offensive and politically inept to say the least, represented a kind of hysteria based on no real facts.

The Labor Party realised much more deeply than the Liberals that Australia had changed. Its leaders believed in non-discrimination in principle, but also saw that elite opinion, not least in the business community, would turn against the Liberals if they pursued race as an issue in immigration. However, sometimes their attempts to exploit the issue were crude. The then foreign minister, Bill Hayden, detonated the issue in parliament in August with a silly and hyperbolic attack on the Opposition. He claimed Australia's good name was being dented by frequent anti-Asian

statements from sources in or close to the Opposition, which was
a reasonable claim, but he then went wildly overboard with a
series of personal attacks. In particular he described Hodgman
as 'vaseline slicked oozing his way into the contemptible barrel
of racist bigotry'.

Howard and another senior Opposition figure immediately
mounted a censure motion against Hayden for his excess. Howard's speech was one of the best, and most influential, he ever
gave. Howard reassured the parliament on the Liberals' commitment to non-discrimination and said the Liberal Party would not
make race an issue at the next federal election. He said that his
party would not be associated with racial discrimination in
immigration or with racial prejudice. He then powerfully
reminded Labor of its own mixed record, that the White Australia
policy had been supported by the Labor Party right up until the
mid-1960s and had in fact been dismantled by a Liberal government. He powerfully recalled Labor prime minister Gough
Whitlam's refusal to accept any substantial number of Vietnamese refugees in 1975 after the fall of Saigon. He reminded Labor
of Bob Hawke's unsympathetic attitude in 1977, when the boat
people issue was first being seriously grappled with. Hawke as
leader of the Australian trade union movement commented that
boat people were not the only ones with claims on Australia's
compassion. He reminded the parliament that it was a conservative Liberal government under Malcolm Fraser which made the
historic commitment to Indochinese refugees, such that Australia
took, per capita, more Indochinese refugees than any other
country. He rejected any proposition that the Liberals should take
a stand against Asian immigration. He made a powerful plea for
bipartisanship on immigration:

> It is very important that we have a bipartisan approach and
> that we completely avoid the kind of cheap point scoring that
> the minister for foreign affairs engaged in today . . . I
> supported the policies of the former coalition government
> which were humanitarian and liberal in the true sense of the
> word. We were prepared to take, with the Labor Party's
> generous support, people from war-torn parts of Southeast Asia
> . . . With those kinds of credentials, what earthly right has any
> member of the Australian Labor Party with its record and

contradictions that lie in its historic past, to come into this House and lecture us about racism?

The reaction to Howard's speech, from his own party and especially from the press, was ecstatic. Howard had effectively rebuked Hayden, killed the Hodgman initiative and greatly buoyed the spirits of his fellow Liberals. But few could resist—not that many tried—making the comparison between Howard's parliamentary mastery and Peacock's shallowness. The headlines the next day said it all: 'HOWARD ROUSING ON RACE ISSUE' declared the *Sydney Morning Herald*, a headline on another of its articles read 'POLL: PEACOCK PROMISES BUT HOWARD STARS,' The *Australian* headlined its report 'THE DAY HOWARD GAVE THE LIBS NEW HEART' and the next day ran the even more flattering headline: 'DEPUTY WHO CAN'T HELP TAKING THE LEAD', still another newspaper headline called it: 'HOWARD'S SHINE MAKES PROBLEM FOR LIBERALS', while my own profile of Howard two weeks later appeared in the *Australian* under the heading 'JOHN WINSTON HOWARD: GREAT WHITE HOPE OF THE LIBERALS'.

It was the best press Howard has ever had, then or since. It transformed him instantly into a leadership challenger to Peacock and made it clear that if Peacock did not succeed, Howard would take his place. As Paul Kelly comments in *The End of Certainty*, the speech confirmed Howard as the clearly superior parliamentary performer to Peacock. He also looked a more honest and attractive politician because his rejection of the race card was so unequivocal, compared with Peacock's earlier flirtation with the Blainey line. It also greatly broadened Howard's image. As a former treasurer he was expected to perform better than Peacock on economics, but to best Peacock on social issues such as immigration was altogether new.

Peacock did well in the subsequent election campaign of that year but still lost comfortably to Hawke. Peacock's deeper weaknesses were exposed, and the tension between Peacock as leader and Howard as deputy simmered. Finally in a remarkably ham-fisted episode, all too characteristic of Liberal Party internal politics, Peacock tried to have Howard deposed as deputy and failed, and felt compelled to resign the leadership of the party. Howard became leader of the Liberal Party, and therefore Opposition leader, on September 5, 1985. He held the leadership until

May 9, 1989, when he was toppled by Peacock in yet another party-room coup.

In the meantime Howard lost an election, narrowly, to Hawke in 1987. Howard was not a successul Opposition leader, although he campaigned well in the 1987 election. He tried to take the party to the dry, deregulatory and socially conservative path he had outlined to me in 1984. But while this alienated the moderate elements of his party it did not satisfy the most conservative sections of Australian politics, associated with the National Party's Queensland premier, Joh Bjelke-Petersen. Conservative forces in Australian politics and business mounted a catastrophic Joh-for-Canberra push which undermined Howard without actually getting the eccentric Queenslander to enter federal politics. This cost Howard heavily in 1987. It was probably the difference between his winning and losing that year.

But there were other problems of Howard's own making. His management style was chaotic. The Liberal Party had become addicted to leadership intrigues and Howard had many party enemies, but he also developed a bad case of political paranoia. He became strangely isolated in his leadership. He could not instil discipline on his unruly front bench. He was perceived as a weak leader and so had to perform crazy–brave actions to prove his toughness. Probably the incident which contributed more than anything else to bringing him down comes under that last category.

Howard might have survived all his leadership travails but for his bizarre intervention once more into Asian immigration, this time arguing roughly the opposite position from that which he took in 1984. Again it was in August, almost exactly four years after he had made his highly liberal original speech on Asian immigration which had done so much to propel him into the leadership. Howard's leadership was under great pressure. He had just returned from London where he had had an audience with Margaret Thatcher, the glamour girl and fantasy object of all right-wing Australian Liberals, who had told him that above all a leader must be resolute, must be tough, must never back down. Howard had faced continued campaigning by Blainey against the level of Asian immigration under the Labor government, he had also faced a similar push from his coalition partners the Nationals, especially the Nationals' leader in the Senate, the former treasury chief, John Stone.

As leader, unlike his brilliant performance as deputy, he had not been particularly dexterous in handling this sort of problem because the challenge to his authority was coming primarily from the Right. But to have taken on the Right decisively on this issue may have eroded his own wobbling base of support, while the party's moderates could never come to love Howard. He tried various compromise formulations but in a series of radio interviews on August 1 seemed to harden his position. Eventually he made the fateful declaration: ' . . . it would be in our immediate-term interest and supportive of social cohesion if it [Asian immigration] were slowed down a little so that the capacity of the community to absorb was greater.' Howard also said, and repeated many times later, that governments had the right to limit immigration from any source to safeguard social cohesion. But the only source he had singled out was Asia.

In trying to understand the reaction to these remarks it is essential to understand their context. The context of the remarks was inflammatory. Australia for much of its history had defined itself partly through its rejection of Asia. The first Act the newly constituted federal parliament passed after federation in 1901 was the Immigration Restriction Act. Slowly, slowly, with infinite pain and care the nation had come to reject that position. In the mid-1960s the White Australia policy was formally dropped but it was not until the late 1970s that Asians in large numbers had been accepted into Australia. These Asians, the Indochinese boat people, were not the highly qualified, English-speaking Asians the country would later accept. If any immigrants were likely to find it difficult at first to settle in it was refugees. There had been a kind of unwritten agreement between the major parties that held for the most part, namely that neither side would mount an all-out assault on the newly racially non-discriminatory basis of the immigration program. This was clearly an area which needed sensitive leadership and where irresponsible rabble-rousing could do great harm.

Moreover there had been a vicious anti-Asian immigration campaign running through parts of Australia in the months before Howard's comments. His own party, and certainly his coalition, was deeply divided on the issue. The issue required not only leadership but adroit management by the leader. It got neither. Many Liberals were deeply committed to non-discrimination as a principle. The former prime minister, Malcolm Fraser, in a comment that was devastating for Howard politically, declared that 'Comments based on race do not belong in the Australian political environment. I do not believe they belong in the Liberal Party.' Howard was immediately subject to devastating criticism from all over the Australian political landscape.

He became defensive and would neither withdraw his comments nor defend them. But his statement begged countless questions. Which Asians were harming social cohesion? What was the evidence that social cohesion was being harmed? Would a coalition government target and reduce Asian immigration? How would it do so without violating the new principle of non-discrimination in immigration policy? What countries did Howard mean in this context by 'Asia'? Didn't his comments merely give heart to those seeking to make sure that Asian immigration was controversial?

I am perhaps overly sensitive to matters of non-discrimination. I have always regarded it as the first principle of political decency. I was travelling through Southeast Asia when Howard made his peculiar remarks and I was sickened and appalled to see them reported on the front pages of newspapers throughout the region. I made my modest contribution by calling in my column on Howard to resign his leadership, convinced not only that his remarks breached canons of decency in themselves, but also that the reaction to them in Southeast Asia indicated the damage he had done Australia. Howard would later tell friends that he had found my columns hurtful.

Howard became belligerent and defensive and highly emotional, the worst combination in trying to defuse a crisis. The Hawke government moved to exploit Howard's travails and it did so intelligently. Late in August Hawke moved a resolution to the effect that no Australian government should use race or ethnic origin as a criterion in determining immigrant selection. The government did not deny the sovereign right of an Australian government to choose who could come to Australia, but made the ethical commitment that it would never base this choice on racial grounds. Howard's position had become so convoluted and confused—he refused either to retract or defend his original remarks—that he forced the coalition to oppose the government's resolution. This the coalition did, many with a very heavy heart. And an historically large number refused to toe the party line. Four Liberals crossed the floor, including a former immigration minister, Ian MacPhee, and a former spokesman on immigration, Philip Ruddock. Two others abstained, including another former immigration minister, Michael MacKellar.

Howard's leadership was shot from that moment on. Senior Liberals have told me that it was this incident, the appalling mismanagement as much as the issues of principle, which convinced them to switch their support away from Howard's leadership. Paul Kelly, whose *The End of Certainty* is the definitive account of Australian politics in the 1980s, records that 'two years later . . . Liberal after Liberal nominated this issue in the winter of 1988 as fundamental in setting the scene for Howard's removal as leader.'

Howard was successfully ambushed by Peacock in May of the next year and said his leadership aspirations were finally at an end. When asked just after the Peacock coup if he still coveted the leadership he came up with one of his more memorable lines: 'Break it down, that would be Lazarus with a triple bypass.' But Howard did learn from the fiasco of his second Asian immigration intervention. He never repeated the remarks and over the succeeding months and years gradually distanced himself from them further and further. Remarkably, he didn't lose his hunger for politics, telling me once in the early '90s that he didn't want to be called an elder statesman of the party because he was too young to be an elder statesman.

He understandably sulked on the back bench for a few months after losing the leadership before coming back as spokesman for industry, technology and commerce in the last months of Peacock's period as Opposition leader. Peacock lost narrowly to Hawke in the 1990 election and Howard entertained the idea of another run at the leadership. But his former adviser John Hewson was elected virtually by acclamation. Howard took on the job of spokesman on industrial relations. He had always believed industrial relations reform was essential to his broader agenda for economic reform and he was a reasonably effective spokesman in that portfolio under Hewson.

Astonishingly, Hewson lost the unlosable election to Keating in 1993. Howard once more ran for the leadership but was defeated by Hewson, who was nonetheless fatally damaged by his election loss. Eventually the Liberals turned to Alexander Downer to lead them. He was a failure as leader, totally mastered by Keating, stumbling through gaffe after gaffe. Finally, in desperation the Liberals turned back to Howard as the only figure of substance left standing among them.

Howard knew, however, that he still had a repair job to do on the question of how people saw his attitude to Asia, now so central a part of Australian life. Before he regained the leadership I published a column calling on Howard to unequivocally recant his previous views if he was serious about another shot at the leadership. Rather to my surprise, Howard took up my challenge. In the way of politics and journalism Howard and I had got back to fairly civil terms despite the strength of my former columns criticising him. That is the way in Australian politics. I did come to admire Howard's pragmatism and professionalism as a politician. Certainly, too, he was always good company. He invited me to have lunch and talk over the Asian immigration issue. Howard had to repair his general standing on Asian issues but he also had a specific political need. The moderates, or so-called 'wets', within the Liberal Party needed to be conciliated if he was to regain the leadership, or certainly if he was to have nearly unanimous support for regaining the leadership. They needed to be convinced that he had changed. At his suggestion I interviewed him for the *Australian* in January, 1995. The interview, undertaken while Downer was still leader and Howard was theoretically restricted to commenting on industrial relations, became a front-page piece and was headlined: 'HOWARD: I WAS WRONG ON ASIANS'. Because I had written the column critical of him Howard was entitled to reply to me. In fact it was a measure of how weak Downer's leadership had become that he could not prevent such an interview taking place.

Never since Paul on the road to Damascus has a political conversion been so thorough. Howard moved beyond his previous admission that his 1988 remarks were clumsy and described them as 'wrong' and 'a mistake'.

He said: 'If they [my remarks] were seen by Australians of Asian descent as suggesting that I regarded them in any way as lesser Australians than any other Australians, then I regret that very much.' In this interview Howard, whose formal position then was merely Opposition industrial relations spokesman, (although it was obvious that he was coming back to the leadership), committed himself absolutely to supporting a racially non-discriminatory immigration policy, describing non-discrimination as the 'cornerstone' of the Liberal Party's immigration policy. He also said that support for Australia's engagement with Asia was a bipartisan 'constant' in Australian politics. He strongly supported Australia's thrust into Asia as well as specific initiatives such as APEC. Echoing Keating, he singled out Australia's relationship with Indonesia: 'I think Australia's relationship with Indonesia is incredibly important. The economic potential of that relationship is great . . . and there's something wrong if we can't sell a lot of our services to that burgeoning middle class.'

He also made the intriguing and possibly profitable suggestion that many Asian immigrants were natural conservative voters and would vote for the Liberal–National coalition: 'A lot of the people who have come here from Southeast Asia, their values are my values—small business, the emphasis on family, entrepreneurial risk taking, the emphasis on education.' He even claimed the Liberal Party was the natural party to take Australia into Asia and that the Keating government's policies in some instances were retarding Australia's integration with Asia. In this category he cited the slow pace of microeconomic reform in general, and the failure to reform industrial relations, in particular, more quickly. He also claimed the government's rhetoric was damaging Australia's standing in the region. By claiming more or less to be the first Australian government to engage with Asia, the Keating government reinforced a negative stereotype about Australia's past. He castigated Keating for what he regarded as Keating's denigration of Australian history. He said: 'One thing many Asians do have a regard for is their history and you don't gain any points for jettisoning your history.'

These views represented an effort by Howard to present

himself as a modern, contemporary leader, fully supportive and understanding of Australia's most important and challenging external engagements and the changing nature of its domestic society. He also attempted to float a new term in Australian politics: 'tolerant conservatism'. He said: 'All my life I've been a tolerant individual. In my personal relations I've been a tolerant person. I'm a tolerant conservative.'

One of Howard's senior front-bench colleagues, after reading the interview, told me that he thought the remarks represented a genuine change of heart by Howard, but that this change of heart was entirely consistent with, indeed sprang from, Howard's deep conservatism. After all, in the early 1980s Asian immigration on a large scale was still quite new. This made conservatives uneasy. Now, by the mid-1990s, Asian immigration was an absolutely routine, long-established part of Australian life. As a result the true conservative position, which resists change but then defends the new status quo once that is established, was now comfortable with Asian immigration. Certainly Howard himself was dealing in his own electorate with the new Australia. Some 7 per cent of his electorate were Asian, he was routinely sending out fund-raising letters in Chinese to constituents with Chinese names.

Howard became leader shortly after this interview was published. In a series of speeches on foreign policy in 1995—to the Asia Australia Institute, to Melbourne University's Asia Link centre, and to the Australian Defence Association—Howard took an orthodox line on contemporary Australian foreign policy, identifying Asia as the number one priority, strongly backing APEC and other regional initiatives. This became the pattern of several of Howard's policy positions as 1995 wore on. The tactic was to minimise differences with the government, to make the government the issue and dissatisfaction with it the driving force in the election. But the process was at times bizarre. The Liberals promised to freeze immigration, for example, at its current level, thus in effect implying the government had got immigration policy right, despite other Liberal criticisms of the government on immigration.

This became the pattern across most policy areas. There was plenty of criticism of the government but overall a commitment to change little. For a man who had once sold himself as a 'conviction politician' this seemed a very narrowly political and tactical route to office, although certainly it was spectacularly successful. The broader question for Howard was whether he had changed and grown enough to really be an effective Australian prime minister in the second half of the 1990s and beyond. In his second incarnation as Opposition leader he showed little real feel for Asia or for the internationalisation of all domestic issues which is one of the great driving dynamics of our time. Typically, when the then Thai Opposition leader, Banharn Silpa-Archa, visited Australia and asked to see his Australian counterpart, Howard was too busy to see him. A few months later Banharn was Thailand's prime minister, someone likely to be important to Howard, certainly to Australia. Had Howard really learned the vernacular of modern foreign affairs, indeed of modern, cosmopolitan Australia? Despite displaying little real feel for the region, Howard did, however, make the basic adjustments necessary to being a credible Australian leader in the 1990s.

Certainly it was important for Australia that Howard had completely accepted the Keating paradigm about modern Australian foreign policy. He did not of course accept Keating's version of the past, especially his attacks on long-time Liberal prime minister, Robert Menzies. But he did accept the Keating government's understanding of the hierarchy of Australia's national interests.

His speech to the Asia–Australia Institute in October 1995, was an important statement of Howard's view of the world. His first significant comments in that speech were: 'The coalition places a strong emphasis on the Asian region. We recognise its vital importance for Australia's long-term interests. We welcome our growing interaction with the peoples of the region.' Later, during the election campaign in early 1996, Howard would issue a formal election foreign policy in which the Liberal Party declared that closer engagement with Asia would be its highest foreign policy priority in government. It repeated this statement many times. In the speech to the Asia–Australia Institute Howard attacked Keating by supporting him, declaring that: 'A deep involvement with the nations of the Asia–Pacific region should be seen for what it is—a bipartisan given in the conduct of

Australian foreign policy.' This was a sensible formulation for
Howard to adopt. It accepted the Keating evaluation of what was
important to Australia, but contested Keating's claim to sole
ownership of the ideas.

Howard continued:

> I have never disputed the importance placed by the current
> government on our regional ties. What I continue to reject are
> the rather tawdry attempts by the prime minister [Keating] and
> his colleagues to depict themselves as those great Australian
> statesmen who discovered Asia. They did no such thing.

The section headings of Howard's speech set out his foreign
policy thinking. First came 'Asia's importance to Australia', then
'Our proud history of interaction with Asia', in which he set out
a coherent (if to this writer ultimately unconvincing) defence of
the Liberal Party's record on Asian engagement. This was followed
by a section headed 'The state of our current regional relationships', in which he made the reasonable point that while Australia's exports to Asia had risen rapidly under Labor our overall
market share in most Asian markets had declined. Howard was
on quite strong ground here. The most important factor influ-
encing Australia's performance in Asia will be its economic
success and the pace of economic reform. By the end the Keating
government was clearly very tired and the pace of reform had
slackened.

The next section was headed, simply, 'APEC'. In this section
Howard made two points. Despite the fact that Hawke had
founded APEC it actually grew out of diplomatic work undertaken by former Liberal prime minister, Malcolm Fraser, he
asserted. Thus he was claiming a share of Liberal ownership for
APEC. The second point, which was designed simply to be
reassuring, was that he recognised the importance of APEC and
would continue to support its development vigorously in government. Again this was orthodox and sensible.

The next section was titled 'the need for strong bilateral ties'.
This was platitudes but again reassuring platitudes. Then came
'Emphases in East Asia' which declared: 'The coalition recognises
that many of Australia's most important bilateral relationships
are with East Asian states' and went on to make obvious and
sensible points about Australia's relations with Indonesia, Japan

and China. There followed a section on 'Regional security priorities', in which Howard strongly supported the American presence in the region, but also showed he was up to date by also strongly supporting the new regional security dialogue body, the Association of South-East Asian Nations Regional Forum. The speech's conclusion restated its major themes.

The importance of all this was that Howard was not going to give anyone, especially in the business community, any reason to vote against the coalition on the grounds that its foreign policy might be either eccentric or anachronistic regarding Asia. In some ways Howard's conversion demonstrates just how thoroughly the new Asian paradigm is established in Australian politics. You cannot now credibly aspire to leadership in Australia without a sensible position on Asia.

During the 1996 election campaign itself Keating and his foreign minister, Gareth Evans, repeatedly said the coalition was either not really interested in Asia or would not be able to cope with the challenges of Asia. Keating even went so far as to say that Asian leaders would not deal with Howard. This was plainly an overstatement and probably did Keating some harm. Asian leaders are extremely pragmatic and would certainly deal with whoever is the legal government of Australia.

There is no evidence that Keating or Evans's remarks earned Labor a single vote inside Australia. What they certainly did was make life more difficult for the Howard government when it came to office. Newspapers all over Asia had reported the Keating and Evans remarks. Asian commentators were used to dealing with the Keating government and tended to accept the remarks at face value instead of seeing them as just domestic electioneering. Moreover a number of coalition parliamentary candidates made racially insensitive remarks during the campaign and then scored well in their electorates. The coalition leadership quickly and decisively distanced themselves from these remarks, in one case the Liberal Party even withdrew the candidate's party endorsement. That, however, was reported in Asia far less than the original offensive remarks.

With the exception of a couple of stumbles Howard was disciplined and effective in the campaign and ultimately won in a landslide. His remark during a campaign interview that he wanted Australians to feel 'comfortable and relaxed' about their past, their present and their future was greeted with derision by media commentators but was exactly the kind of reassuring message voters wanted to hear. His reform proposals were modest but based around values he had espoused most of his life— namely a more flexible industrial relations system, greater support for the traditional family, greater support for private medical insurance and the partial privatisation of the telecommunications giant, Telstra. This was no radical agenda but it seemed to be about the level and intensity of change Australians were looking for. In any event they clearly wanted to clobber Keating and they did just that.

Howard looked nervous during the first television debate and was constantly twitching his shoulders. On one occasion during a radio interview he got confused about the detail of his tax policy but apart from that stuck to his script. Unlike his previous time as Opposition leader he never let the pressure get to him and he never allowed his opponents to dictate his agenda.

Once in government Howard's early months were taken up with domestic issues but he did recognise, as did his foreign minister, Alexander Downer, that he had to counter the impression Keating had created that the coalition government would diminish Australia's commitment to Asia. He and Downer made important statements asserting the contrary. 'If you had a dollar for every time we're going to say engagement with Asia is our number one priority before the end of the year you'd be a very rich man,' one government official told me in April, 1996.

In terms of Asia, Howard did one shrewd thing shortly after the election. He dispatched the former senior Australian diplomat, Richard Woolcott, to Kuala Lumpur with an invitation from Howard for Malaysia's prime minister, Dr Mahathir, to visit Australia on his way to or from New Zealand in March. Happily Mahathir agreed to do this and Howard was able to demonstrate very early the falseness of Keating's claim that Asian leaders would not deal with him as prime minister.

The Howard–Mahathir meeting in Brisbane in March was by no means earth-shattering but Howard did make one significant policy change. He dropped Australia's opposition to Malaysia's proposed East Asian Economic Caucus. This had been a position developed over some time by the Liberals in Opposition (and urged on them by this writer). Howard sensibly did not come out gushingly in favour of the EAEC. But he recognised that there was a developing mood within East Asia for some sort of consultative mechanism as well as APEC and restricted to the western Pacific. If the EAEC were to get going one day Australia might want to join. Our previous high-profile public campaign against the EAEC, which had been primarily driven by Keating, was doing us no good. A more neutral position made more sense.

Howard also raised with Mahathir Australia's desire to be included in the second Asia–Europe summit. Mahathir put his view that the membership of the group should not be expanded. But, as Howard told me privately after the meeting, the atmospherics of the meeting were excellent. At a post-summit press conference Howard made one especially smart remark. He said that he had discussed with Dr Mahathir the tensions between China and Taiwan. As a regional leader of three weeks standing, Howard said, he was interested to hear the views of a regional leader of fourteen years standing. No Australian could regard this as sycophantic or grovelling but it showed a happy deference to the more experienced leader, the kind of deference often shown in Asia. It was a well-advised remark.

Similarly, the fact that Howard, unlike Keating, would not be competing with Mahathir for regional leadership served him well. This may serve him well throughout the region. Despite the undeniable success of Keating and Evans in regional diplomacy there was a feeling that the region was suffering 'initiative fatigue' with the Keating government. A period of intelligent consolidation, caution and consultation in Australian foreign policy, which can later develop into a more activist mode, may be no bad thing.

However, as the months wore on, big question marks emerged over the basic competence of the Howard government in foreign policy. The abolition of a mixed credit concessional loan scheme, though foreshadowed in the election campaign, left a bad taste, and a sense of Australian commitments dishonoured, in several Asian capitals.

Worse, Howard himself delivered clumsy and confused speeches in his first trip to Asia as prime minister. In his first speech in Indonesia, in September 1996, he declared that

Australia was 'not Asian'. In some ways this is true enough but it was an absurdly negative way to frame his first message to Asia. When Keating declared that Australia was neither Asian nor European, but just Australian, it was after four years of intense diplomatic engagement with Asia. It was a mild corrective to what some saw as swinging the pendulum too far. But Howard foolishly chose to make his first message a negative. Instead of re-visiting the dreary debate about whether Australia is part of Asia, he could have used a different formulation, declaring Australia's enthusiastic commitment as part of the Asia–Pacific. Howard's speech did contain plenty of general positive comments on the Australia–Indonesia relationship, but it was a typical Howard failing, and a sign of a lack of familiarity with the rhythms of the region, that he should express his views about Australian identity in a negative, dividing and exclusionary way, rather than in a positive, uniting, inclusive fashion.

Moreover, it raised questions about the coherence of foreign policy under Howard. His comments could not possibly assist the realisation of what his government had identified as a key foreign policy priority, namely getting Australia included, as part of Asia, in the Asia–Europe summit process.

Similarly, in Howard's first speech in Indonesia he said that Australia was not a bridge between Asia and the West. Yet Liberal Party policy in Opposition had described Australia in exactly that way. Moreover, utterly non-contentious official state and federal Australian efforts to convince multinational firms to set up their Asian regional headquarters in Australia had used similar formulations. Eventually, Australian officials travelling with Howard had to explain that Australia was indeed a business bridge, but not a cultural bridge. Again, the question is begged—why use such a narrow, negative, formulation, why indeed express so clumsy, and so gratuitously unhelpful, a concept?

However, all these stumbles appeared to be mere day to day incompetence, rather than any decision by Howard to change the orientation of Australian foreign policy.

But the big story about Howard and Asia is the way Howard, as a professional politician determined to succeed, responded at last to the imperative of his own society. No modern Australian leader could have been less intuitively switched on to Asia than

Howard, yet he has made the adjustments necessary and, as any good politican would, will now try to make the Asian connection a winner for him and his government. This is the reality of the new Australia.

6

A NEW ZEALAND INTERLUDE: A VOYAGE ON THE STARSHIP *ENTERPRISE*

Porirua East is as close to a Maori ghetto, or at least a Maori and Pacific Islander ghetto, as you will find in Wellington, New Zealand's picture-postcard pretty capital and second biggest city. Walking through the area, as I did in September 1995, reveals the paradox of race relations in New Zealand. Most of the houses are timber, and provided ultimately by the government. They are semi-detached with two families per building, in their basic structure much like the houses which figured in the extraordinarily powerful and successful New Zealand film, *Once Were Warriors*. By first world standards I suppose they are fairly modest, but my impression of them as I walked around that day was that really they looked pretty affluent, certainly tidy and well cared for, with only the odd house a bit scruffy, and, as far as I could see, only one house bearing graffiti. The atmosphere in the streets certainly seemed relaxed and friendly. There is a lot of crime here, the locals told me, but much of it is burglaries or domestic strife.

Some of the Samoan kids were huge, and some of the Maori kids looked pretty tough, much like most large teenage males after school, wearing baseball caps back to front and one or two in football jerseys from Australian rugby league clubs. But there was no sense, as a non-Maori wandering about, of being unwelcome or in any danger. The most common expression I came across was a shy and curious smile.

Race relations in New Zealand, for all their recent troubles, are probably better than they are in almost any comparable country with a substantial indigenous minority and a dominant, white, settler majority. Yet New Zealanders seem obsessed these days with race relations, to the point almost where other areas of intellectual life in New Zealand seem somewhat atrophied as a consequence. Certainly Kiwis seem much more exercised about race relations than peoples who have had much more bitter relatively recent racial experiences, such as Malaysians or Indonesians. A peculiar view of their Maori uniqueness also seems to be part of a more general world view of New Zealanders which is increasingly eccentric and unreal.

Partly this is a consequence of the nation's unique aloneness. It is further from anywhere than just about any developed country in the world. Its environment is benign and almost infinitely distant, except for its relatively giant neighbour across the Tasman, Australia. New Zealand, with the partial and very different exception of Papua New Guinea, is the only country in the world actually dominated by Australia, from its strategic environment to its television programs. And, as one official put it to me, 'For every major social trend in Australia there is a pale reflection in New Zealand'.

However, the Kiwis' turn in the 1990s towards Asia, an even more belated turn than Australia's, appears not so much a pale imitation as a full-blooded attempt to follow the same regionalist path that Australia trod in the 1980s. New Zealand and Australia are two of the most similar, most intimately connected neighbours anywhere in the world, with ties of blood, of history and of culture just about as close as those which bind any two nations anywhere in the world. Even in the 1990s influential voices on both sides of the Tasman have fitfully called for full political union (though in reality this is a distant and receding possibility).

But in the 1980s the two nations' paths diverged radically on two fronts. First, New Zealand effectively renounced its military alliance with the United States, which has retained, indeed renewed, its vibrancy at the heart of Australian defence and security policy, and indeed of Canberra's regional aspirations. And in the 1980s Australia intensified to an unprecedented degree its engagement with East Asia, across every field of national life. This, New Zealand didn't do. Instead in the 1980s Wellington combined aggressive free market economic reform with an eccentric, quasi-isolationist, anti-nuclear obsessiveness. Now, decades later than it should have, it has begun the great Asian journey.

By the mid-1990s it stood in relation to this journey at just about the same point where Australia stood perhaps fifteen years earlier. Of course for New Zealand it will be a different journey but the similarities are striking. Not the least among the influences pushing New Zealand down this path is the Australian example, and the broader Australian influence on New Zealand's national life.

New Zealand's trade growth is now overwhelmingly with East Asia, which accounts for 40 per cent of its exports and rising. More dramatically it has at last embarked on a substantial immigration program, one of the largest, per capita, in the world (although these figures can be slightly misleading as New Zealand also often records a large emigration, especially to Australia). About half New Zealand's immigrants now come from Asia. In 1995 it granted visas to about 50 000 immigrants, compared with 98 000 in the Australian program, which makes the Kiwi program bigger in per capita terms, although this is a very recent development and one which may not be able to be sustained politically. Of the 50 000 visas Wellington granted in the twelve months to June of 1995, Northeast Asia accounted for some 21 000 and Southeast Asia nearly 3000. The government has toughened its English language requirements for intending migrants, but this is not considered likely to alter those figures substantially.

The Wellington government and the Auckland business elites are just as ambitious, within the different scales in which New Zealand operates, for its Asian engagement as Canberra is for its Asian policies, but with these crucial differences: the consensus in New Zealand is not shared by the parliamentary Opposition, it is not reflected in the media, and it faces potentially explosive opposition from the Maori leadership. Still, all sorts of similar qualifications could have been made about Australia's Asian engagement at the beginning of the 1980s. You have to start somewhere. The Asian push also acts as a significant counter to the otherwise overwhelmingly isolationist, almost solipsistic, tenor of New Zealand political life. It can be a vehicle for the authentic internationalisation of New Zealand society.

Don McKinnon, the deputy prime minister and foreign affairs and trade minister in Jim Bolger's National Party government, has been the change agent within the government in this area. He does not have the regional standing of his former Australian counterpart, Gareth Evans, but he has been foreign minister for several years and is well known around the region. He is a genuine internationalist pushing his countrymen down the Asian path. He certainly sees the Asian engagement as an historic turning point in his country's history. He explained this idea to me in a long conversation in his spacious office in Wellington's peculiar 'Bee Hive' parliamentary building as his aide (a young woman fluent in Bahasa Indonesian, he boasted) took copious notes.

'There's no question in my mind when you look at the growth in our export income, all the growth in our standard of living is coming out of Asia,' McKinnon told me. He continued:

> For the first time in New Zealand's political and geological history we're in the right place at the right time. But it's a big selling job. New Zealanders do not have the easy knowledge of key Japanese or key Chinese or key Malaysians as they do with Europeans or North Americans. And you cannot just trade with Asia and live off the spoils of trade. You've got to actively involve yourself and engage yourself in the region, and that means trade flows, investment flows, people flows, cultural exchanges, the lot. We've seen a remarkable uptake in Asian languages in our schools, Japanese for example in about 220 of 289 high schools. Chinese is also on the move. Not enough schools are doing Bahasa Indonesian, Korean is just getting off the ground in some places.

But how broadly accepted are these changes? Does the nation more broadly see the Asian engagement as a matter of deep historical change, a turning point?

> I don't think we've reached that stage yet. I'd like to think we would be able to reach that stage. I hope New Zealanders will look back on the 1990s as the decade when we significantly turned towards Asia. I was pleased with a poll the other day which showed that the number of New Zealanders opposed to direct foreign investment from Asia had dropped from 35 per cent to 25 per cent. But I don't think I could convince many

New Zealanders now, without browbeating them for a couple of
hours, that this is where it's all going to happen, it's Asia
which is going to dominate New Zealand in the 21st century.

And how important is the immigration connection? 'Vitally
important. We had a xenophobic attitude towards immigration
in the '60s and '70s. God, we were trawling the streets of Glasgow
and Manchester and Liverpool for citizens who I'm not convinced
were as good as what we could have got if we'd had a wider net.
Then we had a large flow of unskilled people from the Pacific in
the '70s and '80s. Now we have a real chance to get people with
high levels of qualifications, high skills, and half of that's coming
from Asia.' McKinnon argued that these immigrants would eventually provide important trading linkages for New Zealand back
to their countries of origin, a view very similar to that held by
Canberra.

McKinnon argued that the previous Labour government of
David Lange and his successors in the '80s had created an
international impression that New Zealand 'just wanted to sit
alone here in the South Pacific'. McKinnon enthusiastically led
his country's successful campaign in the early '90s for a temporary seat on the United Nations Security Council partly to
demonstrate that New Zealand was back taking an interest in
the world and participating actively in international forums.

Some of McKinnon's ministerial colleagues sounded during
interviews even more enthusiastic about their country's Asian
engagement than he did. I spoke at length to Philip Burdon, then
New Zealand's minister for trade negotiations, who sounded quite
evangelical when he got into his stride:

> New Zealand ambitions for Asia reflect exactly what's
> happening in Australia. Business is leading the process. The
> major cities in both countries are quickly moving to a
> cosmopolitan, multicultural ease as a result of Asian
> immigration. This has been quite revolutionary in Australia and
> similarly so here in New Zealand.

But whereas the Asian engagement has been broadly bipartisan
in Australia, the same cannot be said for New Zealand. Winston
Peters, the Maori former National Party minister and subsequently leader of the New Zealand First Party, doesn't like the

new and large immigration program, of which Asians are so prominent a part. He said to me: 'Last year 50 000 people came to this country and for tens of thousands of them there was no identifiable reason as to why they were let in.' Jim Anderton, a former senior figure with the Labour Party and subsequently leader of the left-wing Alliance Party, has led what would look in Southeast Asia a marvellously quaint and anachronistic campaign against foreign investment. McKinnon has accused both Peters and Anderton of promoting xenophobia.

I found opposition to the government's Asian ambitions also from the leader of the Opposition, the Labour Party's Helen Clark, who explicitly rejected any idea that the involvement with Asia represented New Zealand's destiny. She told me: 'No, I don't see it [NZ] as integrated with East Asia. New Zealand will become something quite unique, but this will have a big Polynesian influence, perhaps 30 to 40 per cent of the population.' Clark said she supported greater involvement with Asia, but criticised the government for sometimes going overboard about this, going soft on human rights in Asia and neglecting opportunities in other parts of the world.

But the most ominous opposition comes from the Maori leadership. Maoris constitute about 13 per cent of New Zealand's population, with other Pacific Islanders another 5 per cent or so. They are much younger, and have a much higher birth rate, than European New Zealanders. Clark's speculation that the Polynesian component of her nation's population could reach 30 or even 40 per cent is not fanciful. It takes not much paranoia on the part of Maoris to see the recently enlarged immigration program as a device by which to keep the Maori proportion of the population at about its present level. Tu Williams of the Maori Congress, an organisation which links Maori tribal leaders, used moderate language to tell me about what could be an explosive looming confrontation. He said:

> There's concern within the Maori community, although the issue still needs further investigation, that the government has embarked on an immigration program that works against Maori interests. In this country it's the Maori population that's increasing. As time goes on this will become a bigger and bigger issue. It's not aimed at any one group, such as Asians,

but it's a matter of working out what the government's real agenda is.

If present trends continue (always a big if) the Asian percentage in New Zealand's population could rise from its present 2 per cent to 5 per cent, similar to the Australian level, by the end of the decade. Extrapolate a bit further and you could get a 10 per cent Asian population by the end of the first decade of the twenty-first century. Of course that assumes that the unusually high immigration levels remain unchanged and that the Asian proportion of that program remains unchanged. But even allowing for all the qualifications, this represents a massive process of change in what was for a long time one of the most conservative and broadly racist (if in an undramatic fashion) societies on Earth.

New Zealand presents by the mid-90s as a fairly schizophrenic society. Its economy has picked up but after a long, long slump. It's hard to know whether its relative economic success in the mid-90s was the result of systematic structural change in the economy or merely the normal bounce at the end of a long recession. In any event its per capita income of around $US12 000 leaves it way down the ladder of Organisation of Economic Cooperation and Development standard of living tables. It may not for very much longer be able to attract high quality Asian immigrants. Its per capita income is way behind such Asian societies as Hong Kong and Singapore, not to mention its trans-Tasman neighbour. Moreover, the intelligent attempt to engage with Asia is running against the still very muddled foreign policy adventurism, isolationism and general nuttiness of New Zealand in the 1980s.

For an Australian foreign policy buff like me, visiting New Zealand in 1995 for the first time in many years made me feel rather like Captain James Kirk of the Starship *Enterprise* in *Star Trek*. It was not that I was boldly going where no man had gone before, nor had I sought out a strange new civilisation. Rather, I felt like Kirk in one of those *Star Trek* episodes in which he finds himself in a parallel universe, one in which everything seems at first exactly like home but something tells you that this is some place weird.

The Australia–New Zealand relationship, as I have noted

earlier, is very intimate. But in truth the two societies have become sharply different, not least over the Asian dimension. But if anything the differences are even more fundamental, and go back to the crisis of the Australia–New Zealand–United States (ANZUS) alliance in the 1980s. There is also, not unusually in such an intimate relationship, a fair amount of friction. Australia patronises, bullies, takes for granted and ignores New Zealand. New Zealand resents being patronised, bullied, taken for granted and ignored. But Australia is now much more powerful vis-à-vis New Zealand than it was fifteen years ago, not only because for most of that period the Australian economy grew more quickly than did the New Zealand economy, but also because of New Zealand's self-destructive foreign policy in the '80s and its late entry into the business of serious regional diplomacy and engagement. It is striking that within Australia whenever the talk is of regional engagement New Zealand is never mentioned, even though for Australia to have another country of similar ethnic, cultural and political background as itself engaged in the region is an obvious advantage in reducing the sense of Australia being the odd man out in the region. But serious Australian discussion of foreign policy never seems to see New Zealand figure as a significant player.

This has some peculiar operational consequences. Don McKinnon recalled the long history of personal acrimony between Australian and New Zealand prime ministers: 'I remember when Menzies (of Australia) couldn't speak to Holyoake, when Muldoon (of New Zealand) couldn't stand Fraser, when Hawke couldn't speak to Lange.' So, when Paul Keating became Australian prime minister McKinnon suggested an annual ANZAC prime ministers' meeting. His point was that this meeting should not be in the corridors of some larger meeting, be it APEC or the Commonwealth, but a separate, dedicated, heads of government trans-Tasman meeting, one year in Australia, one year in New Zealand. The Australians had absolutely no interest in the proposal at all. Although there are significant consultative mechanisms between the two countries the Australians just could not be bothered with a heads of government meeting. It is very difficult to imagine Keating taking that view with a significant Asian leader. Even in the days of trans-Tasman prime ministerial hostility there was less indifference to New Zealand from Australia than there is today.

This is partly because New Zealand is still suffering, rightly in my view, the vast consequences of its desertion from the western alliance in the 1980s. The more you look back on David Lange, New Zealand's prime minister of that time, the more you marvel that such a preposterous figure could ever have been New Zealand's prime minister. Lange effectively took New Zealand out of the ANZUS alliance by refusing to have US ships that were nuclear powered, or capable of carrying nuclear weapons, visit Kiwi ports. Many New Zealanders regard what was really a pathetic abdication of responsibility as the high point of their national self-assertion. Partly as a result, foreign policy discussion in New Zealand, when it moves beyond the narrowest trade focus (which has sensibly been used to drive the Asian engagement) takes on a dotty and unreal air. It's one of the things that made me feel like Captain Kirk.

The New Zealand Labour Party, for example, actually took the view officially that the signing of the indefinite extension of the Nuclear Non-Proliferation Treaty (NPT) was a 'craven' sell out to the interests of the five declared nuclear powers. The NPT has probably been the most successful arms control treaty in the history of the world. It is substantially responsible for the world having to deal with perhaps eight or nine nuclear powers instead of thirty or forty. To have sabotaged the NPT would have been monstrous folly. To get its indefinite extension was a huge victory for those forces trying to contain the spread of nuclear weapons technology. But the position of the New Zealand Labour Party, the official opposition and alternative government, now seems to dwell in the dreamland of green fantasy and undergraduate anti-nuclear protest. It is essentially the outlook of the irresponsible and the powerless, of people who will never have to pay any price in the real world for their words or actions.

Abandoning ANZUS was irresponsible and dishonourable, but it also greatly damaged New Zealand's interests and greatly reduced its influence and independence, in the process paradoxically making it much more subject to the will of Australia. What is truly bizarre is that at a time of great fluidity in international relations, when the whole world is seeking a purchase on the

diffuse power system in the United States, when the new democracies of Eastern Europe are desperately seeking entry into the
NATO alliance, New Zealand decided to destroy its long-standing
and previously intimate relationship with the world's dominant
superpower, the United States. As a result New Zealand brings
nothing extra to regional diplomacy beyond its own small economy, whereas Australia brings all the weight of an intimate
relationship with Washington, an asset which Keating at times
deployed brilliantly.

New Zealand instead has virtually abandoned any distinctive
influence. Its gesture of poking its tongue out at the US diminished its influence and therefore its real independence. It has
become in effect an appendage of Australia, reduced to saying
that, while it does not always agree with Australia's regional
diplomacy, it has a great deal at stake in the success of that
regional diplomacy. The same is even more true of defence and
security policy. While Canberra always made it clear that it could
not substitute for the US in defence terms, in effect New Zealand
has had to seek an even more intimate defence relationship with
Australia. Thus the New Zealand government was virtually forced
by Canberra to buy ANZAC frigates in the 1980s. Similarly,
Canberra, while dominating New Zealand's defence policy, actually argued privately to Washington that it should take a hard
line with Wellington over the ANZUS dispute lest the 'New
Zealand disease' spread to the Australian Labor Party.

More generally New Zealand could effectively bug out from
the western alliance because it felt no threat and it felt no threat
because it knew that Australia would ultimately take care of its
security. New Zealand makes little independent defence effort,
and has no US alliance, because it knows that to threaten New
Zealand any potential aggressor would have to get by Australia
first. Thus Wellington can abandon the demanding business of
making any effort to provide for its own security. It is similar to,
but worse than, what used to be Australia's attitude to the United
States. It is what is known in Australia as the bludger's option
dressed up in the rhetoric of national independence.

The National government of Jim Bolger made great efforts in
the 1990s to recover a friendly relationship with the United
States, and, after Bill Clinton became president, it succeeded to

some extent. But the US makes an absolute distinction between military allies and non-allies, and New Zealand is definitely a non-ally. Thus, at American insistence, New Zealand is excluded from the major US–Australia Kangaroo military exercises. This is a particular irony because numerous Southeast Asian nations participate in these exercises at one level or another.

The situation of Canada is in some ways comparable with that of New Zealand. Canada faces no external threat. Ottawa could easily have decided that its involvement with NATO made it unnecessarily a nuclear target, and that whatever the state of formal alliances, the United States would never allow a hostile foreign power to threaten Canada. And so Canada could have abolished its armed forces and dropped out of the alliance. But Canada wouldn't do that out of simple self-respect. Real national independence involves dealing with reality, seeking influence where you have responsibility, accepting responsibility for your own situation, maximising your effectiveness and pulling your own weight. That New Zealanders decided not to do this in the 1980s was not a sign of independence but insouciance and irresponsibility. When Australian Labor leaders such as Bob Hawke, Bill Hayden, Kim Beazley and Gareth Evans were convincing the Australian Left that there was a moral dimension to the Cold War and that you had to take sides, and that you also had to do what you could to provide for your own security, the New Zealand Labour Party was substituting environmental pamphleteering for foreign and security policy.

The US no longer has nuclear weapons on its ships. In 1993 the Wellington government conducted an inquiry to determine whether there could possibly be any environmental danger in having nuclear-propelled ships visit. The inquiry answered in the negative so convincingly that the Pentagon sends out this document by the truckload. But the National government was travelling very badly in the polls at the time and although some senior ministers privately favoured changing the policy there was no prospect then, as there is none now, of the New Zealand parliament sensibly reconsidering its ban on even nuclear-propelled ships visiting its ports.

Even if it did there is no guarantee the US would revive the alliance. New Zealand defected for no reason when the Cold War was raging, when friendships and commitments needed to count. An irreplaceable skein of credibility and respect was torn in Washington and in Canberra. As a result New Zealand is now more dependent on Australian foreign and security policies, more subject to Canberra's whim, than ever before. That's a very strange form of independence.

Meanwhile New Zealand seems increasingly obsessed with its internal race relations which, despite being basically good, are deteriorating and perhaps entering a new period of confrontation. The races are not yet bitterly opposed and certainly not physically segregated. As Doug Graham, the minister in charge of Treaty of Waitangi negotiations, told me: 'Most New Zealanders regard Maoris with great affection, even if it's paternalistic affection. And we're very proud of Maori culture. But if you get a real big fella, with tatoos on his face, shaking his fist, it frightens the bejeesus out of people.' Nonetheless, Graham remained optimistic: 'Most New Zealanders have a large dollop of commonsense.'

But the negotiations which have dominated New Zealand over the 1990s do suggest the country is entering a uniquely dangerous phase of its history. Basically an attempt is being made to give effect to the 1840 Treaty of Waitangi, which ceded sovereignty over New Zealand to the British Crown, but said that Maori chiefs would continue to exercise chieftanship and control over their lands. The process will involve handing back to Maori control substantial tracts of land, and where this is not practicable, handing over substantial sums of money. Most white New Zealanders in the 1990s seemed happy enough with this in principle but the debate, by the mid-90s, was showing signs of dangerous polarisation.

First, the process produced a lot of division among Maoris, who do not have a unified national leadership. About 85 per cent of Maoris are urbanised and most of these have lost touch with their tribes. How are urban Maoris to benefit from Waitangi settlements? More broadly, who speaks for Maoris? But the dangers of polarisation come also from the increasingly radical claims of sovereignty which some Maoris argue arise from the Treaty of Waitangi. This line of argument has it that Maoris never intended to give away total sovereignty in perpetuity and, focusing on chieftanship, develops ever more radical demands for control over various aspects of New Zealand life.

In September 1995, after a six-month occupation by Maori activists, a school building was burned down in New Zealand's north island. No one was hurt but it was a highly traumatic incident which received absolute saturation media coverage throughout New Zealand. The Maori activists who make the most radical claims, and take the most radical actions, do not appear to represent huge numbers of people, but more mainstream Maori leaders are not prepared to condemn or disown them outright. Winston Peters blamed the media, in part, and said that the media are more interested in the views of radical Maoris 'who couldn't fill a phone box' than they are in the views of elected Maori members of parliament.

But for all that, mainstream Maori leadership has become more radical in recent years. Aroha Mead of the Maori Congress told me:

> We've always said there has to be constitutional reform because the current system is not appropriate. We're developing as a race a clearer idea of what our rights are in this country and internationally. We used to be focused on needs, now it's rights. The Crown [the New Zealand government] has signed international treaties, for example the GATT treaty, without consulting Maoris.

The idea that the government cannot conduct normal international relations without special consultations with Maori leaders is unrealistic, to put it mildly. Yet the widespread currency of such ideas both reflects the irresponsible nature of much New Zealand debate and will also pose a specific problem. When these unrealistic aspirations are inevitably unfulfilled, there will be frustration and anger. This could lead to something nasty. You wouldn't need many activists convinced of the righteousness of direct action to turn New Zealand into an unpleasant place. Will there be more school burnings and the like? 'Yes, probably,' said Doug Graham. 'The first thing they [Maoris] want is to get it out in the open, because the feelings, that no one's listening to them, have been building for generations. It can be cathartic. it will be difficult. I only hope we're tolerant enough to get through it.' The first stirrings of a white backlash are evident in books such as *The Travesty of Waitangi*, although as yet this is not a particularly threatening development.

New Zealand is one of the oddest places in the world. It is endowed with great natural gifts yet until recently its economic performance has been extremely mediocre. It has a tradition of great martial valour, yet it has turned its back on traditional alliances which are essential to nearly every nation's security, with the government recently resorting to participation in UN peacekeeping exercises as a desperate attempt to make the armed services respectable again. Its racial situation is growing increasingly complex and testy. It seems to have only just discovered that something of great historical moment is happening in East Asia, and that this can hold out significant opportunities for New Zealand. The biggest opportunity of all is the chance to internationalise a very provincial society, to get it involved in the great games of the world, and of our region.

7

MAHATHIR AND ANWAR: THE MALAY MAGICIAN AND THE SORCERER'S APPRENTICE

'Please come to our rally tonight. We are expecting trouble. The government will try to cause an incident so they can provoke racial tension in the country. The more foreign reporters who come to our rally the better.' The words came from an earnest young man, Chinese, bespectacled, face pock-marked from recently departed adolescent acne, painfully thin. He was a volunteer worker for the Opposition Democratic Action Party in Penang, Malaysia's only state with an ethnic Chinese majority. We were talking at the scruffy, crowded little shopfront headquarters of the DAP right in the middle of downtown Georgetown, Penang.

Penang is a beautiful little island off the northwest coast of the Malay peninsula. It is like a little brother of Singapore—Chinese, rich, industrious, fast moving. Thirty years ago it was a backwater but today it bustles with the happy intersection of three genuinely global industries—tourism, high-tech electronics manufacturing, and seafood, in all of which it excels. When you visit Penang for the first time you can see why Singapore was booted out of the Malaysian federation in the mid-1960s. Two islands of fabulous Chinese industry at either end of the Malay peninsula, whose combined population would almost even up the racial scales between the majority Malays and the minority Chinese, was just one Chinese island too many. Singapore had to go. Penang stayed.

Now Penang is a rival, and increasingly a successful rival, to Singapore for foreign investment, especially in computer electronics manufacturing. It offers many of the same advantages as Singapore—a highly motivated and disciplined Chinese work force, a plentiful supply of engineers and technicians, excellent general amenities, a sympathetic government regime for foreign investors, good infrastructure, a range of networks and contacts through the Chinese community back into mainland China itself, but at a fraction of the cost of Singapore. Like Singapore Penang has its own rich British colonial history, its own version of Raffles Hotel, the best preserved and liveliest old-style Chinatown in Southeast Asia (unlike Singapore which has effectively demolished the old shophouses) and figures in seemingly countless Somerset Maugham stories. But Penang also supplies one of the most remarkable of Malay politicians, Anwar Ibrahim, deputy prime minister and heir apparent to the prime minister, Dr Mahathir Mohamad. The prospect of an Anwar prime ministership fills Penang's vigorous entrepreneurs with delight. The island holds happy and sentimental memories for me. My wife Jasbir and I honeymooned, at Penang's Batu Ferringhi beach, years before. But this visit, in April 1995, was for business, to cover Malaysia's general elections that year.

As the only Chinese-majority state Penang was expected to be on the front line of any racial trouble. Officials of the DAP, like the young man who spoke to me, were alleging in advance that they had a chance of winning in Penang and that if it looked as though they would win the national government might provoke racial trouble, either to scare voters away from the Opposition or to justify repression. In the end I went to the DAP rally as my young interlocutor had requested. I cannot judge crowd size very well but there must have been 20 000 people at the DAP meeting that night. The vast majority of those attending were Chinese but the crowd lacked any feeling of intensity, certainly of political intensity. DAP leader Lim Kit Siang spoke well enough but people were polite and interested rather than wildly ecstatic. Certainly there were no incidents of any kind, and certainly no racial hostility. Penang was plastered with election posters, thousands of rockets, the DAP symbol, thousands of justice scales, the symbol of the ruling Barisan Nasional (National Front) coalition of Dr Mahathir's, a few circles in green representing the Islamic fundamentalists, Parti Islam SeMalaysia, PAS. It must have required an almighty clean-up job after the elections were over.

I saw the pattern in Penang repeated all over the country as I travelled around for the elections, although most places, apart from pockets of the capital, Kuala Lumpur, had somewhat fewer DAP posters. But the pattern of the campaign nationally was also similar to that which prevailed in Penang. There was a little racial huffing and puffing, a very distant echo of previous troubles, but overall the conduct of the poll was peaceful and orderly. It was also clean. The defeated parties and their leaders accepted the integrity of the poll itself and made no claim to any ballot rigging. And the result was utterly crushing and unexpected. The government of Prime Minister Mahathir was returned with a record majority and a record popular vote. The national elections, and the simultaneous elections in eleven of Malaysia's thirteen federal states, represent the pinnacle of Mahathir's career, and a decisive turning point in Malaysia's history. They represent too a probably decisive reassertion by one of the most feisty, articulate, strong-willed, challenging—and for westerners at times disconcerting—of all of Asia's leaders, Mahathir Mohamad.

Malaysian elections are not rigged. The Opposition is denied a fair go in the mainstream media. It is also subject to petty inconveniences such as being denied permission for some of its public rallies and it cannot match anything like the financial resources of the ruling Barisan coalition. But the polls themselves, the voting and the counting, are clean, as virtually all the significant players acknowledge. As a result Malaysian elections are important. Mahathir's achievement in 1995 was beyond the expectations of any of the pundits, local or foreign. He took the Barisan's popular vote up beyond the 65 per cent mark, a record high since independence in 1957. At the previous national election in 1990 Barisan had scored a record low of 53 per cent. In 1995 Barisan took 162 out of 192 seats in the national parliament. Mahathir first became prime minister in 1981. In his previous three elections at the helm Barisan's vote had declined each time. After the 1990 elections the Opposition controlled two of the thirteen state governments. Now it controls just one, Kelantan, where the PAS runs a decaying regime. In the eleven state elections held simultaneously with the national election in April 95, Barisan actually took its share of the vote to 67 per cent.

I interviewed Mahathir at length a few weeks after his remarkable election triumph. He is one of the most extraordinary leaders I have ever met, yet that day he was certainly sounding and acting like any political leader, recovering after the exertions of a bruising campaign schedule. He described himself as 'relieved' after the win, saying:

> We expected to win but expectations are never sure things. Upsets can happen, so there was as much tension as there might be in other circumstances. There was a complete turnaround as far as the urban voters, mainly the Chinese voters, in favour of the government. They [the Chinese] are very sensitive to the economy. If the economy is doing well, they generally feel very happy. Also, they have come round to think we are not anti-Chinese, as we have been made out. It is true that we want to give the Malays a stake in the economy, but it is not at their expense.

Mahathir's landslide victory holds all kinds of implications for other figures, for his deputy Anwar, and for Australia. Paradoxically as rumblings in early 1996 demonstrated, the election win was not necessarily decisive in shoring up Mahathir's position vis-à-vis Anwar, for it emerged that Anwar had effectively taken control of the United Malays National Organisation (UMNO; the dominant party within Barisan), even though Mahathir effectively ran the country, although the smart money said that the two would likely avoid confrontation, that Anwar would be patient enough to let the succession occur at a time of Mahathir's choosing, and with dignity.

On the night his victory was declared, about 3 o'clock in the morning, Mahathir came into UMNO's downtown Kuala Lumpur headquarters, flushed with confidence, elated at victory, exhausted after his campaign efforts, happy to give a few rough backhanders to longtime foes (especially the foreign press, especially Australia's state-owned broadcaster, the ABC), and trenchantly declared that the election victory would confirm and strengthen, among other things, Malaysia's assertive foreign policy.

At the UMNO headquarters Mahathir claimed the win was an endorsement for his stand on the Asia Pacific Economic Cooperation forum, and his proposed East Asian Economic Caucus, issues about which he has often clashed with Australia. He pledged to pursue his foreign policy positions even more aggressively in the future. This particularly involves the EAEC and APEC. He has proposed an Asians-only EAEC (East Asia minus the caucasians as some wags put it) and has been suspicious of the growing strength of APEC. He said:

> The willingness of the voters not only to support the government but to enhance their support for the [ruling] parties reflects their support for the policies of the government and certainly the policies of the government include our foreign policy. And everyone in Malaysia knows how strongly we feel about things like the EAEC, our participation in APEC, our concern about the oppression of the third world countries and a whole lot of things. We will certainly continue with these policies and if possible we will make ourselves heard even louder because we think that what the voters have done is endorse our foreign policy. They have not in any way rejected what we have done. We are therefore strengthened by their endorsement.

He also hit out once more at the foreign press, accusing it of being grossly unfair to his government. During the campaign he singled out the Australian ABC several times, accusing it of unbalanced reporting, a theme he would return to in interviews with me on a number of occasions. (The other major Australian reference I noticed in the campaign was equally doleful—the DAP's leader Lim Kit Siang accused Dr Mahathir of descending to the level of Paul Keating in his personal attacks on Lim.)

Beyond the sheer size of Mahathir's victory in 1995 two aspects of the election were particularly notable. The first was the apparent endorsement of the government by Malaysia's Chinese community, for the first time at anything like this level. Malaysia's ethnic composition is roughly 60 per cent Malay (including indigenous peoples in East Malaysia), about 30 per cent Chinese and 10 per cent Indian. The main Chinese party in the ruling coalition, the Malay Chinese Association, was seen as a declining force in recent years. This decline stems partly from Mahathir's success in generating a Malay business class, which can support UMNO financially, and in his government forging its own links between UMNO leaders and the Chinese business class, thus rendering obsolete the MCA's old role of raising election finances for the Barisan parties. In any event, the Chinese have never been majority Barisan supporters before. However, in the 1995 election the challenge of the predominantly Chinese DAP, at state and federal level, collapsed utterly. The DAP was routed in Penang, where at state level the Barisan is led by the Chinese party, Gerakan, and by a Chinese chief minister (this is the only state where this occurs). Nationally the DAP was also decimated, its numbers in the federal parliament dropping from twenty to just nine. Similarly Kuala Lumpur is traditionally a Chinese majority city. Barisan, for the first time at the 1995 election, won a majority of federal seats in Kuala Lumpur. It took six out of ten in KL, reversing a previous deficit of three for Barisan as opposed to four for the Opposition, in the old, smaller parliament.

Why did the Chinese swing so heavily behind Mahathir's government? It may be a recognition, as Mahathir suggests, of how well Malaysia is doing economically. It may be that the DAP's optimistic pre-election forecasts had the unintended effect of scaring Chinese voters, who may have feared upsetting Malaysia's delicate racial harmony if Chinese opposition parties did too well, or it could have been a bid for greater Chinese influence within the government.

The other interesting and important aspect of the 1995 election was the setback it dealt Islamic fundamentalism. Too often western perceptions of Islam are stereotyped, inaccurate and out of date. They tend to equate Southeast Asian Islam with the Islam of the Middle East, and to make this equation in political as well as religious terms. This is, of course, ridiculous, as Malaysia's election demonstrates. PAS is by international standards a pretty mild sort of fundamentalist party. Nonetheless it has all sorts of Middle East connections and does, formally at least, want to implement Islamic law as state law, so it is probably fair enough to label it an Islamic fundamentalist party. The only state PAS controls is Kelantan, which it held in the 1995 state election. But Mahathir's coalition won both state and federal seats in Kelantan whereas in 1990 it was shut out of the state altogether. Similarly the Islamic challenge did not emerge in the Malay heartland state of Trenggannu, next door to Kelantan.

Of course the elections in 1995 were about much more than just Mahathir. They were about Malaysian modernisation, urbanisation, embourgeoisement—and the primary wish of the bourgeois man everywhere is for stability. Voter turnout was remarkably high, above 70 per cent, indicating that Malaysians took the choices available seriously. And as in so many East Asian elections where one party is associated with stability, stability won.

Mahathir was not always associated with the status quo. Like so many Asian leaders who preach the virtues of stability, he had a period as a dissident and rebel. He has also overseen profound and revolutionary changes in his society. His whole career has been turbulent, unpredictable, risky and adventurous. The most consistent continuing political strand throughout his career has been that of Malay self-assertion and self-respect.

Mahathir was born on December 20, 1925, in Alur Setar, in the Malay heartland state of Kedah. He was the youngest of nine children. His father was a school teacher, the first Malay head-master of an English school in Kedah. At the time of Mahathir's birth Malaya was a sleepy British colony. The social system the British set up was fundamentally degrading to the Malays. The British were on top as rulers and the most senior administrators, the Chinese in the middle as merchants and with the exception of the Malay aristocracy, the Malays on the bottom. The char-acteristic British view of the Malays was unflattering, to put it mildly. This is evident in the colonial literature, especially the stories of Somerset Maugham, where the Malays are little more than exotic props and have no social identity at all, and even in Anthony Burgess's Malayan trilogy, in which the Malays are seen as universally untrustworthy and indolent.

Mahathir's first education was at a local Malay school but he did sufficiently well to obtain enrolment in an English school. He survived the Japanese occupation during the Second World War, witnessing further Malay humiliation at the hands of a foreign power. He studied medicine at the University of Malaya in Singapore, one of the first Malays to do so, and again

experienced a social environment in which Europeans were presumed to be on top, Chinese to come next and Malays to come
last. As a young doctor he worked first for the government in
various Malay provinces and then later went into private practice.
Mahathir entered politics in 1964, becoming an UMNO representative in the national parliament for the seat of Kota Setar
Selatan. Malaya had achieved independence in 1957 but its first
prime minister, Tunku Abdul Rahman, was in many ways like the
British rulers of old. The British were happy to hand over rule
to the Malay nobility, whom they took to be more politically
reliable than the Chinese (with so many Chinese communists in
Malaya) and of course there was no other indigenous leadership.
The Malay nobility, of course, represented a tiny fraction of the
Malay population.

But Mahathir was impatient with the old-world courtesies and
racial status quo under the Tunku. Mahathir instead espoused a
radical form of Malay chauvinism, demanding both that Malays
be given a greater stake in the economy and that Malay culture
and language should dominate. He was a fiery young leader, and
from his university days a fierce and effective debater. He was
very un-Asian in his disinclination to defer to his elders and
seniors. He had also been a fiercely partisan journalist, writing
pseudonymous political articles even from his school days. The
most sustained statement of his views came in his first book, *The
Malay Dilemma*, which he wrote in 1969.

The first time I met Dr Mahathir for a lengthy personal
discussion, in 1993, I told him that I had read *The Malay Dilemma*
the night before. He seemed just faintly embarrassed, smiled and
reminded me that it had been written a long time ago in very
different circumstances. It was, even at the time of its writing, a
fairly fruity effort and was banned from publication for a time.
What was seen as Mahathir's excessive Malay nationalism also
got him expelled from UMNO in 1969, and he was not read-
mitted until 1972. To read *The Malay Dilemma* today is to be
exposed to a strange mixture of frank but amateur racial theoris-
ing, painfully honest descriptions of the social situation in Maly-
sia, some shrewd analysis and much special pleading for the
Malays. It is at one level a plea for recognition that Malays, in

Mahathir's view, are about to lose their primacy in Malaysia. He wrote, for example:

> The Malays seem to be teetering between the desire to assert
> their rights and arrogate to themselves what they consider to
> be theirs, and the overwhelming desire to be polite, courteous
> and thoughtful of the rights and demands of others. Deep
> within them there is a conviction that no matter what they
> decide to do, things will continue to slip from their control;
> that slowly but surely they are becoming the dispossessed in
> their own land. This is the Malay Dilemma.

In one sense then this is a fairly orthodox nationalist tract from an intellectual leader of an indigenous population which feels hard done by. But *The Malay Dilemma* is extremely unusual in this kind of literature in not pretending that the writer's indigenous group is the possessor of all virtue. While there is plenty of lament about what has happened to the Malays, Mahathir's book is actually full of tough analysis of his people's failings. Perplexingly it also relies on racial and environmental theories to explain Malays' relative poor economic performance. He argues, for example, in lengthy genetic passages that in-breeding, which he says is typical of rural Malays, has weakened Malay stock. Similarly he argues that the abundance and fecundity of the Malay soil allowed Malays to grow lazy and did not lead to the survival of the fittest but in effect to the survival of all. Thus weak Malays were dispossessed both by stronger Chinese immigrants and by British policies of divide and rule. In a not untypical passage he argues:

> The Malays whose own hereditary and environmental influence
> had been so debilitating, could do nothing but retreat before
> the onslaught of the Chinese immigrants. Whatever the Malays
> could do, the Chinese could do better and more cheaply. Before
> long the industrious and determined immigrants had displaced
> the Malays in petty trading and all branches of skilled work.
> As their wealth increased so did their circle of contacts. Calling
> on their previous experience with officialdom in their own
> homeland, the Chinese immigrants were soon establishing the
> type of relationship between officials and traders which existed
> in China.

Thus, while the book paints the Chinese and British as

conniving against Malay interests it also contains stern lessons for the Malays themselves. This has always been a theme of Mahathir's political life, not only to defend and promote Malay interests but to urge Malays on to greater achievement. The book is also notable for its doleful, basically pessimistic assessment of the racial situation in Malaysia. He writes, for example:

> In Malaysia we have three major races which have practically nothing in common. Their physiognomy, language, culture and religion differ. Besides, how is any one race going to forget race when each is in fact physically separate from the other? For the vast majority of the people in Malaysia there is no dialogue. Many of them are not even neighbours. They live apart in different worlds—the Chinese in the towns, the Malays in the *kampungs* [villages] and the Indians on the estates. Nothing makes anyone forget the fact of race.

It would be asburd to suggest that Mahathir's views have not evolved and grown over the years since *The Malay Dilemma* was written. It is no small part of Mahathir's historic achievement that the Malaysia of today is a society transformed from that which he described nearly 30 years ago in *The Malay Dilemma*. However, putting all these ideas as bluntly as he did in the 1960s got Mahathir expelled from UMNO. Tragically, however, his pessimistic analysis was accurate. In May 1969 the non-Malay Opposition performed unexpectedly well in elections. A complex series of events unfolded but in May of that year a terrible race riot broke out in Kuala Lumpur and hundreds of people, mainly Chinese, were killed. All of a sudden the policies Mahathir had been promoting to give Malays a stake in the Malaysian economy did not look so radical or unreasonable. The government was utterly shattered by the race riots, which have become the defining event of modern Malaysia. Just as Indonesians never again want to experience the admittedly much greater terror that followed the attempted coup in 1965, so Malaysians of all races and all parties are determined never again to have a situation develop in which, as Mahathir described it: 'murder and arson and anarchy exploded'.

The government of the day eventually responded to the riots with the New Economic Policy in 1971, designed to favour Malays and bring them up to an economic status nearer that of the Chinese. Getting Mahathir back into UMNO in 1972 was an important part of the symbolism of the new policies. Mahathir had also lost his parliamentary seat in 1969, tellingly to an Islamic fundamentalist candidate, and had gone back to practising medicine. By 1973 Mahathir was again gaining government appointments (he was appointed to the Senate in that year) and in 1974 won a seat in parliament uncontested. His rise thereafter was extremely rapid. Within a year he was education minister, a post always seen as critical in Malaysia, not only for its importance to national development but because of the traditional community and political leadership role played by school teachers in *kampungs*, and thus their influence in UMNO.

Two years later he was elected deputy prime minister, one of many parallels between his career and that of Anwar Ibrahim's. By 1976 Mahathir was fully occupied in making the system work, making the NEP work to maximise the position of Malays, ensuring there was no racial violence and defeating the political challenge of Islamic fundamentalism—which, had Malay ambitions been frustrated, could conceivably have won majority support among the Malay population. Mahathir's then boss, Prime Minister Hussein Onn, was a peaceable sort of a fellow. In 1981, two years before an election was due, he announced his retirement due to ill health and Mahathir became prime minister. His prime ministership has been even more eventful and turbulent than his previous career. He decided he wanted his own mandate and so went to the people a year early, in 1982, and won a huge victory, garnering 110 of 154 parliamentary seats. He set forth to build up heavy industry as a means of giving *bumiputras* (literally 'sons of the soil' or Malays) greater economic opportunity. In many ways this proved a false track for Malaysia and it was later abandoned. A pragmatic attachment to whatever works has been a hallmark of Mahathir's administration. As Dr Noordin Sopiee, head of Malaysia's Institute of Strategic and International Studies, has commented; 'We are doctrinaire in our commitment to pragmatism.'

But despite Mahathir's success opposition to him within UMNO was gathering. He was the first commoner to become prime minister of Malaysia. His style was unlike that of any of his predecessors. He had to struggle for his power, no automatic deference was afforded him as had been given to the Tunku. He had constant conflict with his first deputy, Musa Hitam. Then Malaysia endured a tough recession in the mid-1980s. In 1987 Mahathir was challenged as UMNO president, and therefore as prime minister, by his finance minister, Tunku Razaleigh Hamza. In a fierce contest among 1500 UMNO delegates Mahathir beat off Razaleigh's challenge by 40 votes.

Then in 1990 Mahathir faced in some ways his toughest test. The Opposition united for the first time and for the first time presented some kind of credible alternative to Barisan. By this time Mahathir had made many course corrections. In the mid-1980s he had abandoned low limits on foreign investment and begun what has been a hugely successful and sustained attempt to attract foreign investment into Malaysia. This has been important not only in providing Malaysia with capital but, perhaps even more importantly, providing technology transfer and training. After beating off Razaleigh in 1987 Mahathir also revived the Internal Security Act and cracked down heavily on political opposition. In particular Islamic fundamentalists, Chinese nationalists and UMNO dissidents were targeted. Reaction against this move, which saw more than 100 political detentions in 1987, led to the Opposition's strange and temporary unity in the 1990 elections.

The Malaysian Opposition consisted of essentially four forces. After his defeat in UMNO Razaleigh founded Semangat 46 (Spirit of 46), a breakaway from UMNO which seeks to invoke the spirit of UMNO. It has declined over the years but is strong in parts of Kelantan and Trenggannu. In 1996 it appeared to be heading for reunion with UMNO. The second force is the Islamic fundamentalist party, PAS, which holds government in Kelantan, and is strong in Trenggannu and parts of Kedah. The third is the Democratic Action Party, which although it claims to be non-communal is basically a Chinese-based oppositionist party with a vaguely left-wing past although little program beyond a professed desire to end communal politics and policies of racial preference. And the fourth Opposition force is an ethnic Kadazan-based party in Sabah, in East Malaysia on the island of Borneo. These four forces have almost nothing in common. PAS wants to institutue Islamic law which is totally inimical to the interests of the DAP's constituency, non-islamic Chinese. Neither Semangat 46 nor PAS has anything of interest to say to the Sabahans, many of whom are Christians. Within the Opposition there was a fairly stable and understandable alliance between Semangat 46 and PAS, who can both emphasise their Malayness. But the unity of 1990 was substantially attributable to the widespread, hostile reaction to the crackdown of 1987. In 1990 Barisan still won but it achieved its lowest vote ever. However, this proved a case of one sparrow not meaning summer for the Opposition which was completely unable to maintain its fragile unity after the election. Nonetheless Mahathir, though by now thoroughly entrenched as his nation's leader, was hurt by the 1990 election result.

Then in 1993 the charismatic Anwar Ibrahim challenged the affable but ineffective Ghafar Baba for the position of deputy president of UMNO, and therefore also of deputy prime minister. It is still not clear whether Mahathir sanctioned this challenge from the first. He did not exert himself to save Ghafar but that is not to say that he was delighted with Anwar's total dominance of the Malaysian political scene in the run-up to the UMNO elections. Anwar represented the new wave of Malaysian politics, Ghafar the old. Anwar was young, glamorous, the finance minister, an internationalist with excellent Chinese business contacts. Urban professional Malays tended to identify with him. At the same time Anwar had a strong Islamic identity. He had been a leader of the radical Islamic Youth Movement, ABIM. He had been seen as a dangerous radical in his student-leader days and was detained under the Internal Security Act in 1974. But then in 1982, in a significant political coup, Mahathir announced that Anwar was joining UMNO. Anwar later became deputy minister for religious affairs and greatly assisted UMNO in its perennial struggle with PAS for the loyalty of the Malay heartland. He was significant in getting UMNO to express itself in an Islamic idiom and also in specific initiatives such as founding an Islamic university. He gave UMNO both a modern face and an Islamic face. More particularly he seemed to incarnate a theme that Mahathir had long himself been preaching, namely that orthodox adherence to Islam was not inimical to success, including economic success, in the modern world. Indeed in his long-standing

'Look East' policy Mahathir had tried to fuse Islamic values with the traditional East Asian work ethic and economic success. Ghafar Baba on the other hand was the classic grass roots *kampung* campaigner, at his best in his shirt sleeves chatting to school teachers in the thousands of Malaysian *kampungs*.

There was plenty of talk, though none of it came from Anwar, that Anwar would be impatient to succeed Mahathir sooner rather than later, that there could be conflict between the two men. However, the 1995 election appears to have transformed that dynamic and strengthened Mahathir. Anwar had developed an enormous profile over the previous two years. He was seen as the wave of the future. He was especially the favourite of the international community. Anwar's rhetoric on international issues, and especially the vexed Asian values debate, was softer than Mahathir's. As one Kuala Lumpur insider joked to me: 'If this was the 1960s, the CIA would organise a coup for Anwar.' Towards the end of 1994 an astonishing poison pen, or rather poison fax, campaign had begun against Mahathir. Although this certainly did not come from Anwar it heightened a mood of some unease between the two. Certainly there were those in Anwar's camp who wanted a rapid leadership change. But the election landslide appeared to transform all that.

Although I had been covering Mahathir off and on for some years, the first time I had a long private discussion with him was in 1993, at his Kuala Lumpur office. The office was spacious, formal and Malay in style. Mahathir wore a name badge on his lapel, a droll touch given that he appears on the front page of almost every newspaper every second day, and on most evening television newscasts. If you didn't know who this man was you shouldn't be in Malaysia. But it's a rule he has set for his country's civil servants, that they must wear name tags and not hide behind any bureaucratic anonymity.

Our meeting is something of a mild diplomatic event. Mahathir has not granted a full-scale, one-on-one, ask-any-question-you-like, interview to an Australian newspaper in years. Australian–Malaysian relations were soured in the 1980s by the execution of convicted Australian drug traffickers, Kevin Barlow and Brian Chambers, in Malaysia, and later by the television series, *Embassy*, which was shown on the ABC, and by the feature film, *Turtle Beach*, which was made partly with taxpayer assistance and contains a wholly historically inaccurate scene depicting east-coast Malay villagers massacring Vietnamese boat people. Mahathir is said to see both *Embassy* and *Turtle Beach* as examples of the western media, in this case its Australian variant, using its financial muscle and international English-language-based distribution power to defame and condescend towards developing countries, particularly Malaysia. I was forewarned by some Malaysian friends of Mahathir's renowned combativeness when dealing with the western press, that at times he can be something of a scold.

Instead I found an endlessly polite, solicitous even, interlocutor. The interview began on time, always an unusual courtesy for any politician to extend to a journalist, and went seemingly as long as I liked, although I judged after an hour or so that I had taken enough of the prime minister's time. I also found to my surprise that in private at least Mahathir is a very quiet man, very considered in what he says, naturally very softly spoken, such that it is hard later to pick up his voice on the tape. This aspect of Mahathir is too little remarked. The former Australian prime minister, Bob Hawke, recounts in his memoirs that he met Mahathir shortly after learning of his own daughter's potentially fatal drug addiction. He broke down and wept in front of Mahathir, unable to continue with the formal agenda for their meeting. Mahathir was immensely sympathetic to Hawke in this episode, responding both as a fellow parent and a doctor, and going to considerable personal lengths to get information which he thought might help the Hawke family. Mahathir had even wanted to use this as a basis for a personal relationship, but alas, as we know, it was not to be. But the solicitous and sympathetic side of the Mahathir personality is evident to anyone who knows him.

However, when I reviewed the tape and the notes of my first interview with Mahathir I found his remarks, if not the style of their delivery, were just as trenchant and uncompromising as I had been led to expect. In substance the views were also unconventional, beyond what most East Asian leaders would say publicly, to say the least. Virtually alone among Southeast Asian leaders, for example, he would not endorse the conventional wisdom that the United States military presence was necessary for regional stability in the post–Cold War period. Instead he said, 'I don't see a major role for the US as a balancing force. We always thought that the American bases in the Philippines were not necessary. It's not going to make a difference whether the US is there or not. The presence of the Seventh Fleet on and off is OK.' So, was he worried about the consequences of any potential US withdrawal? 'No, I'm not. It's inevitable, anyway.' In any event, he argued, should you measure regional engagement by how many tonnes of steel the US has floating around the Pacific or whether important people in Washington really have their minds focused on the Pacific? But his critique of America and its international role goes well beyond this:

> Americans tend to be deflected by what seems to them to be
> their righteous roles. For example, they cannot get on with
> Vietnam because some of their soldiers are missing. When you
> fight a war some people are bound to be missing. The
> Vietnamese have been unable to trace something like 30 000 of
> their own people. To hold that as a reason for not establishing
> relations is to miss the forest for the trees. In the case of
> China this insistence that China must follow American
> perceptions of what is right and wrong is wrong. You can't have
> relations on the basis of your values and not other people's
> values. Because of issues like these the US seems to forget the
> bigger issues—like the importance of the region, the role the
> region will play in the future and even now.

Mahathir that day gave expression to bitterness, though as I say the tone of delivery was sweet and mild, at what he saw as America's role in preventing the formation of a Malaysian initiative—the East Asian Economic Caucus. He argued with considerable persuasiveness that America's opposition to the EAEC—based on the idea that it might divide the Pacific—was a bit hard to take, was indeed hypocritical, given its own formation of the North American Free Trade Agreement. After all, if the EAEC is going to divide the Pacific, can't the same argument be made much more strongly about NAFTA? He was particularly incensed about the role of the former US secretary of state, James Baker, in stymieing the EAEC:

Baker went so far as to tell the Japanese that when he met me
I was wearing Malaysian dress. I don't see what that has to do
with it. But he's so biased he told the Koreans that Malaysia
didn't fight for them in the Korean War. Of course when that
happened we were still a colony. That kind of attitude, that
intolerance, is very worrisome.

He claimed that America's chief worry with the EAEC was
that Japan might eventually take a leading role in it. However
he said he would keep pushing ahead with the EAEC:

We'll keep pushing it. We see a trend of protectionism in both
Europe and North America. In order to prise open the markets
we need a strong voice. The wholehearted support of all the
ASEAN countries is very important. We believe America is
trying to pressure some ASEAN countries into not supporting
it. The role of Japan and South Korea is also important and
these are also being pressured.

Although he didn't use the word it's clear that Mahathir saw
the US as a bully, saying:

When we realised the Soviet Union was not going to be a
world power and America would be the sole, dominant power
in the world, we feel, like in all things, when just one party
becomes over powerful there is the tendency to be overbearing
because there are no checks, no balances.

He criticised what he saw as a US double standard for
intervening in Iraq but failing to act over Bosnia: 'When the
Cold War ended the whole idea of non-interference in the internal
affairs of other nations was disregarded.' However, he was prepared to use the United States as one positive validating comparison point—for his policies favouring Malays over the other
races in Malaysia, saying that such policies were comparable to
American policies of affirmative action: 'How anyone could say
we are discriminating against the non-*bumiputras* is hard to
believe. The well-off in this country are the non-*bumis*. We are
trying to bring up the *bumis* to the same level, not to bring
anyone else down.'

When we spoke North Korea was umm-ing and ah-ing over
whether it would abide, even formally, by the agreements which
limit the spread of nuclear weapons. Mahathir described North

Korea as 'very worrisome'. He continued: 'But I doubt if even North Korea would try anything ridiculous like starting a nuclear war. They might go for some kind of conventional attack.' This in itself I thought an alarming enough prospect, but Mahathir was prepared to identify what he saw as the chief security problem confronting East Asia: 'In the region the most worrisome thing is the growing strength of China. China must re-equip itself and this may cause Japan to balance the strength of China.'

He made one prediction in that interview which turned out to be wrong. He did not think there would be a settlement of the Uruguay Round of the General Agreement on Tariffs and Trade: 'I doubt whether the political leaders [of the US and Europe] have the will to do what is right. They will always pander to their voters.' As we now know, there was eventually a conclusion to the Uruguay Round, although it was a fairly modest deal compared with what the world had earlier hoped for.

When I spoke to Mahathir that first time it was before the great Keating–Mahathir row which followed the APEC summit in Seattle that year. However he was even then extremely sceptical of APEC: 'We have been very wary of APEC, simply because there have been so many powerful members who dominate it.'

Nonetheless, at that time he was prepared to be quite positive about Australia's regional diplomacy, although always given the context of the burdens he felt Australia carried in its engagement with the region because of its history. He said:

> We are practically over the hump [in bilateral relations]
> perhaps. But there is still a lot that needs to be done. Australia
> has now expressed a desire to be more identified with Asia
> than with Europe. Now Asia has a certain culture which
> Australia does not have. If Australia wishes to be identified it's
> not simply because there are a lot of economic benefits to be
> had by being identified. But also you have to identify with the
> culture of the area. It's like when you live in a society you
> have to accept the values of that society. You can't just come
> into that society with your own ideas and values and expect
> that society to accept you. Australians, pardon my saying so,
> have been very abrasive in many instances and quite arrogant
> in making value judgments as if we don't know what we are
> doing. We resent the kind of things like the *Turtle Beach*

picture, although Australians also rejected that picture. But to
depict us as barbarians who kill the refugees is grossly unfair.

He did, however, accept that Australian attitudes were undergoing 'a very welcome change . . . I think it's a good thing for
Australia to realise it is of this region, it's not part of Europe.
And gradually policies have been changed but attitudes must also
be changed and some of the Asian culture, as I say, should be
accepted if not adopted.'

These remarks are vintage Mahathir. Australians should not
feel particularly singled out by them. They form part of a general
assertion on his part that the old assumption that western
societies were inherently and always superior to Asian societies
is no longer true. But it is too easy to caricature Mahathir's views
as simply a reverse assertion that Asia is now superior to the
west. That is not what he is saying to people who bother to
listen to him, although certainly there are aspects of most
contemporary western societies, such as drugs, violence, promis-
cuity and family breakdown which he very much wants his
society to avoid. But his message about the historic new interaction between the west and Asia is far more complex and
nuanced than his detractors normally allow. He is sometimes
blunt and hurtful about the failings of western societies but this
is, in his view, in an historical context in which the west has
been lecturing Asia for literally centuries. Nonetheless it is also
obvious that much of what Mahathir has to say about modern
western societies is true, a point that should be of no minor
significance. He often enough articulates what enormous numbers
of East Asians are thinking and saying privately.

When you actually take the trouble to read through
Mahathir's sermons to the west you are forced to admit there is
a great deal of force in what he is saying. Part of the disconcerted-
ness of western responses to Mahathir, as to Lee Kuan Yew, is
the unconscious assumption in western audiences that it ought
to be westerners lecturing Asians, not the other way around. In
December 1994, Mahathir addressed a conference on human
rights. He upbraided the west for its hypocrisy. After all, he
pointed out, for several hundred years western nations were
colonial powers. Yet the whole concept of colonial power was a
denial of the universality of human rights. Equal rights never

extended to the races being colonised. Even the most elevated concept of colonialism involved at least deferring the rights of the colonised while they were being 'civilised' and brought to order. Yet today the west regards as unacceptable any Asian argument about delaying certain expressions of civil rights. Similarly, Mahathir was critical of contemporary western practice on human rights, both within the west and internationally. He made a familiar Asian critique of western societies: 'Hedonism and absolute immorality are the norms of absolute freedom for one and all.'

Yet while many western audiences react with automatic cynicism to Mahathir saying such things, it is really only the same critique as American neo-conservatives such as Norman Podhoretz, William Bennett and many others have been making for two decades and more about their own societies. Reading a lot of Mahathir is at times reminiscent of reading speeches by Newt Gingrich, the US Congressional Republican leader.

The problem is that while it is salutary for the west to be read such lessons from time to time, it doesn't necessarily lead anywhere positive, although in several important speeches Mahathir has also made the point, as have East Asian thinkers like Japanese journalist Yoichi Funabashi, and Singaporean minister, George Yeo, that both Asia and the west have important things to contribute to the discourse of human civilisation, that each can learn from the other, and that what is interesting about the Asia–Pacific is that it has the opportunity to adopt and adapt the best of both traditions.

An intriguing counterpoint to Mahathir comes from his deputy, Anwar Ibrahim. Anwar certainly shares his boss's overall point of view but his rhetoric is softer and more self-critical. It may be generational. Mahathir, who is in his 70s, was born into colonial rule and lived through Japanese occupation, British overlordship and Chinese economic success. His whole career has been about Malay self-assertion. Anwar, who is in his 40s, grew up in a successful, independent Malaysia. In a fascinating speech in Hong Kong in late 1994 Anwar traced the changing view of Asia by the west and called for an authentic relationship of equals. But he also had some tough messages for Asian leaders who might be tempted to misuse the legitimate debate about Asian values. He said:

> If we in Asia want to speak credibly of Asian values we too must be prepared to champion those ideals which are universal and which belong to humanity as a whole. It is altogether shameful, if ingenious, to cite Asian values as an excuse for autocratic practices and denial of basic rights and civil liberties. To say that freedom is western or un-Asian is to deny our own traditions as well as our forefathers who gave their lives in the struggle against tyranny and injustice. It is true that Asians lay great emphasis on order and societal stability. But it is certainly wrong to regard society as a kind of false god upon which altar the individual must constantly be sacrificed. No Asian tradition can be cited to support the proposition that in Asia the individual must melt into the faceless community.

These two speeches are not contradictory, though their emphasis is different. The response to these intelligent arguments in the western press, including the Australian press, has been too often dismissive, too unwilling to listen and take the arguments seriously.

Mahathir's critique of the western press goes beyond arguing that it lectures Malaysia and other developing countries and doesn't listen enough. In his dispute with the British press in late 1994 over their campaign about aspects of British aid funding for a dam project in Malaysia one of his strongest themes was an unwillingness to accept a political agenda laid down by the British media. Mahathir's point is that the propaganda contest is unequal. A major international newspaper like the *New York Times* is influential all over the world. It is not only read by millions in the American elite but is syndicated and reprinted around the globe. What it says affects a country's reputation, not least with investors and potential investors. Malaysian newspapers do not have this kind of clout and Mahathir makes the fair point that there is a disparity of power here, such that western journalists judge and affect his country but no one in his country can judge and affect western societies. None of this is to argue against a free international press fairly scrutinising the Malaysian and any other government. But it is to point to genuine disparities of power and the pressing need for accuracy, responsibility and balance by the international media.

Mahathir's most dramatic clash with a representative of the west in recent years was his argument with Paul Keating after the Seattle APEC summit. The episode began on November 22, 1993. Keating was asked by reporters in Seattle to react to, among other things, remarks by Mahathir in the *New York Times* to the effect that he had got more attention by staying away from the APEC meeting than he would have received if he had attended. Until that moment Keating had had a relatively good relationship with Mahathir who, like Indonesia's leaders, had grown heartily sick of Bob Hawke's combination of regional neglect and moralising lecturing. Mahathir and Keating had had a long and successful private meeting at the Commonwealth heads of government meeting in Limassol in October of that year. They had discussed APEC, among other things. They had also discussed Australia's bid to sell patrol boats to Malaysia, a giant commercial bid. The personal chemistry between the two of them had been satisfactory and Mahathir had seemed reasonably positive to Keating.

This was only one of a series of steps Keating had taken to improve the relationship with Malaysia. His office had explored with Mahathir's office the possibility of a Keating visit either in 1994 or '95. Keating had gone out of his way to meet the redoubtable Malaysian trade minister, Rafidah Aziz, when she visited Australia. But it was all blown away on November 22. Keating, clearly irritated with the reporters' persistent questioning, said he could not care less whether Mahathir attended APEC meetings or not. He also said: 'APEC is bigger than all of us—Australia, the United States, Malaysia and Dr Mahathir and any other recalcitrants.' The Malaysian reaction was quick. The next day a spokesman for Mahathir said he was 'not concerned' about Keating's comments. But Nazri Aziz, the deputy chairman of UMNO Youth, demanded Keating apologise for his remarks.

Thus began a great series of slowly escalating statements and actions by Malaysian officials, journalists, Opposition figures and later ministers harshly critical of Keating. Virtually no one in Australia thought that Keating had not blundered in his initial comments. A leader with a sensitivity to Southeast Asian ways or even to the great difficulties in the Australian–Malaysian relationship in the past would not have made such remarks. Nonetheless the Malaysian reaction was clearly an over reaction. It seemed deliberate and out of all proportion to the original offence. All of this, even from this distance on, offers a real problem of interpretation. It is impossible to know even today how much of the reaction was orchestrated by Mahathir and how much was just 'surface noise'. A Cabinet reshuffle was looming, there was no end of ministers and would-be ministers keen to demonstrate their loyalty to their boss. Also, as senior Malaysian friends pointed out to me at the time, there was a genuine feeling of annoyance in the Malaysian population.

Keating was furious, but went partly into a useless denial mode, his office claiming that the Australian media was beating the story up. But there was plenty of genuine confusion in the Australian media in that first week after Keating's remarks. The Malaysian government on the one hand through official spokes-men was sayiing that it had made no official protest while individual ministers within the government were making increas-ingly tough statements and taking actions that directly harmed Australia's interests. Although Mahathir himself stopped short of actually demanding an apology from Keating he did acknowledge that he would take seriously calls for action against Australia from within UMNO. On Thursday, November 25, when asked whether Keating would still be welcome to visit Malaysia, he replied: 'It is up to him . . . we'll look at the situation.' But specific actions proceeded apace. Australian-made television shows and commercials were banned from Malaysian television. It was announced that a group of scholarship students would not be coming to Australia. The minister for posts and telecommu-nications announced that he would get his department to review its dealings with Australian companies. All through this crisis Australian businesses in Malaysia were screaming in pain. The offices of the minister for foreign affairs, Senator Gareth Evans, and the then minister for trade, Senator Peter Cook, were inundated with faxes from Australian companies demanding that action be taken to bring an end to the crisis.

On Monday, November 28, Keating made his first serious attempt to repair the damage. He went on ABC television that night and talked about the problems. He refused to apologise and said there was no need for an apology. His remarks about Mahathir, he said, were part of the 'rough and tumble' of international politics. He tried to be positive, saying he wanted a good relationship. But Keating fluffed his lines on the ABC. After endless agonising and consideration his advisers had come up with a form of words which was thought might just possibly mollify Mahathir. Keating was meant to stick to the agreed script and not say anything else about the Australia–Malaysia problems. Unfortunately, showing that occasional lapse in discipline which bedevilled his career, Keating did not get the words right and his remarks did nothing to soothe the situation. In Kuala Lumpur the Malaysian Foreign Ministry made an informal protest to the Australian High Commission. This was not a formal protest, it was not the Australian high commissioner being called in and dressed down, but it was a protest nonetheless. On Wednesday, November 30, the Malaysian defence minister, Najib Tun Razak, said that Malaysian ministers were unhappy that Keating had not apologised and relations were likely to move into a 'very difficult period'. Najib said: 'It is difficult to say but there will be implications across the board.' He also made some ambiguous comments about the bid by Transfield to supply the patrol-boats. These were interpreted by some Australian newspapers as indicating that the Transfield bid was now in trouble because of the diplomatic row. When Keating saw Najib's coments in the next morning's newspapers he was incandescent with rage. He instantly sent a personal message to Najib demanding an immediate explanation. The Australian position was starting to harden and minds in Canberra were turning to retaliatory action that might be taken. Canberra let Kuala Lumpur know that scaling down defence cooperation under the Five Power Defence Arrangements was on the table, that the FPDA altogether could even be under threat. Najib subsequently informed Australian officials that his remarks had been misinterpreted by the Australian press and that he had meant to do nothing more than restate the official Malaysian Cabinet position and that nothing more should be read into his remarks.

The Malaysian Cabinet also decided on that Wednesday that it would make no formal protest to Canberra over Keating's remarks and that it would not engage in official action against

Australia. However, the anti-Australian rhetoric did not abate. The Malaysian Cabinet, via Foreign Minister Abdullah Badawi, also made it clear that it felt the Australian government should take some further initiative in resolving the dispute. The next day Keating issued a public statement saying inter alia that he had not meant to give offence. Keating's public statement was polite enough but not at all apologetic. The most conciliatory thing he said was that his remarks in Seattle 'were not calculated to give offence to Dr Mahathir'. He also said that both governments needed to avoid a situation in which the media were 'setting the tone of the relationship'. He said that the issue had been 'blown out of proportion' and that both governments should 'act in a way which clearly draws a line under what has happened and avoid any further deterioration in the relationship or any slide into tit-for-tat retaliation'. Those last words were a clear warning of a looming Australian response.

However, at this point Keating also made his greatest single blunder in the dispute. He wrote a private letter to Mahathir. Keating's foreign minister, Gareth Evans, was out of the country and Keating did not show him the letter before it was sent. A copy was shown to the defence minister, Senator Robert Ray, who had never got on personally with Keating, and who sent a message to Keating's office saying he thought the letter was rubbish. Keating did consult the trade minister, Peter Cook, who was acting foreign minister, but who was diplomatically inexperienced. There is no evidence that he consulted the former defence minister, Kim Beazley, who, along with Evans, was the intellectually best-equipped internationalist in the Cabinet. Instead, Keating's own hand was dominant in the drafting of the letter and it was a starchy, disagreeable missive, in the view of some who saw it clearly bad mannered as between two individuals. One of Keating's colleagues who later saw the letter would describe it as 'the most ill-advised diplomatic communication since Evatt wrote to Molotov', a reference to a famous episode in Australian history in which the leader of the Opposition in the 1950s, Labor's Doc Evatt, wrote to the Russian foreign minister to ask whether the Soviets had any spies in Australia. Evatt's actions were regarded with despair by his colleagues and earned him near-universal ridicule.

Eventually Evans intervened, Keating made some slightly further conciliatory remarks, a number of Australian Cabinet ministers made as soothing remarks as possible, the FPDA and other threats of Australian retaliation were made privately and finally the Malaysian Cabinet decided to call the whole dispute off. It ended crisply, leaving few apparent permanent results and the next year Mahathir was speaking kindly of Australia in launching the Malaysian Australian Foundation. The episode is nonetheless acutely instructive. Keating is one of the most formidable politicians Australia has ever produced but he was completely outplayed in this game of regional diplomacy by Mahathir. Despite the fact that Malaysia over reacted there was enough fault on Australia's side, both in the original remarks and in the subsequent mishandling of the dispute, that regional sympathy generally went Malaysia's way. Moreover the regional press represented the dispute as demonstrating Australia's 'otherness', its outsider status, in Asia, and was heavily critical of Australia in the episode. A smart Asian leader would never have made the initial remarks Keating made. The dispute reinforced a sense that Australia could not manage tricky Asian relations very well. Further, Keating was subject to extensive and trenchant criticism within Australia while Mahathir mobilised his own political culture entirely around himself and in favour of his leadership, such that even the Malaysian Opposition leader, as noted earlier, when later looking for a line to criticise Mahathir said he had sunk to the level of Keating. The episode also reinforced Mahathir's aggressive regional diplomacy. It emphasised to everyone in the region once again that Mahathir was not to be trifled with. It also, domestically, took the spotlight off Anwar and placed it firmly back on Mahathir. Anwar, like the rest of the Cabinet, had no alternative but to back his leader. And then, when it looked as though the dispute could actually start to do some measurable harm to Malaysia's interests, Mahathir just switched it off. Australians may not have appreciated the episode, but it was masterful. It was exactly the kind of manoeuvre Keating himself might pull in a domestic context but as this episode showed, Mahathir was much more experienced and tactically adept in playing regional politics than was Keating.

Australians may not like to hear it but it was one episode in which Mahathir completely outplayed Keating.

I asked Mahathir about the incident in our second extended discussion in May 1995, which also took place at his Kuala Lumpur office. Feeling both self-confident after his election win and apparently magnanimous, Mahathir said he was prepared to 'forgive and forget' Keating's labelling him 'recalcitrant' for not going to the APEC Seattle summit. But he repeated his long-held view that for Australia to become fully engaged with East Asia would involve some cultural change on our part, a point Australians would do well to consider. He said: 'If you want to become Asian you can't just say, well, we are Asian because geographically we are close to Asia. You should say we are Asian because we have an Asian culture, an Asian mentality.' Does Australia's western background prevent it from becoming a full partner with the countries of East Asia? 'No, I don't think this is something that is incurable, so to speak. If you are willing to accept that you are not placed there to pass judgment on others I think you'll be readily accepted over time.'

However, he said, there were occasions when parts of the Australian media told 'deliberate lies' about Malaysia that he found 'very hard to swallow'. In this Mahathir clearly distinguished between TV and newspapers (about the latter he had no general complaints), and specifically between the ABC, which was the object of all his complaints, and the rest of the Australian media:

> For example, the reason I was very annoyed with the ABC was that they interviewed me as I was going to a function and asked me, how is the situation in Malaysia? I said, well it's fine, everything is going OK. They showed me saying that and immediately after took a picture which was of the riots in 1969 and showed it together, making me sound like a very big liar.

But at the government-to-government level, he said, 'We didn't have many difficulties even at the time of Bob Hawke. I could get along with him except when he called Malaysians barbarians. [Hawke described the execution of two convicted Australian drug traffickers as barbaric.] Perhaps the culture of Australians is different from ours. We don't say things like that about other people.'

I asked Mahathir about the episode, mentioned earlier, in which Hawke broke down during a meeting with Mahathir and wept over his, Hawke's, daughter's drug addiction. Mahathir replied:

> Because of that it sounded very odd for him to take that kind of stand. That his own family was affected by drugs, he should understand how we feel about people who distribute drugs. We have more than 250 000 drug addicts registered. And we have any number of deaths. To us, a person who distributes drugs is no better than a murderer because he has caused death.

However, Mahathir was being remarkably conciliatory in our interview that day on another score as well. In a dramatic reversal of his past position, and in something that was to become quite a little international story, Mahathir reversed his previous hard-line stand against Australia eventually joining his proposed EAEC. Excluding Australia, and America, had always hitherto been a central aspect of the EAEC proposal. It was what so upset Canberra and Washington about the idea. But on this day Mahathir said:

> I think it [Australian membership] is a distinct possibility. Of course, as Australia becomes more Asianised, certainly in terms of geographical relations but also in terms of outlook, there is no reason why they cannot be a part of the EAEC. But true identification with Asia is important.

This was a radical departure from Mahathir's previous position. When Thailand's former deputy prime minister, Dr Supachai Panitchpakdi, had suggested Australia might eventually become an EAEC member, back in 1993, Mahathir had dismissed the idea completely, had ridiculed it even. In his interview with me he did not see Australia as an immediate member of the EAEC but thought we could join a couple of years down the track. This was similar to the thinking being pushed by a number of Australia's Indonesian friends, who wanted Canberra to drop its opposition to the EAEC in exchange for an assurance that we would be allowed in within a couple of years.

Unfortunately, shortly after his interview with me Mahathir was in Japan. My story had been carried on the international wires and the Japanese journalists assumed that Mahathir had caved in to pro-Australian pressure from Tokyo. Phrasing their questions in this way produced a predictably combative response from Mahathir, who, while acknowledging the accuracy of my report, then seemed to retreat from its substance. Nonetheless, our interview was a sign of the flexibility he was prepared to bring to these issues. However, on APEC he was still extremely wary. While saying he saw a 'constructive role' for APEC, his disillusionment with its progress was clear: 'Frankly, when APEC was first proposed we were very worried about it. From the start we protested but now it's a very big organisation. We are not even consulted. We have become minor players in this whereas in ASEAN we were equal partners.' He would like countries to be able to pursue trade liberalisation at their own pace and he would like APEC to focus more on development cooperation.

On the great issue of the day, and in some ways the issue which has been one of the dominant issues of the region over the last four years, the Japan–United States trade dispute, he sided unequivocally with Japan and was, as usual, harshly critical of the US. The Japan–US trade row, he said, was

> very, very serious. The main effect we see is the appreciation of the yen and all of us borrow in yen. We borrowed yen when it was 100 yen to the Malaysian ringgit, now for every 100 yen we borrow we have to pay three ringgit. So you can imagine how costly it has been for us, this quarrel between them. The objective, of course, is to make Japanese goods less competitive but, in the process, we have to pay more money for Japanese goods, which we have to buy. There is no alternative. If I were a Japanese I would buy all those American cars even if I had to dump them on the scrap. Because it costs much less to buy those cars than it costs to overcome the increasing value of the yen. It has affected them very badly. What are 200 000 cars to the amount they have to pay because of the yen appreciation. Of course, maybe it's a matter of principle for them, a matter of pride for them, that they cannot give in to that kind of pressure. The US doesn't seem to care what happens to the rest of the world. It's only interested in its own relations with Japan, that is all. You can see that there are a lot of attempts to manage trade rather than to let trade be free. At the time when they were the biggest manufacturer there was a lot of talk about free trade, access to markets and all that and we in

Malaysia for example bought everything from outside. But now
we are in a position to compete and I'm quite sure in time
there will be barriers against us. It's easy to talk about free
trade when you have a lot to gain from it but once you see
you are at the losing end the whole principle goes overboard.

He also argued that the structures of so-called free trade are
sometimes weighted in favour of the powerful: 'People talk about
level playing fields but a giant versus a small person is still not
a fair fight.' Mahathir had in mind in particular the pressure on
Malaysia to open up its financial sector to foreign competition.
Giant American banks, he argued, would then dominate that
sector of the Malaysian economy, while the reciprocal freedom
for Malaysian banks to operate in the American economy would
be meaningless because they are so small.

Once again Mahathir claimed that US 'arm twisting' was the
sole reason why Japan had failed to sign on to his proposed
EAEC. He also objected, once more, to what he said were
American attempts to impose American-style democracy on the
region:

Democracy sounds very good but democracy has contributed to
a lot of human misery. In some countries hundreds of people
die every time there is an election. If you ask those people
whether they would like to die for that . . . Malaysia is a
democracy but we have a type of democracy that suits us. The
US is thinking up new ways of arm twisting. There is still this
idea that the west has nothing to learn from anybody. You
must not presume that yours is the only correct way. Other
people exist and they have ideas too. To us, results are
important, too.

This is the heart of the argument of governments from Kuala
Lumpur to Singapore to Jakarta. Their way may not be exactly
the same as the American way, or even the Australian way, but
it is working. And that's what counts.

Mahathir repeated his view that he saw no value in the
American military presence in the region, saying, 'I have never seen
the need for it. By having forces there you tend to define potential
enemies of the future. But by defining enemies for the future, you
make enemies now. If you define a country as an enemy it will
make sure it can take care of you.' His scepticism about the utility

of military alliances, perhaps reflecting the aftertaste of the 'recalcitrant' row, extended even to the Five Power Defence Arrangements, about which he said: 'As far as exchange of intelligence and expertise, it (the FPDA) is very important.' But he did not think that the FPDA (which links Australia, New Zealand, Britain, Malaysia and Singapore for the purposes of the defence of the Malay peninsula and Singapore) provided any security guarantees for Malaysia: 'Malaysia thinks if we get into trouble we cannot rely on anyone to come to our assistance. Our best bet is to have good relations with our neighbours.'

He had substantially softened his view of China from our previous interview, saying: 'I think China has realised the best way to grow is by economic development. If you look at the history of China they have never invaded neighbouring countries.' This is a considerably more benign view of China than he gave at our interview two years ago. Does it reflect a growing confidence in China's commitment to economic reform? A growing comfort and familiarity with China's role in the region? Could it paradoxically be caused by China's increased assertiveness and belligerence, and a desire therefore not to say anything which might offend China?

In the course of this extensive discussion Mahathir also spoke with surprising frankness about domestic Malaysian politics. He openly acknowledged the phenomenon of 'money politics' in Malaysia. 'Money politics is a big problem,' he said.

> I would like to state this very clearly. It all started in 1987, during the contest for the UMNO presidency, where I succeeded against Tunku Razaleigh. He was known to have said that spending $20 million to become prime minister is cheap. That was when a lot of money was used to gain support for himself. According to the nominations at the division level I had more than 80 per cent of the nominations. He had less than 20 per cent. And yet when it came to actual voting by the delegates I won merely by 43 votes, which means I got about 54 per cent of the votes. The only explanation is that these people who came as delegates have been bought. Since then delegates have come to expect that their favours will be paid for. This is the trouble now because a lot of Malays have a lot of money. More business people are getting into politics. Before, most of the leaders of UMNO were Malay

schoolteachers and they didn't have any money to spread around. Now we have successful businessmen going into politics. Because of the demands of the delegates, the expectations of the delegates, they think this is an easy way out. It's not so easy to stop it. Sometimes it is in the form of giving them trips abroad or some perks, all kinds of things including, of course, cash. It's not so easy to catch these people. But we know this is happening and we are doing our best.

This is as frank as Mahathir has ever been with the international press on questions of money politics. UMNO, one of the great mass-based political parties anywhere is, something like the Kuomintang in Taiwan, trying to remake itself, and certainly modernise its image. It has divested itself of much of its corporate wealth, which it acquired in the 1970s and '80s really as a consequence of government licensing arrangements, although these corporations, now in private hands, remain extremely sympathetic to UMNO and continue to ensure it is very well financed at election times. But, while maintaining its dominant position, it is trying to modernise itself. This is in some ways the typical challenge to long-term ruling parties in East Asia.

Part of Malaysia's uniqueness is that it is likely to be the first Islamic country to enter the ranks of the developed world, in the full sense of the word (as opposed to the misleading per capita economic statistics of some oil-drenched Muslim nations whose populations are not well educated and do not enjoy a full range of amenities, in a developed-world sense). When I asked Mahathir about the implications of the 1995 election in beating back the political challenge of Islamic fundamentalism, he bristled at the use of the term: 'I really don't agree with the term Islamic fundamentalist. I believe I am a fundamentalist myself. If you are a Muslim fundamentalist I think you are a very reasonable person.' His argument is that a true understanding of the teachings of Islam leads you to become a moderate and tolerant person. Islamic extremism of the kind found in the Middle East has little support among Malaysians, he argued, 'although I must say they are sometimes attracted to this kind of interpretation.'

Islam is a subject I have had a chance to discuss at length with Anwar Ibrahim as well. 'We are fortunate,' Anwar told me,

because from our history, and our present, the perception of
Islam is that it should be a force for progress and
modernisation. We have a different history. We have learnt to
live and work with non-Muslims for hundreds of years. Any
semblance of intolerance for non-Muslims would hurt both
Muslims and non-Muslims.

Nonetheless, he argued, Islam can in part inform the political
culture: 'We talk of the inculcation of Islamic values in government. We see it partly as a question of greater discipline. There
are pockets of extremist tendencies but the government draws
the line very firmly.'

When the Shah was overthrown and the Ayatollah Khomeini
took power in Iran, the effect was at first electrifying in Malaysia,
especially among student activists, as Rehman Rashid describes
in his scintillating book, *Malaysian Journey*. But as the true nature
of this regime, and its utter failure to deliver a decent or peaceful
life to its people, became obvious to all, Iran, and all the slum
societies of the Middle East, lost all appeal to Malaysians.
Nonetheless Iran, Saudi Arabia and some other Middle Eastern
Arab powers have been active in trying to spread their kind of
political Islam in Southeast Asia. Southeast Asian nations on the
whole have good relations with the Islamic nations of the Middle
East but they don't see them as a model and they don't want
them meddling in local affairs.

I asked Anwar about this: 'We follow events closely,' he said,
'but what we see is not always something to be proud of. We
know Islam promotes learning yet there are rich societies that
tolerate illiteracy. There are also military dictatorships.'

Anwar said that one of the things that drew him into politics
was the example of Dr Mahathir who, he said, represents the
'new Malaysian', oriented to the future. Culturally the task now,
he said, was to 'select intelligently what is best in the west and
what is best in the east. But must we sacrifice our basic values
and morality? The fact is family values have declined in the west
but now you have Bill and Hillary Clinton emphasising family
values. Must we just wait for a lead from the US?'

There is no doubt that in most of the ways that count
Mahathir has delivered for his society. In the decade 1980 to
1990, notwithstanding the mid-decade recession, the economy

grew by an average of more than 5 per cent a year. Between 1987 and 1991 it grew by 8.3 per cent a year. By 1995 it had been growing at 8 per cent a year for eight years, an impressive record of sustained improvement and shared prosperity.

At the same time the races have come to an accommodation. There may not be perfect racial harmony in Malaysia but there is less racial tension there than in the United States, there are no race riots and no discernible racial violence. The races are working together effectively. Social stability has been maintained in the face of the often psychologically disorienting experience of rapid economic growth and modernisation. Social change has occurred in Malaysia but within the parameters of a consensus on certain key social norms. Most intriguingly the nation is trying to realise a vision of Islam which can accommodate a large non-Islamic minority population, and which can help economic and even political modernisation.

These are huge, historic achievements. It is nothing short of surly for foreigners to sell them short. And they have been driven by Mahathir, a complex mixture of ego and pragmatism, cussedness and determination, perhaps altogether the most extraordinary Malaysian the world has yet seen.

Of course Mahathir is a bundle of paradoxes. He complains about the diminution of ASEAN's role because of APEC, yet it is his own confrontational and non-consensus oriented approach which effectively makes ASEAN caucusing within APEC impossible. More than any other Southeast Asian he argues for Asian values of consensus, face and stability yet his own style is confrontational, dialectical, extremely western. He is the guardian of Malay tradition yet the chief force pushing Malays into accommodation with modernity. He lambasts the west culturally yet imports its culture, via its technology and investment, into Malaysia. He is the celebrator of tradition, yet he has striven to cut the power and prerogatives of Malaysia's sultans.

But these are the larger paradoxes of development and rapid modernisation. They apply in different ways in many modernising societies. Above all Mahathir is a leader, whose leadership has been effective and delivered the results. He occupies a giant and secure place in his nation's history.

8

CLINTON IN ASIA: PRIMARY COLOURS IN PRIMARY DISARRAY

 It could have been the jazz age presidency—Bill and Hillary Clinton, Al and Tipper Gore, baby boomers, yuppies, laid-back scholars and funky politicians. Perhaps the defining moment of Bill Clinton's 1992 election campaign, a campaign so dominated by trivia and advertising images and personal impressions, came when he played the saxophone on Arsenio Hall's television program. The style of the new White House looked clear. It's going to be jazz, I thought— plenty of improvisation, plenty of mood indigo.

It would have been a perfect style for someone like Clinton. Jazz is populist, democratic, quintessentially American but not overly nationalistic. It's also sophisticated but free-wheeling, and the outsider often cannot tell whether the band is playing the scheduled melody or not. All American politicians from the deep south need to demonstrate that they are not rednecks. Much was made, remember, of Jimmy Carter's being a nuclear engineer as well as a peanut farmer. But southern politicians don't want to look too bookish or remote either. Jazz would have been the right motif.

But it would be too charitable to attribute so classy and complex a mode as jazz to what the Clinton White House became. Instead, the campaign's theme song, 'Don't Stop Thinkin' About Tomorrow', by Fleetwood Mac, provides a better clue. It was a soft-pop administration, treacly, saccharine and insubstantial, with an underlying attachment to mild hallucination.

Bill Clinton, the man, was a radical departure from all the

previous postwar presidents. For one thing, all of them before Clinton had been soldiers. Some, like Dwight Eisenhower and George Bush, had been authentic war heroes. While it would be wrong to describe the US as a militaristic society, it has been accustomed to finding leadership virtues in military experience, to expecting its leaders to have had some personal and beneficial association with the military. George Bush in a way was the epitome of this characteristic. His résumé was awesome and included heroic Second World War service. While he had certainly displayed what some might regard as an heroic flexibility on many domestic issues, he had been consistent on the great issues of the Cold War. From the point of view of Asia–Pacific countries, those nations in Northeast Asia, Southeast Asia and Australasia, Bush had been an essentially sympathetic character in other, more personal ways as well. He had served in the Pacific war and formed a deep attachment both to the Pacific and to the notion of peace in the Pacific. In Bush's relationship to Japan there was something of the quality of the relationship between Germany's Chancellor Konrad Adenauer and France's President Charles De Gaulle. He had seen the horrific consequences of messing this relationship up and he was determined it wouldn't happen again.

His relationship with China was even closer. He had been de facto US ambassador in Beijing when he served as head of the American liaison mission in the early '70s, before the US restored full diplomatic relations with China. When president, he had been jokingly described as being in effect the State Department's desk officer on China. Moreover he was an instinctive and convinced internationalist. He was a former head of the Central Intelligence Agency. He was an old Cold War buddy of many of the successful leaders in East Asia. He was a free trader. Bush was said to have problems with the 'vision thing', but only in terms of domestic politics. In international relations he was very, very good, way above the average for US presidents. He handled the intricate end game of the Cold War deftly. He and his formidable foreign policy and defence team were comfortable in the use of American power. He was masterly in assembling a domestic and international coalition to fling Iraq's Saddam Hussein out of Kuwait. Taken all in all, while the East Asian region had its share of complaints about Bush, he was in every sense an acceptable American leader who provided a sense of safety and stability in American foreign and security policy.

Clinton was the reverse of Bush in almost every way that mattered personally. Whereas Bush had been a war hero, Clinton was a draft dodger. Whereas Bush had been a businessman before going into politics, Clinton had been a professional politician from his twenties. Where Bush's greatest strengths were his foreign policy expertise and leadership, Clinton in 1992 more or less campaigned against the very idea of foreign policy. He was going to concentrate, he said, with 'laser-like intensity' on America's domestic problems. He accused Bush of spending too much time and effort on foreign policy and neglecting America's problems at home. This was a brilliant political judo trick, turning Bush's greatest strength, an area of central presidential competence in which he was clearly vastly superior to Clinton, into a weakness. At the same time Clinton accused Bush of immorality in foreign policy, of being too soft on dictators, too cautious on Bosnia and too tough on Haitian refugees. But once in office, Clinton would reverse himself on all these positions.

From his earliest days in office Clinton spooked much of East Asia. There were too many contradictory signals. In the early days it was not necessarily that policy was bad so much as that it was incoherent. How much of this can be attributed to Clinton's personality and background, what a Marxist might term the subjective factors of Clinton, as opposed to the objective international circumstances of the end of the Cold War and the need to rethink America's role in the world, especially in the Asia–Pacific?

This is not an easy question to answer. But America's presidential system confers enormous power on the nation's leader, and invests in him enormous sentiment and national identification. In a great national enterprise such as America's engagement with East Asia, where it has this century fought three huge and terrible wars, the personality of the president is going to be important. In Clinton's case it has perhaps been decisive.

William Jefferson Clinton was born in Hope, Arkansas, on August 19, 1946. His father died before he was born and his stepfather, Roger Clinton, was alcoholic and abusive. In the

creepily confessional fashion of modern American celebrity politics, Clinton has often spoken of these traumatic beginnings.
Nonetheless he was a bright kid and successful at the public
schools he attended. Meeting President John Kennedy was one
of the inspirations for his decision, made while still a schoolboy,
to become a politician. He graduated from Georgetown University
with a degree, ironically enough, in international relations. After
that, he went to Oxford University as a Rhodes scholar, where
he became friendly with Strobe Talbot, later to be a famous
journalist and Russianologist whom Clinton would appoint
deputy secretary of state.

Clinton was not a particularly happy Rhodes scholar. It is a
melancholy if impressionistic feature of Oxbridge education that
fewer of its overseas alumni seem to form the same affection for
Britain as a result of their educational experience than similar
overseas students who have studied at Harvard or UCLA form
for America. Clinton seems to have been very much a child of
his times. At this period he was involved on the fringes of the
anti-Vietnam movement and his time at Oxford was otherwise
unfocused. It was as a student, as he later famously testified,
that he tried a joint of marijuana, but did not inhale.

After Oxford he became more serious and subsequently graduated from Yale Law School. He was already deeply involved in
Democratic Party politics. He had been director for Texas of
George McGovern's failed presidential campaign against Richard
Nixon in 1972. The McGovernites were the baby-boomer
stormtroopers who took over the Democratic Party and gave it
a new paradigm, overthrowing its previous cultural conservatism
and establishing the primacy of the causes nearest to the hearts
of the boomers—anti the Vietnam War, pro feminism, the environment, childcare and the rest.

In 1974 Clinton ran unsuccessfully as a Democrat against a
Republican incumbent for an Arkansas congressional seat. His
involvement in Democratic politics deepened. In 1976 he was
Jimmy Carter's Arkansas campaign manager in the gentle Geor-
gian's successful presidential bid. He was also elected state attor-
ney-general and championed a raft of popular causes including
environmentalism and consumer rights. In 1978 he won a handsome victory over a large field to win the Democratic nomination

for the governorship of Arkansas. In those days in the old south winning the Democratic nomination was as good as winning the election itself, which he duly went on to do. At 32 Clinton was one of America's youngest ever governors. He was full of ideas and energy and rapidly began implementing all his promises, including an, as it turned out, unpopular initiative to raise taxes to provide better highways.

In those days Arkansas was on an absurdly short two-year cycle for the governorship. To his astonishment, Clinton lost the governorship in 1980, partly over the tax rise issue, partly because of the Republican landslide which accompanied Ronald Reagan's election to the presidency in the same year. Throughout his career Clinton has shown one of the great characteristics of the successful democratic politician—resilience and an ability to come back. While out of office, he practised law but worked hard at plotting his comeback. He had to work harder to win the Democratic primary in 1982 and then confronted his past failures head-on. He apologised for the tax rises, said that he had made 'the mistake of a young man' and asked for a second chance. He won the general election well and remained governor until his bid for the presidency in 1992.

As a governor Clinton represented the so-called 'new south', the south which repudiated its racist past. He ran for the most part a competent and modernising administration. He was associated with the centrist Democratic Leadership Council. Those who know him say he was deeply scarred by the experience of losing the 1982 race and determined never to lose touch with electoral sentiment again. His most controversial reform as governor was to insist on periodic minimal competence testing for the state's teaching force. This was energetically opposed by the teachers' unions but was popular with parents.

It was clear throughout the 1980s that Clinton was aiming for national office. In 1987 he went to the trouble of announcing that he would not run for president in 1988, ostensibly for family reasons. At the 1988 Democratic Convention he was given the plum job of making the speech to nominate Governor Michael Dukakis of Massachusetts as the party's presidential candidate. Clinton has always had problems with time, with keeping to schedules, making appointments on time, with managing his time.

His nominating speech went way over schedule and was regarded as unimpressive. One of his main themes was the fragility of the affluence America was experiencing under Ronald Reagan.

Most of the Democratic Party's big guns did not contest the presidential primaries in 1992. This was because George Bush, whose approval rating had reached a dizzying 92 per cent in the wake of the Gulf War, had looked invincible. Democratic Party heavies like New York governor Mario Cuomo, Senators Sam Nunn, Bill Bradley and Al Gore, and Congressman Richard Gephardt did not enter the primaries. Even Jesse Jackson stayed out of the race. Even so, Clinton's chances were nearly destroyed when Gennifer Flowers came forward with details of an alleged affair between the two of them. This was early in the primaries and had Clinton faced a real heavyweight he would probably have been finished. Instead he earned himself the mantle of the 'comeback kid'. Hillary stood by him, they admitted their marriage had been rocky at times and Clinton, benefiting from rule changes which favoured a southern candidate, ultimately won the nomination.

Those who know him say Clinton's appetites had indeed been a problem for him. In mid-1992 one of America's most seasoned political observers told me he thought Clinton unelectable because of the allegations of personal scandals in which he'd been immersed. That this judgment was wrong indicates that Clinton's election represented something new in American politics. There had certainly been presidents who had been womanisers before, but none had had his dirty linen aired so publicly, especially before the election. Does Clinton's triumph mean that Americans have become more 'mature' about their leaders' private lives, like the French, or does it mean that the baby boomers have been able at last to debauch the standards of American public life? In a nation racked by teen pregnancy, illegitimacy, absent fathers and family breakdown, is an absence of moral example in leaders something to be absolutely relaxed about? Is it merely a reflection of contemporary social mores or a further coarsening of public life? These questions will remain long after the presidency of Bill Clinton is over.

It was during the actual campaign itself that Clinton demonstrated just what a formidable politician he was. He turned Bush's greatest strength, his expertise in foreign policy, into his greatest weakness. He heavily underlined the generational choice. He turned foreign policy into the enemy of domestic renewal. He was also greatly helped by Bush's lack of a clear domestic agenda. Bush had been in power, as vice-president or president, for twelve years. Even a more naturally domestically oriented, reform-minded politician than Bush would have found it difficult to be convincing in arguing for any new political agenda for himself. Clinton was also greatly assisted by the hardline speeches at the Republican convention, by an extremely sympathetic media, which identified with him both on political and generational grounds, and by the third-party candidacy of Ross Perot, which attracted far more disgruntled right-wing Republicans than it did Democrats.

Clinton won fewer than 50 per cent of the votes but he was the clear winner in the election nonetheless. His victory was like a liberation for the baby boomer generation, especially those in the media or those involved in political activism. His victory over Bush was the triumph of the boomers over the World War 11 generation at last.

Because I watch Asia intensely, I have watched the Clinton presidency intensely. America is, after all, the most important player in Asia. That is why there is a chapter on Clinton in this book. An American president is certainly an Asian leader. But I have watched Clinton from the particular viewpoint of the Asia–Pacific region. And the sight has not been pretty. Most of the movers and shakers in East Asia initially had an open mind about Clinton. They were, even at great geographical distance, caught up in the excitement of the new young president and the possibilities he offered. There was a certain fatigue with the long Republican reign, even as its long-term stability was appreciated. But from the first Clinton was a worry to the region. For a start, everything associated with him, his campaign and his office, seemed to reek of chaos, indecision and procrastination. Months went by after his inauguration and thousands of sub-Cabinet posts had still not been filled. Australia, which had had political appointees as ambassadors from the US under Reagan and Bush, was typical of many countries in still not having an ambassador from the US at all by mid-'93. In the first half of 1993 visitors from East Asia, and from elsewhere, couldn't see anybody of significance in Washington because most of the significant jobs were still unfilled. It does not seem to be drawing too long a bow to consider that in this endless procrastination Clinton's administration was reflecting his personality.

The US presidency is not only the most powerful, but potentially the most transforming, of offices in the world. Harry Truman, one of the great presidents, was after all not only a haberdasher but a failed haberdasher. Yet he was a great president. Herbert Hoover was perhaps the best qualified, and best regarded, man of his generation. Yet he was a dud as president, whose chief claim to a place in history is that he ushered in the Great Depression. Clinton, however, seemed at his core to be strangely untouched by the presidency. He spoke and acted much as he always had, conducting long, meandering meetings that led nowhere, talking endlessly, endlessly consulting the opinion polls, taking up every possible position on most issues before arriving at some awkward and unsatisfactory compromise. He did not seem to be transformed by the presidency but rather to impose his own personality on the office.

His senior foreign policy appointments were particularly disappointing. They were dominated by retreads from the Carter White House and lacked any sense of a unifying Big Idea of what they wanted to achieve, or even who they really were, in foreign policy. Warren Christopher, as secretary of state, was particularly ineffective and dithering. The French came up with the cruelest line about him, that he represented a triumph of American technology—he was so lifelike. Clinton would later try to replace him, offering the job to General Colin Powell. Les Aspin, Clinton's first defence secretary, whom Clinton ultimately fired (or, more gracefully, whose resignation he accepted), was a genuine policy intellectual but again hugely ineffectual. He presided over the great early Clinton fiasco of the broken promise of lifting the ban on gays in the military. He was afflicted with heart problems (which ultimately killed him) that limited his overseas travel. He had a halting, hesitant TV style and politically was always out of his depth. The ultimate spark for his political demise was the revelation that the US field commanders in Somalia had requested reinforcements, only to be denied them by Aspin. Anthony Lake, as national security adviser, was almost invisible.

In late 1993 the *Economist* magazine dubbed them—Christopher, Aspin and Lake—one of the least impressive foreign policy troikas in postwar American history. It was a hugely influential piece by the *Economist* and captured a mood that had been growing in Washington, a mood of impatience and frustration with the mediocrity and lack of sparkle in Clinton's top foreign policy team. For a president who liked to think of himself as Kennedyesque there was no way these grey, grey men could be thought of as the best and the brightest. Yet they truly reflected Clinton's personality. They were process men all, policy wonks and great consultors and deliberators. But they were not men of action. They were extremely uncomfortable with power, with America's power and its competent, decisive use. They contrasted poorly with the Reagan and Bush teams, which were exceptionally heavyweight and effective. True, Reagan had started off with Al Haig as secretary of state, an authentic flake whose mangled syntax guaranteed a confused message. But then he moved to the immensely reliable George Shultz, while Caspar Weinberger, as defence secretary, was extremely effective in testifying before Congress, was beloved of the military and successfully oversaw Reagan's strategic modernisation. Under Bush the at times crude but powerful Texan James Baker, one of the toughest wheelers and dealers in American politics, was secretary of state while the even more impressive Dick Cheney was defence secretary. Cheney turned out to be one of Bush's most inspired appointments. His sense of calm and command throughout Operation Desert Storm was a great strength of the Bush presidency. No one in Clinton's foreign policy team, on the other hand, communicated either vision or command. And this was a feature which only got worse as the months went on. Later Strobe Talbot was appointed deputy secretary of state. I saw him perform and had conversations with him in Bangkok and Canberra. While he was obviously a clever fellow, he clearly had very little background in East Asia and appeared to be just what he was, a scholarly journalist, whereas what the Clinton team needed was figures of gravitas and authority.

Clinton's early failure to appoint any neo-conservatives to his foreign policy team was a deep disappointment. The neo-cons were instinctive liberals, originally Democrats all, who had been anti-communist in the Cold War and had come to view the liberal critique of America, which grew out of the Vietnam War, as exaggerated and distorted. Some of them defected to Ronald Reagan. Others, such as New York congressman Stephen Solarz, remained Democrats. They had tended to be hawkish in the Cold War and strongly supported the use of American force against Saddam Hussein. They were comfortable with American power and accustomed to thinking in strategic terms. But Clinton found no place for the likes of these in his administration.

Stories of the administration's incompetent internal procedures leaked out. Later, Colin Powell's memoirs would record National Security Council meetings in the Clinton administration conducted like 'graduate bull sessions', going on for hours, with no clear agenda, no resultant action, intermittent and changing attendance, note takers talking back to principals—in other words, chaos.

But it was Clinton's own words and actions, which gave the greatest cause for concern in foreign policy in the early months of his presidency. Indeed just before he was inaugurated he sent shock waves around the world by talking, in an interview with the *New York Times*, of 'normalising relations with Iraq'. Clinton was a southern Baptist, he told the interviewer, and he believed in death-bed conversions. All around the world, foreign affairs departments, military intelligence analysts, governments and commentators believed this meant some new and radical departure in American Middle East policy. Instead, it turned out to have meant nothing more than that Clinton was speaking in an undisciplined way without having thought through his words. He and Al Gore had to spend the next week clearing up what he had meant and reaffirming that they were planning no change in American policy.

Insofar as Clinton had made any foreign policy commitments during the campaign, these were scratched once he took office. He promised, for example, to stop turning back Haitian boat people. Yet when he came into office he continued the policy of turning them back. Eventually he solved the Haitian problem by peacefully invading Haiti to install Jean-Bertrand Aristide, but that was years later. In the mean time his word, the word of the president of the United States, was severely devalued.

During the campaign Clinton made Bush look like a wimp on the Balkans. He criticised what was then the primary peace plan, the Vance–Owen plan, because it gave too much to the Serbs. He strongly suggested he would use force to prevent Serb aggression being rewarded. Soon after Clinton was elected he ended up offering to enforce the Vance–Owen plan. Then came the so-called 'lift-and-strike' option—lift the arms embargo on the Bosnian Muslims and strike at Serb artillery. Secretary of State Christopher was dispatched to convince the Europeans of the wisdom of this plan, a task in which he was completely unsuccessful. The episode fully demonstrated Clinton's incompetence on foreign policy. The idea of Christopher effectively arm-twisting America's European allies into any action they didn't want to take was laughable. Clinton did nothing to convince the American people, or Congress, or anyone else, least of all the Europeans, that any action was necessary. At one point he even lamented the amount of time the Bosnian crisis was taking from domestic concerns. This is no way for the leader of the free world to talk. It is certainly no way to obtain a result in foreign policy. Eventually, years later, Clinton would dispatch American forces to Bosnia to help implement a peace agreement. But there was no rhyme or reason, beyond the opinion polls and Clinton's ultimate need to look presidential, as to when or why he would take action.

There seemed to be no strategic map in Clinton's head. As one former senior US official put it to me: 'It's the classic state governor's approach. There is no such thing as foreign policy, only domestic consequences of foreign actions.' Nowhere was this more clear, or more dangerous, than in Clinton's approach to the other two great Asian powers—Japan and China. The triangular relationship between the US, Japan and China is the most important in the Asia–Pacific, perhaps in the world. They are the three giants of Asia, in some ways the three giants of the globe. Finding a sensible *modus vivendi* with Tokyo and Beijing is always going to be one of the central challenges for any American president. With Japan, Clinton never seemed to understand that he was dealing with an ally, and that every alliance needs political nourishment. He engaged in inconsistent and bullying trade policies while ignoring the strategic dimension, thus harming the alliance and earning the US enormous opprobrium throughout the region. With China, he was dealing not with an ally but with a difficult emerging superpower whose behaviour is going to be of first order consequence for all the nations of the East Asian hemisphere. While it would certainly be wrong to hold Washington responsible for all the vagaries of Beijing's behaviour over the last few years, the litany out of Washington of astonishing policy reversals, mixed signals, incoherent posturing, inconsistency and weakness mixed with bullying has been about as bad as it could be, and has contributed significantly to the difficulties the region is having with China. Similarly, it has eroded America's prestige.

Comprehensively mishandling Japan and China has been a sign of a deeper failure, however. Clinton, while sometimes talking of building an Asia–Pacific community, has given no indication of understanding the underlying structure of politics in the Pacific. This is a structure designed almost entirely by the US and it has been of great benefit to the US. It may well need substantial redesign in the post-Cold War era but changes will almost certainly be better accepted and more successful if they are introduced gradually and if continuity with the best elements of the previous structure are continued. But Clinton gave no indication of even understanding the previous structure.

The personalities of presidents have been crucial in setting up the broad Pacific security and economic structure. Indeed America became an Asian power really as a consequence of the personality of one of its greatest presidents, Theodore Roosevelt. As assistant secretary of the navy Roosevelt almost single-handedly engineered the Spanish–American war at the end of the nineteenth century which led to the US acquiring the Philippines as its one great and distant colony. Colonialism is intrinsically flawed as a moral system, and the Americans made their share of mistakes in the Philippines, but Filipinos were certainly better off with America as a colonial master than they would have been under continued Spanish rule. For one thing the Americans understood that eventually colonies would become independent. They were also far more inclined to believe that subject people could aspire to equality with their colonial overlords in time than were European colonial powers. In any event responsibility in the Philippines was one of the factors which ensured that the US would be a significant Asian power.

At the end of the Second World War the US was pre-eminent in Asia, ruling Japan, freeing the Philippines, and with its navy dominant throughout the Pacific. The dynamics of the Cold War quickly led to the US imposing a blanket security structure. It provided for Japan's security such that Japan did not have to bear the cost of rearmament. Similarly the rest of Asia did not have to bear the psychological and strategic cost of coping with Japanese rearmament. The US was resolute in the security guarantees it gave in Asia. It ultimately committed itself to formal security alliances with Japan, South Korea, Thailand, the Philippines, Australia and New Zealand. It demonstrated its authenticity in the Korean War, when it sacrificed more than 50 000 of its own dead to secure independence for South Korea. The Vietnam War, however poorly executed, was essentially conceived in the same strategic design, to stop the spread of communism and secure a non-communist future for South Vietnam. In this, America was temporarily unsuccessful (the Vietnamese themselves finally throwing off communism in everything but name). But the Vietnam commitment bought precious time for the other Southeast Asian states—Thailand, Malaysia, the Philippines, Indonesia and Singapore—to conquer their own insurgencies and grow their economies to such a stage that they were no longer under challenge as states by the time of Saigon's fall in 1975.

Moreover, the United States also provided the essential conditions for the East Asian economic miracle. The US did not perform the miracle, the East Asians did that for themselves. But the US did provide the two absolutely critical preconditions—military security and access to the American market for East Asia's exports. In a development full of ironies, the Vietnam War itself, and the need to supply the vast American forces in Vietnam, was important in generating much economic growth in Japan, South Korea and other East Asian states. Every important development in the region was either engineered, or hugely influenced, by Washington. Even the re-emergence of China into the global community, and the vastly consequential process of

Chinese economic reform, was substantially a result of far-sighted American foreign policy, namely Kissinger and Nixon playing the 'China card' against the Soviet Union.

All of this was done partly to serve American strategic and economic interests. But it was also done with a genuine desire to help East Asia. It was one of the most benign, effective and important acts of global leadership which the world has seen. In 50 years it transformed a region of poverty, conflict and with an utterly bleak outlook, as East Asia was in 1945, into a region of prosperity and peace, into the world's most dynamic economic zone, into what will probably be the dominant economic force in the twenty-first century.

But America's interests were also served. America's trade across the Pacific is now 50 per cent greater than its trade across the Atlantic. Its exports to East Asia are growing 50 per cent faster than its imports from East Asia. America is brilliantly placed to pursue a trading future with the most dynamic region in the world because of its own past enlightened policy.

Obviously, some of the structures need reworking in the post–Cold War environment. But the structure of Asian security, based as it is on a web of bilateral alliances with the US rather than one multilateral alliance like NATO, is probably easier to adapt than the structure of European security. Some things will need to change, of course. East Asian nations will need to share more of the burden and equally achieve greater parity in decision making. Already this is happening. The US has 100 000 troops stationed in East Asia. Nearly half are in Japan. Tokyo now pays such a high proportion of their non-salary costs that it is in some ways cheaper to have US troops there than in Iowa. Similarly, the cost to the US of its Korean commitment is declining. But the value of these bilateral alliances is huge, to the US and the region. What is needed now above all else, however, is some constructive US leadership in creating the new security and economic order. Professor Don Hellmann, who formerly headed the US APEC Studies Centre at the University of Washington, has argued that this leadership is manifestly lacking, that the Cold War is the first major conflict to come to a decisive conclusion in which the winning party made no effort to influence decisively the structures of the ensuing peace.

As a result, leadership has passed to smaller nations, such as Australia, which founded the Asia Pacific Economic Cooperation forum, and South Korea, which midwifed the entry of China, Taiwan and Hong Kong into APEC. There is nothing wrong with middle powers exercising leadership, but America's psychological absence is highly disturbing. A great power which doesn't pay attention can be dangerous and destabilising. The US at first opposed a multilateral security dialogue body for the Pacific, something which has now taken root. Thus the key components of the new international architecture in the Asia–Pacific came about either without significant American input or in the face of early American opposition.

In the field of security Clinton, following the late conversion of the Bush administration, declared himself dedicated to pursuing new multilateral cooperative initiatives in security, to complement America's bilateral alliances. The most significant such new body was the Association of South East Asian Nations Regional Forum (ARF), which was set up in Singapore in 1993. The annual ASEAN ministerial dialogue session is one of only two occasions when the US secretary of state must turn up to a scheduled multilateral event in the Asia–Pacific (the other is the APEC ministerial meeting). The new ARF was to be set up at the ASEAN meeting in Singapore in 1993. Its whole purpose was to bring together, for a security dialogue at foreign minister level, all the key governments in the Asia–Pacific—China, Japan, South Korea, all the ASEAN states, Russia, Vietnam, Australia and of course America. But what happened? Clinton's secretary of state, Warren Christopher, was busy with the Middle East and didn't show up to the Singapore ARF meeting (although he attended part of the ASEAN meeting preceding it). What was worse, the following year the ARF meeting was held in Bangkok with a full working agenda of security issues to be discussed. Again all the foreign ministers from around the region gathered for this unique body. This time Christopher didn't show up at all.

This was one of the most maddening features of the Clinton administration. It would on occasion say all the right things but the words had no meaning or consequence. Worse was Clinton's own dereliction in not turning up himself at the APEC leaders' meeting in Osaka in November 1995. Clinton had inaugurated the APEC leaders' meetings in Seattle in 1993 and on that occasion had uttered his many platitudinous commitments to forming a Pacific community. Having APEC leaders meet personally each year was a vital innovation in Asian politics. Never before had there been a gathering of East Asian heads of government. That is extraordinary but true. There was no forum at which the president of China, the prime minister of Japan, the president of Indonesia, the prime minister of Thailand, the prime minister of Australia and all the others had occasion to meet. To have them meeting at all was an extraordinary development which would greatly augment APEC's power and prestige, and significantly influence general policy outcomes in Asia. But to have them meeting with the American president should have been seen as a beautiful structure by Washington. It was the perfect symbol of inclusion, collegiality, cooperation. Calling this meeting was the one act of leadership in Asia which Clinton has performed. He deserves full credit for it, although it is a small thing to set beside the general abdication of American leadership in his presidency.

Clinton also managed to get himself along to the next APEC leaders' meeting in Indonesia in 1994. But in 1995, at the last minute, he pulled out of the Osaka meeting because of a ridiculous budget dispute he was having with the congressional Republicans. What underlined for everyone at Osaka just where APEC stood in Clinton's priorities was that a week later he was able to stitch up a temporary deal to enable him to make a visit to Ireland. Everyone at Osaka knew anyway that had it been a visit to Ireland at stake Clinton would have managed to attend. But APEC, Japan, the Asia–Pacific community all apparently meant nothing. The whole business reeked of cynicism and irresponsibility. Clinton was finding, to his delight, that he was registering improvement in the polls because of the Budget crisis. It was in his interest to keep it running.

Almost worse than boycotting the APEC meeting, however, was Clinton's cancellation, at the last minute, of the associated full state visit he was supposed to pay to Japan. This was a visit which was supposed to focus on the positives, to celebrate and underline the strength of the US–Japan alliance, to put some political ballast back into the relationship. The Japanese had of course planned to roll out the red carpet for the American president. It was to be not only a head of government visit but a head of state visit. The emperor of Japan was to host a goodly portion of the Clinton visit personally. The Japanese, who put great store on courtesy, face and hierarchy, regarded Clinton's abrupt cancellation of the visit as deeply insulting. It further eroded support within Japan for the American alliance.

Clinton did later have a good visit to Japan. Wherever Clinton travels his apparently consuming desire to be loved leads him to exert his formidable charm and produce good atmospherics. But the temporary good atmospherics cannot make up for past neglect, nor do they have any permanent hold or effect on Clinton's mind. Following the tragic rape of a Japanese school girl on Okinawa, the Clinton administration did negotiate some improvements to the US–Japan security treaty, and reaffirm its importance. But by then much damage had been done.

Clinton's insouciance towards Japan has been bewildering and irresponsible. It characterised his administration from its earliest days. Again it was as if there was no brain at work in the Clinton administration. The inability to see America's most basic interests and the damage his administration was doing to them was astonishing.

Clinton began badly with Japan and got consistently worse. From the beginning his administration gave the impression that it had thoroughly internalised the revisionist view of Japan associated with writers such as Karel van Wolforen and Chalmers Johnson. In effect the revisionists hold that Japan is a unique economy more or less immune to the forces of the physical universe, that it has achieved its economic success through unfair, mercantilist policies which must be combated with brute force. Clinton's administration quickly slipped into a routine of extremely sterile trade confrontation with Japan. It argued that America's trade deficit with Japan was a result of Japanese invisible barriers to imports and that only by agreeing to cut its trade surplus, in other words by agreeing to specific trade targets, could Japan demonstrate good faith.

Clinton himself gave the most crude and offensive version of this crude and inaccurate theory during then prime minister Kiichi Miyazawa's visit to Washington in early 1993, not long after Clinton was inaugurated as president. In the hearing of press microphones, Clinton described the Japanese as pathological liars, claiming that they 'say yes when they mean no'.

From his earliest meetings with Miyazawa, Clinton established the pattern of the United States, the most powerful and successful nation on Earth, demanding that Japan agree to buy a certain proportion of its imports from America, a proposition which contradicts both notions of free trade and the specific, rules-based trade system underpinned by the World Trade Organisation. The Japanese, while making concessions, always refused to accept binding targets or 'managed trade'.

There was one flicker of hope in the early months of Clinton's presidency. In July 1993, Clinton went to Tokyo for a meeting of the Group of Seven leading industrialised nations and then to South Korea. He got a meaningless but face-saving trade agreement from Miyazawa during that visit but more importantly behaved with grace and dignity. This is one of the many paradoxes of Clinton. He loves to be loved. He really would like to be loved by everybody, no matter how contradictory their separate agendas. He is thus led to say whatever he thinks his audience wants to hear. He is personally charming and places a great store by good personal relations. This is all very well but means it is very dangerous to take him at his word. Henry Kissinger has wickedly described the situation in which Clinton always agrees with him within five minutes of a conversation beginning. Within 10 minutes he has promised to do much more than Kissinger has asked in the direction he is suggesting. The problem is the next fellow goes in to see him with entirely contradictory suggestions and gets just the same response. In any event Clinton had a good visit to Tokyo and an excellent visit to South Korea. In uncharacteristically clear language he told North Korea that if it attacked South Korea with nuclear weapons, 'your country will cease to exist'. Ah, what a wonderful, unrepresentative and misleading moment that was in the Clinton presidency. What clarity! What resolve! What purpose!

Similarly he set out a comprehensive view of American security policy in East Asia, saying it rested on four pillars. The first was continued forward deployment of American forces in the region. He specifically assured Korea there would be no further reductions of US troop numbers on the Korean peninsula. Second, the US would strengthen its efforts to combat the proliferation of weapons of mass destruction. Third, the US would encourage and take part in new regional dialogues on the full range of security issues. And finally the US would support democracy throughout the region. The president declared: 'The bedrock of America's security role in the Asia–Pacific must be a continued military presence. In a period of change we need to preserve what has been reliable. Today we therefore affirm our five bilateral security agreements with Korea, with Japan, with Australia, with the Philippines and with Thailand.'

The problem with these commendably clear statements is that they were so uncharacteristic. They didn't mean anything. While Clinton was physically in Asia he performed in a way that would make him popular while he was there. But as soon as he got on the plane to go home it was as if he took off his remarks like taking off an overcoat. There was no consequence from them.

Indeed all through 1994 the US moved towards crisis in its trade relations with Japan. The Super 301 trade legislation was revived which would enable the US to impose harsh, punitive trade sanctions on Japan. At the time Japan was running a trade surplus with the US of about $US60 billion and the US attributed this entirely to Japan's restrictive trade barriers. In fact, American paranoia did not square with the facts. All through the '90s Japan imported, per head, about the same value of products as many affluent Western European nations. Moreover, Japan was consistently moving towards becoming more import friendly and the level of imports into Japan was rising rapidly. According to a study issued in 1994 by the East Asia Analytical Unit of the Australian Department of Foreign Affairs and Trade, Japan's manufactured imports tripled between 1985 and 1991, rising to $US113 billion and falling very slightly the next year because of Japan's recession. In the '90s Japan's imports reached as high as 8 per cent of its Gross Domestic Product, compared with 9.5 per cent for the US.

The real story of the seond half of the 1980s and the early '90s was not Japan's resistance to imports but America's declining share of the Japanese market, which reflected problems in America's competitiveness generally. The US share of the Japanese market for manufactured imports fell from 35 per cent in 1985 to 27 per cent in 1992. America's performance in the Japanese market was particularly poor compared with Europe's. Japan's trade surplus with Europe fell by a third between 1992 and 1996, the period of Clinton's presidency, whereas Japan's surplus with America only began to decline, and then only slightly, and perhaps temporarily, at the end of Clinton's first term. Real leadership would have meant Clinton telling America about competitiveness and its poor domestic savings rate, not trying to get Japan to solve America's problems by guaranteeing to buy a certain percentage of its goods.

In October 1994 Japan and the US had one of a series of almost annual trade crises. Full-scale American sanctions were only just avoided as Japan made the bare minimum of concessions to avoid triggering Super 301 sanctions. As usual, the air was filled with rancour and the two allies engaged in a competitive campaign for international support. This was another aspect of Clinton's foolishness. Japan undoubtedly won the propaganda battle internationally, not so much because of any Japanese propaganda efforts but because of the clear unreasonableness of America's actions. Australia, a strong ally of the US, clearly backed Japan. Indeed Australia's prime minister Paul Keating had publicly congratulated Japan's Prime Minister Kiichi Miyazawa, for resisting American pressure for 'managed trade'. Even in Europe, where paranoia about East Asian economic success is hardly less intense than in America, official sentiment favoured Japan. The European Union trade commissioner Sir Leon Brittan, accused the US of being 'discriminatory' in its policies towards Japan. He also raised the question of American hypocrisy over its own substantial impediments to free trade. Brittan said Europe had 'a very long list of US trade barriers' that it wanted America to remove. He also commented: 'Any attempt to force Japanese markets open through numerical targets risks above all being counterproductive as well as being incompatible with Europe and America's mutual commitment to free trade and multilateralism.'

Other officials were more blunt, especially concerning the performance of the US trade representative, Mickey Kantor, a former Los Angeles lawyer who had risen to prominence in Clinton's presidential campaign but who had little Asian or diplomatic experience. Fairly typical was a remark by David Howell, chairman of the British House of Commons Foreign Affairs Committee. 'What the United Kingdom and Japan are engaged in is trade, whereas what Mickey Kantor is seeking is a deal.'

It is not often that Britain has preferred Japan to the United States. It is a mark almost of genius that Clinton could fail to hold even European opinion. But it was within Asia that America's name suffered most. There was not a single Asian opinion leader of consequence who thought America was in the right. As Australia's then trade minister, Bob McMullan, commented: 'I don't know of a single country in the world that actually agrees with the mechanism the United States is using even though it is undoubtedly correct that the Japanese should open up their economy more to imports.'

In Japan itself, America's name was on a steady downward trend. In 1993 a poll showed only 35 per cent of Japanese thought of America as a friendly country, down from 53 per cent before Clinton came to office and 73 per cent in 1985. Clinton himself was regarded favourably by a dismal 6 per cent of Japanese. This was a reputable poll sponsored by the American CBS network, Japan's TBS and the *New York Times*. American policy makers are extremely foolish to ignore the long-term consequences of throwing away, in either country, the hard-won base of political support for the relationship.

But if things were bad in 1994 they got much worse in 1995, when the relationship reached meltdown point. It was May of 1995 and as usual the US and Japan were having their annual trade crisis over Japan's refusal to embrace numerical targets in a trade deal. The US, as usual, was threatening punitive trade sanctions against Japan. But then came what must rank as one of the most fantastically irresponsible statements by a presidential spokesman in decades. Clinton's official spokesman formally linked the trade dispute to the defence relationship, something which Washington had never done before. This contradicted 50 years of established US strategic doctrine in East Asia, and for absolutely no benefit. Without making any direct threats to terminate the security relationship, Clinton's spokesman said the impasse over auto trade could become an 'impediment' to other aspects of the relationship.

These words, though by no means emotive or florid, and later substantially clarified, caused shock waves across the Pacific. The US–Japan alliance has a long history, and officials in both countries knew the forms of words to be used and those to be avoided. For decades American and Japanese spokesmen had always insisted that trade disputes would not affect the alliance. It was, as usual, impossible to know what weight to give to the Clinton spokesman's words. Not the least maddening aspect of Clinton was that you never knew whether a new formulation of words meant a radical change in policy or merely transitory incompetence, whether the administration was as usual just saying whatever came into its silly head or actually had a deeper purpose.

The trade sanctions the US threatened against Japan in this dispute were of staggering proportions. The US said that unless Japan complied with its demands on auto trade it would raise from 2.5 per cent to 100 per cent the tariff level on thirteen makes of Japanese luxury cars imported into the US, imposing a record sanction of $US5 billion, although with a projected knock-on effect on the Japanese economy of $US15 billion. Once Washington announced a formal thirty-day notice for the imposition of these tariffs, the Japanese began formal proceedings under the World Trade Organisation to have the American tariffs declared illegal. Had the case proceeded before the WTO, the US would almost certainly have lost on the merits. By imposing sanctions before the WTO dispute reconciliation procedures were exhausted, or indeed even begun, Washington seriously weakened the moral and political force of the WTO. However, it threatened the WTO in a more subtle and insidious way as well. Had the US lost a case at the WTO it would in all likelihood have ignored the ruling. This would effectively have blown the WTO's authority apart. Yet had the WTO made a blatantly biased decision in favour of the US this too would have destroyed its credibility. In other words the US, under Clinton's leadership, was prepared to put the entire global trading system at risk unless it could get its way.

At the very last minute Kantor and Japan's then trade and industry minister, Ryutaro Hashimoto, worked out a deal. Clinton was very closely involved in all this personally, receiving at one point hourly telephone updates from Kantor and later extravagantly praising Kantor's work. The deal was the typical fudge. The Japanese promised to buy more US autos and auto spare parts, and to deregulate their own spare parts industry. The Japanese described the numbers in the agreement as mere industry forecasts, the Americans described them as binding numerical commitments. In substance Kantor had backed down and Hashimoto's popularity soared in Japan as a result of his being seen to have stood up to Kantor. Hashimoto later became prime minister of Japan.

Kantor and Clinton, on the other hand, could sell the cobbled-together agreement to an American public deeply ignorant of trade policy as a great victory. But it was an appalling and futile way to conduct world trade. Four years of Clinton have damaged the US–Japan alliance, the most important alliance, indeed the most important bilateral relationship, in the world. That a Japanese politician could become popular through mild anti-Americanism is sad and worrying. Later, when US servicemen in Okinawa were accused of raping a Japanese schoolgirl, polls showed for the first time a majority of Japanese against maintaining the alliance. Clinton has squandered 50 years of political capital, and a large part of America's pivotally important standing and position in East Asia, for absolutely no gain amidst a welter of folly, malice and incompetence.

But as if that were not bad enough his management of the China relationship was perhaps even worse. China has been compared to nineteenth century Germany, an immensely powerful nation, newly emerging onto the world stage, determined to have the standing of a great power, but unused in recent times to exercising great power and coming into an international system completely unused to coping with it as a great power. It took two world wars and countless millions dead before Germany was incorporated into the international system constructively. Managing China's emergence will be an immensely complex task. Yet again, the leader of the free world seems to be without the slightest clue as to how this might be accomplished.

During the presidential campaign Clinton criticised Bush for being too soft on China. He said he would link China's Most

Favoured Nation status, that is, the normal trading status which America affords to almost every nation on Earth, with its human rights performance. In office this became a commitment to demand from China progress on decreasing its trade surplus with America, progress on preventing the proliferation of weapons of mass destruction, and progress on human rights as a condition for renewing MFN. Early in 1993 Clinton delinked the first two of those. Eventually in 1993 he conditionally renewed China's MFN status, saying that for it to be renewed the following year China would have to show clear and demonstrable proof of improvement in human rights.

American concern for human rights is laudable and often effective. But it can be a cloak for protectionism, for the promotion of vested interests and for old-fashioned quasi-colonialist meddling. What was clear about China was that the economic reform program instituted by Deng Xiaoping at the end of the 1970s had produced the greatest increase in wealth that China had ever seen. An increase in wealth does not always increase human freedom. Japan and Germany in the 1930s demonstrate this. But in today's world where so much of wealth is concerned with international trade and with information technology, which is inherently subversive of dictatorship, it almost always does. Certainly every serious observer of China agreed that while it remained a politically repressive place, the amount of personal and even political space its citizens enjoyed was greatly increasing because of the economic reforms. The appalling massacre in Tiananmen Square, horrible as it was, did not invalidate this conclusion.

Decision time for Clinton on China's MFN loomed as June 1994. In the early months of that year it became clear that China was not going to do anything specific to meet Clinton's demands. The Chinese leadership was in any event outraged at America's meddling. Virtually every country in Asia, virtually every country in the world, condemned the American approach. Clinton was subject to devastating criticism from his fellow Americans. The former defence secretary Dick Cheney declared, 'We risk doing enormous damage to the positive forces for change inside China by going through this process every year of threatening to withdraw its most favoured nation trade status.' Former assistant secretary of state for East Asian affairs Richard Solomon said:

> It's illogical. Why? Because I think there's a general realisation there has been really dramatic improvement in the situation if one takes a ten- or twenty-year perspective. Economic growth and the trade that's been a driving force behind that has been a real force for positive improvement. To threaten to pull MFN is to undercut one of our major sources of positive influence for improving the situation in China.

Cheney and Solomon were Republicans, but Clinton was hearing the same message from US business a thousand times over: this policy was dumb, dumb, dumb. It would do nothing for human rights in China. Indeed, if it injured the economic reform program it could very well harm them. At the same time it would damage US interests. Of course, eventually Clinton caved in and did a complete reversal on his China policy. He renewed China's MFN status and delinked it from human rights.

There were several key points to emerge from that humiliating volte-face. First, in his foreign policy Clinton marches to the edge of the precipice, then walks back. As Winston Lord, Clinton's assistant secretary of state for East Asia, told me, the administration's foreign policy might be compared to Wagner's music, in Mark Twain's famous comment: it's not as bad as it sounds. But in waltzing to the precipice and stumbling back Clinton does immense harm along the way. The policy he finally arrived at regarding China's MFN status—delinking it from human rights— was certainly the correct one. But it is inconceivable that he could have got to it in a more destructive, humiliating and dangerous fashion.

The method of getting there also compromised the quality of the policy itself. Managing China, as I say, is going to be a desperately important and complex business. Threatening and then caving over the MFN issue greatly increased the ill-will between the leaderships of the two countries. But it had a far worse result as well. It dangerously emboldened the Chinese leadership and led them to believe that their dogmatic, inflexible, uncompromising style would always prevail over the feeble antics of democracies like America. It devalued the prestige of democracy and increased the risk of serious Chinese miscalculation. It is in everyone's interests to incorporate China constructively into a functioning international order. But there may be times when China's ambitions or actions will need to be checked. Such times are less likely to occur, and less likely to be explosive when they do occur, if Beijing believes in Washington's resolve. But Clinton demonstrated no resolve. He greatly damaged the standing of America and the credibility of the word of the American president. This is no small achievement.

In the second half of Clinton's term China did become a very difficult neighbour over some issues, notably Taiwan. China's inclination to behave in a bellicose and unreasonable fashion must have been encouraged by Clinton's performance over MFN. But if anything much of his performance over Taiwan was even worse. The tension between China and Taiwan is Asia's most serious security flashpoint outside of the Korean peninsula.

Taiwan's president, Lee Teng-hui, applied for a visa to visit the United States to accept an award from his alma mater, Cornell University, in June 1995. The US, like most countries, observes an official 'one-China' policy under which it gives diplomatic recognition to Beijing but not to Taipei, under the fiction that Taiwan is a province of China. Nonetheless it has extensive relations with Taiwan, including a commitment, under the Taiwan Relations Act, to its security. Taiwan of course has been effectively independent of China since Chiang Kai-Shek and the Kuomintang fled there from the mainland in 1949. As part of its one-China policy Washington has in the past refused to grant visas to Taiwanese leaders.

However, this time it granted Lee a visa. Beijing's reaction, after a couple of weeks thinking things over, was hysterical. It protested furiously, recalled its ambassador to Washington, ran a campaign of virulent personal denunciation of Lee in the official press and began firing allegedly test missiles within 130 km of Taiwan's northern coast.

The people responsible for this gross bullying are of course the Chinese politburo. It is axiomatic that the Chinese are responsible for their own behaviour. But we are concerned here with Clinton's role.

The way this episode was handled was almost a textbook case of why Clinton cannot run foreign policy. Warren Christopher was authorised to tell his Chinese counterpart, Qian Qichen, that Washington would not give Lee a visa because to do so would contradict the one-China policy. Qian convinced the Chinese president, Jiang Zimen, of the Americans' good faith and together they told the politburo that no visa would be forthcoming.

Meanwhile the pro-Taiwan lobby in Washington had got busy and organised huge congressional majorities in favour of resolutions supporting a Lee visit. This sentiment was entirely understandable. Taiwan had turned itself into a democracy and Lee led a democratic and successful government. But in the face of this congressional pressure Clinton once again caved in, overruled Christopher and decided to allow a visa for Lee, thus leading to the furious reaction in Beijing.

Again, the final policy position, extending Lee a visa, was entirely defensible. Rich Armitage, the former assistant secretary of defence, described to me how he would have handled it: 'Just out of courtesy I would have told the Chinese a few weeks in advance that we were going to give Lee a visa. Not asked them, just told them. No drama. No big deal.' Had that sensible path been followed, the Chinese may or may not have reacted but they would have had no excuse to react. Instead Clinton produced the absolute worst possible result for everybody.

First, he offended Lee Teng-hui by being so obviously reluctant to give him a visa in the first place. Thus in giving the Taiwanese their maximum political claim Clinton still managed to offend them. Much more importantly he greatly humiliated his own secretary of state. Christopher's word was worth very little.

More importantly still, he gave both Jiang and Qian every reason to feel personally betrayed by the whole process. But perhaps the most consequential result of all was once more to convince the Chinese that he, Clinton, will always cave in to the greatest pressure. This time the greatest pressure came from Congress. The lesson for the Chinese therefore is that in future they should put even greater pressure on Clinton, so that he will cave in to them. Thus in carrying out a defensible policy Clinton managed to offend everyone and provide everyone with a strong incentive for dangerous behaviour in the future. Throughout the years 1992 to 1996 there were fitful, sometimes quite intense, efforts by Washington at rapprochement with Beijing. These were constructive but they were intermittent at best and overwhelmed by the larger mismanagement.

Of course Clinton did do some good things in Asia. With an approach as random as his it would have been impossible not to. The best thing he did was host the first APEC summit. He also played a role in completing the Uruguay Round of GATT and getting NAFTA passed. Clinton's apologists regard these as great achievements. In fact they were 90 per cent done by George Bush and were passed for Clinton essentially by the Republicans in Congress. It is inconceivable that an American president in 1992 could have abandoned GATT, from which America stood to gain so much. Clinton deserves credit for fighting for NAFTA. Not that NAFTA represents good trade policy. As a preferential, exclusionary trade bloc it distorts trade and investment and represents a partial retreat by the US from the global, rules-based trade system. But a defeat for NAFTA would not have been a victory for free traders but for isolationists and protectionists. In defeating them Clinton did well by doing good.

But the rest of his trade agenda was a mess. In particular, his trade policy ambition of having future trade agreements linked to environmentalism and labour rights was greatly resented in Asia, where it is seen as a form of disguised protectionism and neo-colonial meddling. It is also grossly hypocritical. What was the state of US labour laws when its per capita income was equal to that of Indonesia's today? Indeed far more than any Republican president Clinton has convinced Asia that as America's relative power is declining its desire to impose its will, by bullying and throwing its economic weight around, is increasing.

The other positive achievement of the Clinton administration in Asia was the mostly competent handling of the periodic Korean crisis. It may be that that was partly because it was handled primarily by US foreign policy professionals, who are as good as any in the world, and hardly at all by the White House. Clinton's general foreign policy performance did become less bad as he went along. He finally grasped the seriousness of the situation in the Balkans and committed the US to participating in a peacekeeping mission. He got a good result in Haiti although it is absurd that Haiti ever became so dominant a problem in

American foreign policy. Similarly the US was a constructive, though by no means decisive, influence in the Middle East.

One episode where the US provided decisive, beneficial and utterly admirable leadership was its response to China's attempt to intimidate Taiwan just before the Taiwanese presidential election in 1996. China conducted live missile firings at the north and south ends of the Taiwan Strait, just tens of kilometres away from Taiwanese cities. This was a shocking provocation by China and gravely disturbing to the region. It may well be that the Chinese leadership was emboldened to take this kind of action because of the weakness and capitulation it had experienced from the Clinton administration previously. This time, however, it was met with a measured but decisive reaction. America sent two aircraft-carrier battle groups into the waters around Taiwan. This was an awesome display of firepower. In accordance with the Taiwan Relations Act, Washington told Beijing in no uncertain terms that it was committed to safeguarding Taiwan's security.

At the same time it did not write a blank cheque for Taiwan's leaders. It let them know that a formal declaration of independence would not gain American support. The American action was successful and reassuring. Of course, it doesn't necessarily tell us too much about any increased resolve by the Clinton administration, because in this case Clinton was acting with public and congressional opinion. The line of least resistance, in terms of domestic politics, was for Clinton to be firm with China.

The American military is the best in the world, not only in terms of technology and firepower, but in terms of strategic thinking as well. The 1995 Nye Report, in which the Pentagon set out its security thinking for East Asia, was a model of lucidity, sensible proportion and commitment. The problem was trying to decipher whether it told us anything substantial about the Clinton administration.

An altogther different event in 1996 told us rather too much about Clinton and the Clinton team. That was the publication of the novel *Primary Colors*. This is a *roman à clef* about the Clinton primary campaign for the Democratic presidential nomination in 1992. There is a definitive line of dialogue early in it in which the Hillary Clinton figure says of her husband that he could be

a great man 'if he weren't such a faithless, thoughtless, dis-
organised, undisciplined shit'.

Primary Colors is riotously funny and unputdownable. But in
a way it is deeply shocking. It presents the Clinton outfit as
unbelievably sleazy. The book became a huge success in the US
partly because everyone tried to guess who its author was, but
also because so many of its incidents were drawn from real life
and contained authentic dialogue. The Gennifer Flowers escapade
is fully recorded. Even worse is an incident, and this one I
presume is really fictional, in which the Clinton character seduces
and impregnates the teenage daughter of a black cafe owner in
the state of which he is governor. When the girl turns up seeking
support he forces her to undergo amniocentesis and then fakes
his own blood test results in order to deny paternity.

What I found most shocking about the phenomenon of the
book was the absence of a clear and overwhelming denial from
the Clinton camp that this was the type of person the president
was. The other interesting thing about the book is the wider view
of morality it has. The book criticises, but partly succumbs to,
the view ascribed to the Clinton character that his many failings
are redeemed by his 'empathy' with the voters, the famous 'I feel
your pain' quality. This is a nearly total reversal of traditional
notions of morality, that morality consists of doing what you
know is right even when you feel like doing something else.
Instead the view of the author and characters of *Primary Colors*
seems to be that any action you take, no matter how appalling,
is redeemed so long as you have good feelings in your heart. If
this book is widely read in East Asia it will certainly reinforce
views (which I think are ultimately wrong) about America's
decline. In any event, Asia does not want 'good feelings' from
the Clinton administration, it wants sensible and dependable
policy.

Overall it is impossible to be positive about Clinton's record
as president. In domestic policy he delivered little that he promised, in particular health care reform. He veered wildly from right
to left and back to right again. He attempted one of the biggest
single extensions of government in American history, the partial
nationalisation of health insurance, but periodically claimed to
be in favour of small government. He came to office full of the

possibilities of government action but after the Republican slaughter of the Democrats in the 1994 congressional elections was happy to declare that 'the era of big government is over'. His appointments were highly liberal yet in the conservative second half of his term he railed against Hollywood pornography and violence. His philosophy was really summed up in his exquisite line of unconscious self-parody in his 1995 State of the Union address: 'My fellow Americans, every single survey shows . . .'

After the Republican congressional victory he seemed less a president and more a leader of the Opposition, not trying to govern in any conventional sense, merely to discredit the other side. His personal style was a very odd mixture. He was part 'bubba', part self-improvement guru and talk-show host. In the end he transformed himself into a kind of conservative Republican president. He began his presidency championing gays in the military and ended his first term signing a bill to outlaw gay marriage. This was a politician without discernible core beliefs beyond re-election.

But it was in foreign policy, the area he never wanted to pay attention to, that he was really at his worst. Overall, Clinton was perhaps the feeblest president since the awful Republican trio of the '20s, Harding, Coolidge and Hoover. The *New Republic* is a consistently pro-Democrat political magazine, one of the best in America. It labelled the Clinton term 'craven and uncaptained years' in American foreign policy. As a region accustomed to gallant and decisive American leadership, East Asia found Clinton extremely perplexing, to say the least.

This is a tragedy because no region in the world is more readily open to American partnership than East Asia. In significant degree modern East Asia is a creation of America's, but of a different America, the postwar America led by men like Truman and Eisenhower, who knew what they were about. The baby boomers do not compare well with the World War II generation. Clinton, a sum of shiny surfaces without apparent depth, is a perfect representative of his generation. Perhaps Generation X will do better.

9

MARTIN LEE: THE MARTYR IN WAITING

 The first time I visited Hong Kong was in 1986. On my first day there the Crown colony conspired to give me two typical and emblematic examples of its enduring character. I had caught the Star Ferry across the harbour to the island and taken a taxi downtown to lunch with Melanie Kirkpatrick from the *Asian Wall Street Journal*, for whom I used to do a little work. We met at one of the seemingly countless palatial city hotels and ate the normal Chinese banquet on the menu for lunch. After lunch, strolling back to the ferry, a sudden storm came on. One minute it was hot and sticky and not raining, the next it was hot and sticky and pouring. From nowhere countless umbrella sellers appeared. It seemed suddenly that every corner had an umbrella stall, stocked with a marvellous array of umbrellas, from the very cheap to the not so cheap.

It was an entirely trivial incident but it seemed to be part of the web of Chinese Hong Kong life. There is rain, there is opportunity, opportunity equals a market—let's sell. In most western cities of similar affluence to Hong Kong there would be a phalanx of regulations to stop such spontaneous fulfilling of market needs.

I was staying during that visit at a cheap hotel in Sha Tin, out in the New Territories, on the tip of mainland China itself. That night I went out for a stroll in the muggy evening air. I turned down a little side alley and stopped to chat to one of the shopkeepers. A fit, muscular-looking man who looked to be in his late twenties or early thirties, he and his wife were working together in the shop, a little supermarket, the TV on in the background, his two pretty little daughters running around, talking to other shopkeepers or customers at the sidewalk cafes.

He told me his shop opens at 8 a.m. every day. He gets up at 6 each morning to work a full day as a cab driver while his wife runs the shop. Each evening after his full day in the cab he works at the shop while his wife cooks dinner, looks after the two girls and then, for the rest of the evening, works with her husband in the shop as well. For the shopkeeper it's a good life. He spends his evening with his family and he's making money all the time. The shopkeeper is hopeful for the future of his business. He has heard that a big restaurant may soon be opening opposite and that his muddy lane may soon be paved, both of which would mean more customers for his supermarket.

So that was the Hong Kong good life—husband and wife both working the equivalent of two jobs each, working, working, working like the devil, but the whole family together, making money, accumulating assets, building security out of their own efforts.

These two trivial experiences, the umbrella sellers and the friendly supermarket operator, are typical Hong Kong. Every traveller there could recount a dozen similar tales. But they epitomise what has made Hong Kong renowned—the astonishing industry of its people, and its expression in an unfettered market. Nowhere, but nowhere, is the work ethic so deeply instilled, so enthusiastically practised. Moreover, Hong Kong is perhaps the only society in the world that makes you believe in the invisible hand of capitalist economics, à la Adam Smith, working miraculously to achieve beneficial social outcomes.

But this side of Hong Kong is indeed well known. What was more unlikely was that Hong Kong, in the 1980s and '90s, should throw up a figure who would exemplify not only the traditional Hong Kong virtues of industry, family, studiousness and thrift but also political leadership, democratic idealism, resistance to tyranny. As the date of Hong Kong's return to rule by Beijing approached the star of its chief democrat shone with increasing intensity. To some general surprise Hong Kong threw up a leader in the field of political ethics. Perhaps the world had misjudged Hong Kong all along. When its people finally got to vote they voted for committed democrats with one of the most impressive individuals in East Asia as their leader.

Martin Lee Chu Ming, QC, barrister, leader first of the United Democrats and later the Democratic Party, came to be, much more than the governor, Chris Patten, or any of the pro-Beijing business tycoons, the international symbol of Hong Kong. That is not to say that all Hong Kong supported him. Of course not. But in 1991 and again in 1995, when Hong Kong's citizens had a free vote, more of them voted for Martin Lee and his party than for anyone else. That is why Lee is in this book. If Hong Kong were a democracy, he would be its elected head of government. That he has had so little power, while having so much support, in the last years of colonial rule in Hong Kong is an indictment of Britain's rule.

Lee is every inch a politician. For a society without vibrant political traditions Lee has been so formidable partly because he has adapted and implemented the classic behaviours of a politician. He does not set himself up as a saint, or an ancient Chinese mandarin whose manifest scholarly attainments should be automatically respected by all lesser men. Instead he campaigns. He attends endless meetings. He addresses rallies. He talks to journalists. He appears on TV. He organises petitions. He signs petitions. He talks to constituents. He attends endless *yum chas* in Chinese restaurants to talk to the patrons about Hong Kong and its future. And he does all this while proceeding as one of Hong Kong's most successful barristers.

But Lee is uncompromised by the rigours of democracy. He always seems to be perfectly attired, never a hair out of place, he is always straightforward and direct in answering questions. He speaks with passion, but it is always passion under control, just as you would expect from a good barrister. He puts the position directly. He is not lacking in eloquence but the point of his presentations is not showy verbal fireworks but straightforward, reasoned argument.

Lee was born in Hong Kong in 1938. He was the sixth of seven children. His father was a general in the nationalist anticommunist Kuomintang government. Lee's mother was briefly on leave in Hong Kong when Martin was born. Years later Lee would labour, successfully, to prove that he was indeed born in Hong

Kong, although his earliest years were spent in mainland China. Martin's father was, unusually for a senior Kuomintang man, seriously unhappy with the KMT's corruption. He decided not to go to Taiwan when the nationalist leader, Chiang Kai-shek, fled there in 1949 after the communists were victorious in the civil war. Instead he took his family to Hong Kong. This almost certainly meant that the family were less well off than they might have been. In Taiwan, Martin's father would have been part of the ruling structure. As it was Martin's family was by no means affluent during his childhood.

Martin's father taught Chinese language to make a living. According to a profile of Martin Lee in the *South China Morning Post* in 1995, one of the general's pupils was Han Suyin, author of *Love Is a Many Splendoured Thing*, which later became a famous film with William Holden and a rather implausible Jennifer Jones playing Han Suyin herself. One of the general's pupils was a Jesuit priest and through him Martin and his three brothers became Catholics. His Catholicism has remained important to Martin Lee and his father eventually converted to Catholicism in his old age. Lee did well at school and at university but he needed to teach school for three years to save up to study law. In 1963 he went to Lincoln's Inn in London. Lee told the *South China Morning Post* that he had saved $20 000 for three years' living in London, so he had to live cheap. He recalled:

> For me it was nothing but hard work. I lived in a pretty
> shabby location in Kings Cross, on the sofa in a friend's
> council flat. Every morning I would cook my own lunch. I'm
> scared of raw meat so I would use luncheon meat. I would
> chop it up, fry the rice left over from the previous night, add
> some pepper and then an egg. And finally a little brandy . . .
> One thing I got from my old man which I'm very proud of is
> my sense of value about money.

Lee came back to Hong Kong in 1966 and pursued a brilliant legal career. He married Amelia in 1969 and they have one son, a young teenager at school at Winchester College in England, whom Lee is consciously shielding from some of the dangers of post-1997 life in Hong Kong. The marriage is devoted and Amelia plays a big role in organising Lee's countless activities. Lee was a great success at the Hong Kong Bar. He became a Queens

Counsel in the late 1970s and according to local press reports was one of the most successful and highest paid barristers in Hong Kong.

He always had a civic concern with Hong Kong's future. He could easily have organised a foreign passport and salted away enough money to last him a lifetime. Instead he has devoted himself to the cause of democracy for Hong Kong, and the preservation of its way of life after Beijing takes control. In 1985 he ran for and won the position of representative of Hong Kong's legal community on the Legislative Council. In those days Hong Kong's Legislative Council was based on functional groups. There were no direct, popular elections for councillors, only some elections among professional constituencies. In what in retrospect is a doleful irony, the press at the time reported one of his greatest strengths as being his close relationship with the authorities in Beijing. This had been demonstrated in June of that year, before his election to the Legislative Council, when Beijing appointed him to the Basic Law Drafting Committee, a sensible appointment given Lee's standing as a distinguished barrister.

In 1984 Margaret Thatcher had signed with mainland China the Joint Declaration on Hong Kong's future. The Sino–British agreement, which London argued was necessary under the terms of the treaty in which Britain had first taken possession of Hong Kong, provided for Hong Kong to revert to mainland Chinese rule in the middle of 1997. Under the agreement there would be 'one country, two systems' and the people of Hong Kong would be allowed to keep their distinctive lifestyle, based on capitalism and the rule of law. The agreement also provided that Hong Kong would have a high degree of autonomy, with the mainland mainly exercising control over foreign affairs and defence matters. It also provided for an elected legislative council, although there came to be great dispute about what was meant by the term elected. Ultimately, Chris Patten's hybrid was to be a body partly elected by direct, universal adult suffrage and partly elected by 'functional constituencies', that is by particular professional bodies. Although Beijing and London were soon to descend into endless, bitter, indeed vituperative wrangling about the implementation of the agreement, at the time it was well regarded. Certainly Mrs Thatcher was jubilant that she had obtained such a result. There was a widespread view that while the denial of the principle of self-determination to the people of Hong Kong was bad in principle, Britain had got the best deal it could reasonably have expected from Beijing. It was felt that there were more and stronger guarantees for Hong Kong than there might have been. There was also at the time, before the Tiananmen Square massacre, a great deal of optimism both about the direction and the speed with which China's liberalisation would take place. In 1984 and '85 anything seemed possible in China. Beijing had not yet displayed fully its remarkable capacity to maintain overall political control even while it raced helter skelter along the path of economic liberalisation. 1997 seemed a long way away and many people thought communism in China would have collapsed by then.

From 1984 onwards there were protracted negotiations about the terms and text of Hong Kong's Basic Law, the document which would act as its constitution and govern its essential institutions. Lee was a member of the Basic Law drafting committee. The Beijing authorites and the British rapidly fell out. Lee has told Hong Kong newspapers that it was at the moment at a press conference in November 1985, when the head of the mainland Chinese newsagency, Xinhua, which was the voice of official China on Hong Kong, accused the British of deviating from the Joint Declaration by determining that some legislative councillors would be directly elected, that Lee decided he would be the voice of Hong Kong in these tumultuous affairs. He was struck by the meek way British officials took the Xinhua tongue-lashing and the thought that the development of democracy on Hong Kong would be subject to Beijing's whim. He decided he would not stand for that.

And since then that is exactly what he has been—the voice of Hong Kong, or at least that part of it that desperately wants democracy. Like many regional journalists I have had the pleasure of interviewing Lee on numerous occasions—in his barrister's chambers in Hong Kong, in seminar rooms around the region, on Australian television, over the phone. He is accessible to journalists. He understands that an Opposition politician must sell his message. During the last ten years he has been a massive irritation to China, and to Britain. But for China he poses

considerable problems. He has built up such international credibility that if Beijing acts with a heavy hand against him it will
certainly pay a price. This is particularly so in the United States.
In August 1995, the American Bar Association, which has
350 000 members, gave Lee its 1995 International Human Rights
Award. The American Bar Association said the award was 'in
recognition of his extraordinary contributions to the causes of
human rights, the rule of law and the promotion of justice'.

Lee's international acclaim, great as it is, is a pale shadow of
that which he would have liked, as head of a democratic Hong
Kong administration. This, he believes, would have given Hong
Kong much greater leverage in its dealings with Beijing. This has
been a constant theme in Lee's political career over the last ten
years. Give Hong Kong leaders the status and the power and we,
backed by the Hong Kong people, will make the deals with
Beijing, goes his argument. British resistance to this argument
says much about its perennially condescending attitude to the
people of Hong Kong.

But Lee has also argued a bigger point about the nature of
Chinese civilisation and culture, and that is, that it is not
antithetical to democracy and a modern participatory and representative society. The handover of authority over Hong Kong by
the British to the Chinese, in the middle of 1997, is one of the
great defining moments at the end of the twentieth century.
Partly, of course, it is about China's re-emergence onto the world
stage as an absolutely first-rank player. Hong Kong is the most
powerful of the symbols of the 'unequal treaties' between China
and European powers in the nineteenth century. Britain took
Hong Kong over gradually, gradually imposing its will on reluctant
Chinese authorities. The Nanking Treaty gave it Hong Kong
island in 1842. Few British spokesmen today like to recall that
that treaty was a result of a war waged by the British against
the Chinese overwhelmingly for the purpose of selling opium to
the Chinese people. China was humilated in the opium war and
Britain was serving no purpose more noble than that of any drug
trader today. A further treaty gave Britain the Kowloon peninsula,
just across from Hong Kong island, in 1860, and the Second
Convention of Peking, in 1898, gave it the New Territories, the

area on the mainland behind Kowloon. This provided for a 99-year lease on the New Territories which was to expire in 1997.

After the victory of the communists in mainland China in 1949 Hong Kong became a magnet for a million or more brilliant Chinese refugees, who brought to the small Crown colony their passionate commitment to work and family. Closer to mainland China than Taiwan, and for several decades under a more stable and predictable rule of law, Hong Kong became the key listening post for China analysts. The Chinese population contributed their industry, the British the rule of law and the Christian churches much of the educational and social services which ameliorated the potential harshness of life in the freest market society in the world.

Hong Kong became a symbol of many things. It was in one sense a symbol of China's hated colonial past, with British rule having no real legitimacy beyond the colonial inheritance. But it also became a symbol of Chinese success and prosperity, generating fantastic wealth. Latterly it became the most important conduit for foreign trade and investment into mainland China. It became a critical point of contact and dialogue between the west and that fifth of mankind which happens to be Chinese. Not least of its roles here was as a staging post in the increasing Taiwan–China trade. It also developed a remarkable role vis-à-vis Guangdong province, the mainland province next to Hong Kong, becoming the finance, design, services and management centre for the whole of the Guangdong economy. Guangdong's growth rates were astonishing in the late 1980s and early '90s and were the showpiece of China's broader economic reforms. Guangdong led southern China in a sense into becoming the fifth Asian tiger.

Hong Kong then adopted a smaller but similar role to that which it played in Guangdong in several other mainland Chinese provinces. Hong Kong thus became a central element of Beijing's economic reform, which, incidentally, provided Beijing with a powerful motivation for not getting things too wrong in Hong Kong.

But this success in truth had little to do with British thinking on Hong Kong and much more to do with Chinese effort, both on the mainland and in Hong Kong itself. Britain's historic failure in Hong Kong was nothing to do with the quality of administration it provided, which was generally first class, but lay in its complete failure of imagination about the Hong Kong people themselves and their ability to run their own affairs. It was especially a failure of political imagination, in particular a failure to institute any serious democracy in Hong Kong before it signed the Joint Declaration with Beijing in 1984. Even the discussion was always framed in the most negative terms—what would Beijing do to Hong Kong, what would Beijing allow in Hong Kong. Instead, more imaginative policy makers might have wondered about the possibility of Hong Kong exercising a positive influence over the constitutional development of China. If Hong Kong had been a stable, functioning, democratic society long before the handover, it would at least have shown Beijing that democracy was not incompatible with a stable and recognisably Chinese form of social organisation. The more imaginative thinkers in Beijing, especially before the Tiananmen massacre, might have seen in Hong Kong not just a golden goose but a useful, a promising, laboratory for Chinese constitutional development.

I put this line of argument, in particular that Britain should have instituted democracy in Hong Kong long before it made terms with Beijing about ceding rule, to Hong Kong's governor, Chris Patten, during a long discussion we had when he visited Australia in 1993. His response really amounted to little more than blather. There had never been a popular demand for democracy within Hong Kong, he argued. On the other hand when the refugees were coming in in large numbers it would have been extremely difficult if not impossible to institute an effective and stable democracy. And so on. Yet when one thinks of the countless difficult circumstances in which real democracy has been introduced in many societies around the world one can only come to the conclusion that the British really never had any serious interest in implementing democracy in Hong Kong. Patten mouthed these bromides about history's hostility to democracy in Hong Kong even as he was giving himself great plaudits for the modest democratic reforms he introduced to Hong Kong just before the British left. The ability to hold two contradictory ideas in one's head at the same time is a great achievement of modern

colonial administrators. But in real democracy there is little
evidence of real British interest.

This is broadly Martin Lee's view. Neither the British nor the
Chinese have been comfortable with the idea of democracy in
Hong Kong. Like so many others he was outraged and greatly
distressed by the Tiananmen Square massacre in Beijing in 1989.
This was a moment when Hong Kong's people showed what they
truly thought of human rights in China. A million Hong Kong
citizens took to the streets in uncharacteristic protest at what
had happened. Lee led some of the demonstrations himself,
uncharacteristically wearing a protest headband and T-shirt, and
became, from that moment onwards, the Hong Kong citizen most
disliked by Beijing, which later declared that he would be banned
from holding senior office under them in Hong Kong. Indeed
much of Lee's fame even within Hong Kong dated from his
trenchant support of the students of the Tiananmen massacre.
This was certainly also the case overseas. At the time of his
involvement in the anti-Beijing demonstrations he received death
threats and was even given police protection for a time.

Because the Tiananmen massacre was shown on television
around the world it aroused unique international condemnation.
Lee's moral and political status as a courageous opponent of the
Beijing authorities was greatly enhanced by the strongly critical
stand he took in the aftermath of the massacre. To this day it is
unclear if the Beijing authorities knew exactly what they were
doing in that massacre. Certainly it was strange for them to allow
the western media, and especially the television crews, so prominent a presence in Beijing while they carried out the massacre.
This severely damaged China's standing internationally and con-
strained its future diplomatic effectiveness, as well as terrifying
the citizens of Hong Kong and Taiwan, whom in different ways
Beijing was trying to woo. On the other hand the Beijing leaders
were above all good Leninists who understood the dynamics of
power and the imperative of regime survival. In a sense they were
experts at repression, this was something they really understood,
and to judge their actions as clumsy is perhaps to pay them too
little respect. Maybe they intended to send out an absolutely
clear message, mainly to their own population but also to the
people of Hong Kong.

Probably the statements which Lee made which most upset Beijing were those calling for the overthrow of the Beijing leadership. Yet most of the world was calling for this at the time, including many brave Chinese within China. A line of criticism against Lee is that he went too far, breaching the implicit agreement between the British and the Chinese that while Hong Kong would retain its lifestyle and traditional freedoms, neither would Beijing destroy Hong Kong nor would Hong Kong attempt to destroy Beijing. After all Beijing's leadership is vulnerable in its way as are the people of Hong Kong. The fate of the former Romanian dictator, Ceausescu, hangs over the Beijing leadership. By supporting dissidents within China, broadcasting information to them, smuggling them in and out of China and sending them money, Hong Kong's democrats, so this argument goes, went too far. Yet the Joint Declaration determines that Hong Kong will have freedom of speech. If there is no freedom to protest a massacre, just what does freedom of speech consist of? If Lee had said less, he would have been implicitly accepting that Hong Kong was not to enjoy authentic freedom of speech after all. Moreover, the solidarity with mainland Chinese which in other contexts Beijing has promoted, demanded no less. It was of course an impossible situation but it was made impossible by Beijing's brutality, not Martin Lee's intemperance.

In any event Lee's status as Hong Kong's leading politician was established. It was to be borne out most graphically in the 1991 elections. These were the first such elections ever held in Hong Kong. Some 18 of the 60 members of the Legislative Council were elected directly by the people of Hong Kong. Martin Lee's group, the United Democrats, and pro-democracy candidates in associated parties, won sixteen of those eighteen positions, an excellent result. Pro-Beijing candidates supported strongly by mainland China, especially by its de facto consul in Hong Kong, the Xinhua newsagency, were routed. So were other more temperate supporters of taking a soft line towards Beijing, of not rocking the boat. Although the turnout for the election was low it was a great victory for Lee. This was particularly so given that the pro-Beijing forces had engaged in fairly straightforward psychological intimidation, warning that a vote for liberal

candidates could threaten the territory's relationship with mainland China.

Lee naturally tried to maximise his position, and that of his
confreres, in the immediate post-poll period. He effectively argued
that he had won the election and should be given great control
over Hong Kong's governmental affairs. As William Overholt, an
American analyst of Chinese affairs, has put it, in his useful book,
China the Next Economic Superpower, Lee tried to establish himself
as the Hong Kong version of Aung San Suu Kyi of Myanmar,
the winner of fair and democratic national elections who was
being denied power by an undemocratic executive authority. Of
course the people of Hong Kong knew they were not voting for
a government, as such. And of course, the legitimacy of the
election is partly diminished by the low turnout (about 40 per
cent) although this was a higher turnout than some American
congressional elections have produced and their legitimacy is
never called into question. But the weight of the argument rests
with Lee. The people of Hong Kong may not have been voting
for a government, as such, but they knew what Lee's policies
and positions were and they gave him very strong support. Either
elections count or they don't. Certainly, had pro-Beijing candidates been elected there would have been little argument about
their legitimacy.

In a newspaper article just after the election Lee made his
demands explicit:

> The people of Hong Kong have spoken with an unmistakably
> clear voice: we want democracy. The British Government is now
> at a turning point. Is it prepared to respect the wishes of the
> people of Hong Kong, or will it try to frustrate our aspirations?
> In making appointments to the Executive Council, and the
> remaining seats on the Legislative Council, the British
> Government should respect the results of these elections and
> match the proportion of seats won by the political groups.
> Only by appointing individuals who represent the public can
> the British Government ensure that the colonial administration
> retains public credibility and accountability—two qualities that
> the present administration lacks. The British must choose
> between government of, by and for the people and government
> against the people. In 1984 the British Government explicitly
> promised democracy to Hong Kong in order to persuade us to

accept the Sino–British Joint Declaration and the 1997 handover. In the wake of a successful first democratic election, Britain can no longer back away from this promise . . . The British Government must urgently change its policy, in which the Foreign Office makes good Sino–British relations paramount and concentrates on stifling challenges to the colonial administration, rather than establishing durable, long-term democratic institutions.

Needless to say, neither the British colonial administration, nor Beijing, were convinced by Lee's arguments. Most conspicuously, Lee himself was not appointed to the Executive Council. (The Legislative Council mirrored the functions of a parliament, though it had little real power. The Executive Council mirrored the functions of a cabinet, although of course all real power resided with the governor.)

Beijing had told the British not to appoint Lee to the Executive Council. Lee's party was also extremely disappointed with the twenty Legco members the governor nominated. Only one of these came from a list of twenty nominees which Lee and his colleagues had forwarded to the governor, on the governor's invitation, as being people who would be acceptable to the democrats. Overall the governor's choices were regarded as conservative.

When the British Conservative Party politician, Chris Patten, was appointed governor of Hong Kong in 1992 it looked, briefly, as though this might change. Previously, governors of Hong Kong had been Foreign Office diplomats, normally professional Sinologists who spoke Mandarin Chinese (though never Cantonese, which Hong Kongers speak) and knew China well. The criticism of them is that they tended to put too much weight on good relations with Beijing for their own sake and to have not only little enthusiasm for experiments in democracy, but little real empathy with the people of Hong Kong. Britain had been getting a dreadful drubbing in the international press, especially in influential newspapers such as the *New York Times,* for its handling of Hong Kong. Patten, as an immensely experienced politician (he was chairman of the Conservative Party and engineered John Major's shock election victory in 1992, but lost his own seat in that election) but with little direct experience of either China or

Hong Kong, was thought to bring the essential political skills to the job.

Patten entered the job with an apparent determination to stand up to Beijing. But the mainland Chinese told him bluntly that he must not appoint Lee to the Exco. Patten responded with some vigour and testiness that he could appoint anyone he liked to the Exco. But he came up with a way of finessing the situation which was to be not untypical of his period in office. He determined as policy that the Legislative Council should be rigidly separated from the Executive Council, thus creating a situation in which the possible nomination of Lee could not arise. However, this move weakened the democratic development of Hong Kong and in effect further centralised power in the governor's hands.

In mid-1992 I had one of numerous long conversations with Martin Lee. He had already reached that stage of quite openly canvassing his own future security with journalists. It is not, as some have cynically alleged, that Lee seeks kudos from possible future martyrdom but simply that it is a question journalists always ask him. Will you leave after 1997, will you be a political prisoner, will you be safe? His reply was straightforward:

> I'm going to stay after 1997. I'll possibly be in prison. It's naive not to expect political prisoners after '97. Political prisoners are certainly a possibility. I don't think that [imprisoning Lee] will be their first official act. It is possible from what they've been saying recently that they would try to remove some members of the Legislative Council—those they don't like—by pretending they've broken some aspect of the Basic Law.

In 1992 Lee was still trying to convince the British authorities to implement full democracy in Hong Kong before 1997. But surely, the counter-argument ran, if the British did that against Chinese wishes the Chinese would simply wipe it out after 1997. Lee didn't agree:

> This is a basic fallacy. People always assume that if democracy is in place in Hong Kong—if we set up a good system of law with a court of final appeal which we want and so on—because China doesn't like them China would necessarily abolish them. I think that is a wrong premise to go on and it's very

dangerous and that is why these things are happening, because
the British Colonial Office believes in this kind of thinking, a
typical Foreign Office line.

What the British government should do is to give to the
people of Hong Kong what they are clearly entitled to, so long
as they do not constitute a breach of the Joint Declaration,
and then let China do what she likes. I don't believe China
would do all these things in 1997, particularly if these institutions are working well.

I still remember just a couple of days after Margaret
Thatcher signed the Joint Declaration in Beijing on December
19, 1984, she had a press conference in Hong Kong. She was
very enthusiastic about the agreement. She said the eyes of the
world are on us and we intend to make it work. Thereafter she
never even talked about Hong Kong. She certainly did not
come back until she was replaced by [John] Major. I remember
towards the end of '87 I went to London and pressed for
democracy and of course she refused to see me. When I was
interviewed and asked why are you here, Mr Lee, I said I've
brought with me the water with which Mrs Thatcher washed
her hands of Hong Kong.

I put it to Lee that if there were democracy in Hong Kong
at least the people of Hong Kong could make their own deal
with Beijing about the future. He replied:

Exactly. The pity is the British government have not been
allowing us to stand on our own feet. After all, the Joint
Declaration says quite clearly that after '97 it is going to be
the Hong Kong people who will be ruling Hong Kong with a
high degree of autonomy. That is, except for defence and
foreign affairs we would be masters of our own destiny. We
therefore need the British government to let go . . . All the
British need to do is let go and let us negotiate with the
Chinese. But the British always assume they are better. They
have a few Sinologists in the Foreign Office. Somehow they
think they know the Chinese mind better than us, the Chinese.

Otherwise, he said, there was a fair chance that Britain would
'follow the pattern of appeasement and leave in disgrace'. International pressure, he thought, could be quite crucial: 'I hope that
other countries like Canada, Australia and the United States

might exert their influence and at least talk to their British counterparts.'

Hong Kong's prosperity, he argued, could only be guaranteed by democracy:

> It's a myth to me, that if one should have democracy,
> prosperity will disappear. Everyone knows that once you have
> democracy then you can change a government peacefully at
> elections. This is the only way to guarantee stability and
> prosperity even when you need to change a government. It's
> only when you don't have that system that any change of
> government will produce bloodshed and therefore disorder. And
> after all, there are a lot of people leaving Hong Kong for
> Canada, Australia, America, and they always go to a country
> which has democracy.

But surely Hong Kong's huge economic role in China would prevent Beijing from acting too destructively?

> Look at Shenzhen, in Guangdong province, the province closest
> to Hong Kong. Hong Kong factory owners represent 75 per
> cent of foreign investment in Guangdong, and 90 per cent of
> goods produced in Hong Kong factories are for export. So you
> can see the influence we have. Unfortunately since Tiananmen
> Square the Chinese policy has changed. Instead of putting
> Hong Kong's prosperity first and foremost on its list of
> priorities for Hong Kong it has changed. This has now become
> second and the first is its ability to control Hong Kong. In
> order for that to happen it needs British cooperation, which
> unfortunately it has found.

Were British commercial interests influential in these decisions?

> Lots of people think like that. We are not the only people
> accusing the British of selling out. Recently the International
> Commission of Jurists came up with a report which is a very
> strong indictment of the British and Chinese governments.
> Clearly we would like to see a fully democratic legislature
> before the handover, and that's what the British promised us
> during their parliamentary debate on Hong Kong on December
> 5, 1984, when the minister responsible informed the House of
> Commons that they would institute democracy before 1997.

I took the interview down a detour. Lee had taken a generous and somewhat politically courageous stand on the vexed issue of the Vietnamese boat people who languished for so long in brutal camps in Hong Kong. This was by no means a stance likely to win him greater support in Hong Kong. He explained:

> The Hong Kong people have been misled by the Hong Kong government on the boat people issue into thinking that any decision on the boat people is a Hong Kong decision and they will have a say on it. Whereas we know as a matter of constitution and of law that any decision is a British decision because it concerns foreign affairs and foreign relations. We believe it is only right that the people of Hong Kong should be part of the international community. We should honour our obligations. Therefore we believe it is not right for the people of Hong Kong to urge abolishing this policy [of granting first asylum to boat people]. After all, there are millions of people in Hong Kong who want the countries of the free world to take them because they don't want to be returned to a repressive Chinese regime. How can we justify our conduct when we are forcing 50 000 people from Vietnam against their will to return to an even more repressive regime?

Politicians around the world tend to have no great love for the press, even though all politicians depend on it and use it whenever possible. But one of Lee's chief concerns about Hong Kong post 1997 was for the freedom of the press: 'If you pursue a policy of appeasement I'm afraid freedom of the press will be gone soon after 1997. And when freedom of the press is gone I don't think any other freedom can be preserved. All you need to do is not look far away but look at Macau now.'

Lee is an optimist about eventual democracy and freedom of expression in mainland China, but this is optimism over the long term and he doesn't want Hong Kong's freedoms sacrificed in the meantime. But Beijing's leaders, he argued, are pursuing in some ways contradictory policies:

> The paramount leader, Deng Xiaoping, has been pushing a very aggressive program of economic reform. And at the same time he makes it quite clear there will not be any political reform, forgetting perhaps that he himself said about ten years ago you cannot have economic reform without the corresponding

political reform. I hope he succeeds [at economic reform], but the people would like more freedom and they would also like to have a share in their government. It's like a genie being let out of the bottle. You can't let it half out. The question is timing—when will it all happen?

We're all looking forward to reunification with China, but on the terms China laid down herself in the Joint Declaration. Even the leftist students and workers are in Hong Kong, they are not in China. With absolutely no problem in going back to China if they want to, they're still in Hong Kong, because they do not really aspire to the socialist way of life. They want the capitalist way of life, that's why they're here.

As for Taiwan, of course China would appreciate that if Hong Kong is not properly run after 1997, and we lose our high degree of autonomy and so on, and we lose our freedoms, then it will be very difficult for Taiwan to agree to be reunified with China. But we have to be careful in taking that point of view as a ground for optimism. Because the Chinese look from the long term . . . they say at the moment we want to take back Hong Kong first, and when we do we want to make sure Hong Kong is controllable. Therefore we don't like democracy, a high degree of autonomy and so on. Now with Taiwan, if it's ten years, twenty years, 50 years, it doesn't matter.

Interviewing Lee is a slightly peculiar experience. There is passion in what he says, and always there is great precise language. The voice seems taut and lean, and yet the man is plainly relaxed with himself. He is endlessly though not effusively courteous. He is solicitous as well. At the time we met in 1992 I was carrying a few extra pounds. Without being the slightest bit offensive he managed to suggest that I read the book, *Fit for Life*, which he said had done him a great deal of good. You don't ingratiate yourself with reporters by telling them they are over-weight. This was not some politician's tactic of gaining an extra personal connection with a reporter. You had the impression rather that Lee was actually concerned for your welfare, just as a fellow human being.

After that interview Hong Kong's governor did put forward proposals to make Hong Kong's legislature more democratic. But his reforms still fell a long way short of anything approaching real democracy. They were nonetheless loudly condemned by

Beijing which eventually decided it would abolish the Legislative Council and replace it with a new interim body, and later a more permanent body, after it takes control in 1997. Nonetheless the basic equation remained. The governor had the power, the Chinese were about to get the power. Indeed Patten's determined selling around the world of his quite modest reforms tended to focus greater attention on him, (and he would be gone after June 1997), and less on Hong Kong leaders like Martin Lee.

For much of the last few years Lee has concentrated on fighting a battle for the integrity of the Court of Final Appeal, which is now to be set up immediately after Beijing takes control. Hong Kong has lived for decades without democracy but with the stable rule of law, and above all an independent judiciary. In many ways the rule of law is just as important to the maintenance of Hong Kong's distinctive way of life as is the sustenance of any kind of democratic institutions. Indeed, given that Hong Kong has never had real democracy but has for many decades had the reliable rule of law, in terms of the maintenance of Hong Kong's way of life, the rule of law could be regarded as even more important than democracy. Certainly Lee, every inch a proud barrister with a deep love of the law, has always understood that the independent judiciary, and the Court of Final Appeal, are central to his struggle for Hong Kong.

As long ago as 1985 he was trying to get from Beijing the maximum interpretive power, and independence, for Hong Kong's courts. He told me:

> There is an article in the Basic Law which says interpretation of the Basic Law will be vested in the standing committee of the National People's Congress of China, which is a political body. And although there is some delegation of interpretation to the courts they reserve to themselves the right to interpret every clause of the Basic Law. And once it is interpreted by the political body it shall be binding on all our courts. When I was on the drafting committee of the Basic Law I tried to get them to delegate irrevocably this power of interpretation to our courts but I failed.

Lee has spent the last few years waging the campaign for Hong Kong's courts and judicial system more widely. He has done this primarily in Hong Kong. But he has also had a powerful

voice on the opinion pages of some of the most influential
newspapers in the world, in particular the American heavy-
weights—the *New York Times*, the *Washington Post*, the *Wall Street
Journal*. He occasionally gets into a little silly Hong Kong booster-
ism. For example, in the *Washington Post* of June 1994, he claimed:
'Hong Kong is still the freest society in Asia.' That just isn't true,
and contradicts some of Lee's other statements. He seems to be
ignoring South Korea, the Philippines, Thailand and Taiwan—the
four great democratisation stories of East Asia—in making such
an absurd claim, not to mention Japan, the great, stable democratic society of East Asia, as well as the democracies and part
democracies of South Asia, particularly India. To state baldly that
Hong Kong—where, as Lee himself points out endlessly, you
cannot even vote for the government of your choice—is more
free than these societies is silly.

Nonetheless, Lee is right to argue that Hong Kong people
have become far more politically aware in recent years. In the
same article he wrote:

> Hong Kong has changed dramatically in the five years since
> China opened fire on the pro-democracy demonstrators and
> especially since our first democratic elections in 1991. Public
> rallies and street marches in favour of democratic reform are a
> part of daily Hong Kong life. Press conferences, petitions and
> campaigns—dealing with everything from human rights to
> housing costs—are the norm.

Always in these articles he drew attention to the threat to
Hong Kong's legal system, to its Bill of Rights and the Court of
Final Appeal. The court was one of the great victories for Hong
Kong in the Joint Declaration. It was meant to have a number
of judges from overseas countries with common-law systems
similar to that of Hong Kong's, to guarantee its legal continuity.
But under the deal finally worked out between the British and
the Chinese there would be only one foreign judge on the court,
a compromise Lee regarded as a sell-out.

In December 1994, Lee put his case in the *Wall Street Journal*,
in an opinion piece titled 'Why China Needs Hong Kong's Legal
System'. He wrote:

> Hong Kong's independent judicial system acts to curb

corruption and preserve property and contract rights. But China is even now insisting on a right to remove judges from Hong Kong's Court of Final Appeal, the equivalent of the US Supreme Court. Although this violates the Basic Law, our post-1997 constitution, judges who want to keep their seats will be under tremendous pressure to find in favour of the Chinese government in major cases or those involving a lot of money.

In the middle of the subsequent year, Lee was so enraged by the compromise that Britain worked out with China over the Court of Final Appeal that he supported a motion of no confidence in the Legislative Council against Governor Chris Patten. Apart from limiting the number of foreign judges to just one, the deal also involved the court's having 'no jurisdiction over acts of state, such as defence etcetera'. The standing committee of the National People's Congress in Beijing would effectively be able to determine what constituted 'an act of state such as defence etc'. Lee declared: 'The only certainty of a common law with Chinese characteristics is that investors can never know whether or not their opponent in court will have the clout in Beijing to have their cases thrown out.' Once again, this time in the *Asian Wall Street Journal*, he argued the case of what China would be losing by not having Hong Kong functioning properly. He wrote: 'Reformists in China, such as Qiao Shi, who have expressed concern about the lack of a rule of law will not now have a working example of what an independent legal system is.'

The Court of Final Appeal, and China's threats to Hong Kong's Bill of Rights, have figured constantly in Lee's public campaigning over the last few years. Lee once again underlined his legitimacy with the Hong Kong people by the results of the September 1995 Legislative Council elections. Lee's Democratic Party picked up 19 of the 24 seats it contested. Lee himself scored more than 80 per cent of the vote in the seat he contested. Pro-democracy allies of Lee's won numerous other seats as well, but the situation was confused by a raft of independents and the still peculiar methods of electing the majority of Legco members, among them choosing representatives from so-called 'functional constituencies'. There was a good deal of confusion among voters as to which functional constituencies they might qualify to vote in. The official pro-Beijing candidates, despite huge backing from Beijing-linked firms, fared very poorly, as they had done in 1991 (although this time they did manage to pick up a few seats).

Lee naturally claimed that the results were a clear message from the people of Hong Kong to the government of Beijing that they wanted democratic rule and they did not want interference in their lives from Beijing. Lee also condemned Beijing for its 'intimidating behaviour' during the elections. He said: 'Hong Kong people voted with their hearts and their minds for freedom and democracy. The elections, in short, are a mandate for democratic government in Hong Kong, and real constitutional, legal and human rights reform to ensure basic freedoms in Hong Kong after 1997.'

One senior official from the pro-Beijing Alliance for the Betterment of Hong Kong seemed to confirm Lee's worst fears when he commented of the vote: 'The Hong Kong people will have to pay for it.'

In early 1996 I had a number of conversations with Lee. He was as taut and precise as ever but there seemed a deepeningly sombre mood underlying everything that he said. His bleak forecast for the future of Hong Kong was unambiguous:

> The prospects are getting worse all the time. There's no doubt at all that Beijing wants to tighten up the screws. Beijing wants to control Hong Kong and the Preparatory Committee [which Beijing set up with mainland and Hong Kong representatives to oversee the transition to their rule] will be effective to do just that. The recommendations made by the Preparatory Committee were extremely worrying for the people of Hong Kong.

I asked him what was the worst aspect of the situation Hong Kong faced, a little over twelve months from the formal handover of power: 'The worst is the decision to set up a provisional legislature to replace the elected one.' But not far behind that came the 'emasculation' of the Bill of Rights and the intended revival by Beijing of some draconian and clearly anachronistic colonial laws.

What chance then does Hong Kong have of preserving the substance of its free and distinctive way of life?

Basically it's really up to the people of Hong Kong to put our act together, to stand united to defend our much weakened system within the 'one country, two systems' formula. I'm sure other governments of the free world can help but I doubt if they would. It seems every government seems to be only interested in having more China trade, including your government [i.e., the Australian government].

The Hong Kong administration now is clearly a lame-duck administration, waiting to back out. It seems to me they [the HK government] have more or less given up on crucial issues, such as the setting up of the provisional legislature. The British are not going to do anything.

He argued that once the Beijing authorities had made a decision, the advisers the Hong Kong government listened to gave them advice accepting the inevitability of Beijing's actions and merely seeking ways to minimise the damage. 'Surely we should be standing up,' he said.

He still took great heart from the election results.

Every time commentators said the Hong Kong people are intimidated they voted very clearly to show that this is not the case. This happened in September 1991 and in September last year. That shows very clearly that the Hong Kong people have not been intimidated and do not want a supine government.

Much of the problem, he believes, came from the unstable state of the Beijing leadership itself, in the twilight of Deng Xiaoping. 'I don't believe this present administration, this joint leadership in Beijing, feels secure in themselves. Look what they are doing to Taiwan, for example. It is obvious that the leadership doesn't control the army.' This was at the time when Beijing was engaged in heavy-handed military exercises at the northern and southern ends of the Taiwan Strait, designed to intimidate the voters of Taiwan.

He thought that the Beijing leadership may have signed the Joint Declaration in 1984 with 'the best of intentions' but had been transformed by subsequent events, not the least being the Tiananmen massacre of 1989.

At our last conversation in early 1996, Lee's tone was more sombre still, if that is possible, and if anything more defiant. He was deeply pessimistic about the Preparatory Committee's willingness or ability to seriously represent Hong Kong's interests to Beijing: 'A small number of them will speak up for Hong Kong. But because of the secrecy we'll never know who they were or what they said. The problem is also because of the personalities involved, if they're not listened to they won't push again.'

He completely rejected the Provisional Legislature which Beijing intends to appoint: 'The Provisional Legislature is not a legitimate body. It is not provided for in the Basic Law, so we [the Democratic Party] cannot join such a body.'

He fiercely rejected the notion that Chinese Confucian civilisation was incompatible with democracy. He also rejected the neo-Confucianism espoused by some regional leaders such as Singapore's Lee Kuan Yew, which emphasises authority over democracy. 'It's utter nonsense,' he said.

> They should just go to Taiwan to see that democracy and Chinese culture are not incompatible. Taiwan completely explodes the myth. Confucianism is not inconsistent with democracy. Many governments rely on Confucius but Confucius lived many centuries ago when people believed in many feudal things.
>
> How do you think the Singaporeans would react if Hong Kong, after it's been returned to a communist regime, should have democracy and human rights and not the Singaporeans? Some Singaporeans have a vested interest in seeing that democracy be destroyed in Hong Kong, that our people be deprived of their human rights. There's a secret agenda but it's so obvious to everyone.

But Lee was if anything more scathing about western nations which, in his view, had lost interest in democracy and human rights in Hong Kong. Because I am an Australian, he spoke directly to the case of Australia to illustrate his point: 'I remember on my last visit to Australia Keating [the then prime minister] just refused to see me. I think Australia is not different from many other countries as far as policy on China is concerned—trade comes first, which is not suprising in this world, money before honour. Clearly they put trade before human rights.'

But he also saw disarray in the leadership in Beijing, which he thought was obvious from their treatment of Taiwan:

> I think they are certainly struggling. You used to get statement

after statement from Beijing that they do not advocate the use of force on Taiwan, but then the army drummed up a lot of statements [that they might use force] too. The army generals are taking a very hawkish line on Taiwan. They clearly aren't coping with the very reasonable attitude taken by the leadership of Taiwan.

These conflicts and problems he saw as endemic to Beijing's system:

The succession problem will not be resolved just because Deng Xiaoping goes. It will only happen if they embrace democracy. The only way forward is for the Chinese leadership to wake up that the tide is for democracy and human rights. Ours is a great nation but we always feel embarrassed that our people have no say in their government.

And what is the future for Martin Lee under mainland communist rule? 'Martin Lee is not my problem, it's their problem. I'm prepared for the worst. I don't know about my family. As to my wife, she's got to make her own decision. My son is studying abroad and will presumably continue his studies.'

But Lee, sombre as he is, strikes ultimately an optimistic note: 'I believe there's a bright future for our Chinese people and for the people of Hong Kong. I just cannot see our people being deprived of our rights forever.'

Certainly, if that is the case, it won't be for want of trying on Martin Lee's part.

10

MORIHIRO HOSOKOWA: JAPAN'S FALSE DAWN OR TRUE?

It was one of those perfect moments of history. A handful of us, journalists from Asia–Pacific newspapers and magazines, were gathered with about twenty of then Japanese prime minister Morihiro Hosokowa's aides in his private office in his official residence in Tokyo. It was November 16, 1993, the 100th day of Hosokowa's government. We were waiting for the prime minister, who had called us together to outline his, and Japan's, vision for the Asia Pacific Economic Cooperation forum on the eve of its first ever summit meeting in Seattle, America.

The prime minister's office, a rather heavy, formal room, has some slightly bizarre touches, among them a string of statuary along classical Greek lines at the top of the walls. I found this reliance on heavy western classicism puzzling in the official rooms at the top of the Japanese political hierarchy, given that the Japanese aesthetic itself is so attractive and diverse. Yet it is a touch you often find in Japanese (and Korean) formal settings, reflecting, presumably, the period when Japan had a national policy to move 'out of Asia and into the west'. These days Asia–Pacific fusion is more the vogue in Japan, and Hosokowa himself was an excellent exemplar of this trend.

We were welcomed into an anteroom to watch on TV the critical Diet committee debate on Hosokowa's political reform package. The last three speakers, representing respectively the then disgraced Liberal Democratic Party, the Communist Party and then the government, had their say. The LDP's counter-

272

proposal was voted down. The government's passed and the chamber erupted in applause. There were more episodes in the political reform battle still to be fought out, but this was a critical victory. What seemed only a few seconds later a flushed and exhilarated Hosokowa strode into the room, beaming with confidence and full of entirely unnecessary apologies for keeping us waiting.

This had been an important moment for Hosokowa. Just as political reform would turn out to be perhaps his single most important legacy for Japan, so too the passage of that bill was hugely important for Hosokowa's credibility at the APEC summit in Seattle. America's Bill Clinton had been in a similar position. If he had not got the North American Free Trade Agreement passed by Congress he would have looked pathetically weak at Seattle. So too Hosokowa needed to get political reform passed in Japan to appear to his heads of government colleagues as an effective reformist prime minister. The situations of both Clinton and Hosokowa represented the truth of the frequently repeated new orthodoxy that the walls between domestic and foreign policy have come tumbling down, that much of what is expected of national leaders is in effect determined by the global economy. Even though political reform may appear a domestic political issue in Japan its consequences are clearly international. The dynamic of reform itself was driven as much as anything by Japan's need to function more effectively in the modern community of nations.

The times were right for Hosokowa by 1993. The situation Japan found itself in called for a clean break with the past. It was necessary to blow away the cobwebs of a no-longer functional system. In the end Hosokowa's government was short-lived but its significance, as I will argue in this chapter, was long term and Hosokowa an important politician.

When Nissan announced in early 1993 that it would close a plant in Tokyo it deeply disturbed the Japanese people. The motor vehicle industry was the symbol of the country's competitive economic success and the guarantee of its continued prosperity. Not since the Second World War had a car company ever shut down a plant in Japan. The Nissan plant closure was a sign of profound changes working through Japanese corporate culture and society more widely, brought on by the interaction of the global economic slow down of that year and the radical new international environment Japan was facing.

The view from Tokyo was highly disconcerting to a generation of leaders who had prized above all else stability and predictability. Japan was having to confront, by the early '90s, challenges unique in its centuries-old national history. It had become for the first time a genuinely global economic superpower. It had achieved the highest per capita income of any major economy. It had become the world's largest aid donor, doling out more than US$10 billion per year. And it had accumulated a huge trade surplus of more than $100 billion a year.

At the same time, by early 1993 it was clear that Japan's economic power was paradoxical. Japan was gripped by the worst recession it had seen in twenty years. Economic growth had virtually stopped. The real economy had not recovered from the stock market crash of 1990 which burst the so-called 'bubble economy' and destroyed the three great myths of Japanese economic management—that stocks always rise, that the value of property never declines and that the Japanese economy always grows. The recession perversely exaggerated the trade surplus. Consumers stopped spending on consumer goods. Japan's trade surplus with the US punched through the $50 billion mark.

This surplus was limiting Japan's efforts to find a new global role for itself. The Americans feared and envied Japan's trading success. The Europeans were similar but added a fatal touch of cultural condescension. Japan's most important neighbours, China and Korea, remained paranoid about their Second World War experiences. Much of Southeast Asia had similar attitudes. Moreover, Japan was receiving contradictory signals from a post–Cold War world which needed, simultaneously, a new enemy, a new scapegoat and a new saviour. The US, though constantly annoyed at its trade deficit, wanted Japan to take a new role in military burden-sharing. The United Nations, in particular its secretary-general, Boutros Boutros-Ghali, similarly wanted the Japanese, notwithstanding their pacifist constitution, to play a role in UN peace enforcement as well as peacekeeping operations.

But if Japan moved very far down that road it would greatly distress its Asian neighbours—damned if you do, damned if you don't. With the US, Japan would have liked to move the relationship onto a new level of global partnership, a natural partnership of the world's two most powerful democracies. The Japanese Foreign Ministry in particular wanted to move into a 'third-phase' relationship with the US. The first phase came after World War 11 when the US and Japan were respectively 'big brother' and 'little brother', protector and protected. In the second phase, dating from about the late 1960s and running through the entire '70s and '80s, Japan was also seen as a powerful industrial country in its own right and a formidable competitor to US industry. It was also seen as a key US Cold War ally in an area of vital US strategic interests, an area also heavily influenced by the shadow of hostile Soviet and Chinese communist regimes. With the end of the Cold War Tokyo wanted the relationship to move into a new phase—a partnership of equals.

But of course, one of the greatest blockages to this vision of a new Japan in a new world was Japan's panoply of market-closing mechanisms, which kept much of the global economy at bay. This was not so much formal tariffs and other border measures, but non-tariff barriers, the so-called 'invisible' barriers, the complex of regulations, customs and bureaucratic interference which Tokyo used to keep foreign goods out of its markets. In fact, under international pressure Tokyo did liberalise market access substantially and imported, by the 1990s, very nearly as much, per person, as the US did itself. But there were undoubtedly still substantial invisible barriers which overseas producers found intensely frustrating. At a reception in Nagoya trade consuls of numerous countries regaled me with such stories. One I particularly liked came from a would-be towel importer who was prevented from importing western towels because they were offensive to Japanese culture. Why? Because they were too thick to twirl at the ends to clean one's ears. Then there was the trade in live seafood and fresh flowers Australia could have done if the Nagoya customs people did not close half an hour before the Qantas flight landed and had its cargo cleared.

Such stories are endless in Japan but by the early '90s not only foreigners but Japanese were demanding that their system be liberalised and opened up. That did not prevent Japanese resentment at what they saw as sometimes gratuitous Japan bashing by both the Bush and then the Clinton administrations in Washington. But there did develop a sense that the old paradigm of Japanese politics, in place since America left after its period of colonial governance following the Second World War, needed radical surgery if not total scrapping. The times were ripe for a politician like Hosokowa.

In some ways the biggest part of Japan's problem was the type of political leadership the system produced. The Japanese culture, as expressed through its politics, made it hard for Japan to reform and liberalise, but it also made it hard for Japan to argue its case internationally, as any nation as powerful as Japan must do. It is very difficult for the Japanese to generate western public support for their position, partly because so few of their leaders speak English, the language of international public diplomacy, fluently.

Moreover, Japanese civic culture is based on the concept of *wa*, an almost untranslatable Japanese word which means something like harmony, form, order. It tries to avoid argument and confrontation. It relies for communication less on the precise meaning of words than the overall context in which the communication takes place. This makes it difficult for Japan to produce strong international leaders.

All of these factors combined with the increasing resentment among Japanese both at the corruption and unrepresentativeness of their political culture, and a demand for changes reflecting their preferences as both citizens and consumers, to produce the preconditions necessary for a massive upheaval in Japanese politics.

Thus the times called forth Hosokowa. He became not only the eventual beneficiary of that upheaval but an agent of change in his own right. In July 1993, he led a seven-party coalition to an historic victory over the LDP, ousting the LDP from office for the first time in 38 years. Many international journalists, myself included, were exhilarated by the change in Japan and perhaps we over-estimated what the Hosokowa government could achieve. Certainly it was tragically short-lived as a government. But I don't think we were altogether mistaken to see Hosokowa's election as a decisive moment in modern Japanese politics.

Moreover, he achieved three historic feats. He showed that Japan could live without the LDP and that Japan's notoriously conservative voters were prepared to support a realistic alternative; he liberalised the rice trade, perhaps the most difficult and symbolically powerful move in trade liberalisation in postwar Japan; and he enacted reform of the political system which over time should transform Japan's political culture. For these three reasons alone, Hosokowa deserves a distinguished place in Japanese history. And indeed, despite his resignation in semi-disgrace over a corruption scandal from earlier in his career, he remains a powerful figure in Japanese politics and may yet re-emerge as a decisive figure in Japan.

But apart from all these achievements, Hosokowa also represented a completely different style in Japanese politics and the fact that for a time this style was successful may help convince future Japanese politicians that it is at least possible and perhaps worth trying again. Stylistically, Hosokowa was much more like a conventional political leader in a conventional democracy than most of Japan's previous prime ministers. He campaigned on a program, a set of specific policies. He tried to generate support for his policies and he tried to use his personal popularity, which at the start of his term in office was very high, to garner further support for his political positions. He was a much more public and transparent political leader than the arcane factionalism which normally determines Japanese leadership generally produces.

Morihiro Hosokowa was born on Kyushu island, in Kumamoto, on January 14, 1938. He was descended from a long line of aristocrats, who had governed parts of southwestern Japan for hundreds of years. He was born as the eighteenth generation heir of his household. His grandfather, Prince Fumimaro Konoye, had been prime minister of Japan when it attacked Pearl Harbor, Hawaii on December 7, 1941. Despite that, Hosokowa's grandfather was not really counted as a front-rank player in Japanese policy during the war. Like so much of Japan's wartime history the precise role of the prince is shrouded in uncertainty. Japan in that period had the forms of parliamentary government but was very nearly a military regime. Nonetheless, Hosokowa's grandfather was on the list of war criminals the Allies intended to put on trial after the war but he committed suicide at the end of the war, when Hosokowa was just seven.

Despite these tribulations, Hosokowa's family was in no sense discredited or disgraced during the years of his childhood and adolescence. He was a good-looking, infinitely well-connected and successful youth. He studied at the prestigious Sophia University in Tokyo and graduated from its faculty of law in 1963. He worked after graduation for some years as a journalist for the *Asahi Shimbun*, one of Japan's great newspapers. But he was always destined for politics. As Hosokowa would later reflect in a magazine article:

> I have wanted to be a politician since high school. At that time of my life I started thinking about what job experience I would need to achieve this goal. My decision to become a journalist reflected this concern. As a journalist, I felt, I would accumulate more social experience and be exposed to more types of people than in other professions.

In 1968 he resigned from the *Asahi Shimbun* to follow his political path. The next year he ran, unsuccessfully, for the House of Representatives. In 1971 he won a seat in the Upper House of Japan's parliament, or Diet, representing the Liberal Democratic Party. (The Upper House, in Japan's system, is less powerful than the Lower House.) That year he also married his wife, Kayoko. At 33 he was the youngest member of the Upper House, the House of Councilors.

That so many of Japan's political reformers had LDP backgrounds is not surprising given the type of political culture Japan had developed. For several decades there was no credible alternative to the LDP. The main Opposition party, the socialists, were irresponsible and ineffective, obsessed with sterile left-wing ideology, quasi-Stalinist Cold War posturing and emphatic rejection of the American alliance. The LDP on the other hand was a vast coalition of personal fiefdoms, rather than a party in a conventional sense. It attracted all manner of Japanese interested in self-advancement and also those genuinely interested in politics and leadership. Membership of a particular faction of the LDP was often more important than membership of the LDP itself. It was natural that with an interest in politics and an attraction to seeing himself as a leader Hosokowa would enter parliament representing the LDP.

After entering the Upper House, Hosokowa gained a reputation as bright, personable and capable, but he did not rise to any great prominence quickly. He spent a dozen years in various jobs in politics without ever becoming a first division player. He also became quite seriously frustrated with the lack of power, and even of serious policy debate, within Japan's parliament. As he would later recall:

> When first becoming a Diet member I assumed I could achieve something. Unfortunately I found that the legislative branch [the parliament] functioned as an extension of the central bureaucracy, and was controlled by special interests. Restricted by a system in which both political parties and the legislative bodies themselves were dominated by the administrative branch, the national government had no place for voicing individual opinions.

In 1983, considerably disillusioned, Hosokowa left national politics to enter regional politics and was elected governor of Kumamoto. As governor he became increasingly frustrated by the centralisation of power in Japan. He was micro-managed from Tokyo, as were all governors, and he needed permission from Tokyo for far too much of what he wanted to do. Decentralisation of power thus became an enduring theme of Hosokowa's. He would later write: 'I continuously reminded Kumamoto's civil servants that the prefectural office was not an outpost of the central government and that they should dedicate their ideas and energy to managing the local community as employees of the regional government.' In most western countries this sentiment would be a bromide, in centralised Japan it was mildly radical.

Hosokowa was a good governor within the constraints of the limited powers governors have in Japan. One novel, fairly small, but for Hosokowa, characteristic, reform was to change the method of recruiting prefectural civil servants. Less emphasis was given to the formal examination, which was normally the be-all and end-all of recruitment. Instead the pass mark was set low enough to allow twice as many candidates as positions to be selected. There was then a round of interviews and a certain proportion were allowed to go on to a second examination. Some people were given jobs who would not have qualified on the examinations alone. The interviews were designed to look for encouraging signs of individualism in prospective employees. This would be unusual in many bureaucracies—in Japan it constituted a clear break with the consensus of the past.

He also pursued strong environmental policies, producing the strictest environmental regulations in Japan, as well as making a first-order commitment to triple the amount of greenery in the prefecture, declaring that: 'The amount of greenery is one measure of a community's cultural environment.'

In time Hosokowa came to call for a fully federal system for Japan, with vastly increased local autonomy. He argued that the Edo period in Japan's past should be re-evaluated, with the competition between the various feudal domains of the time having aided development. He saw it as a factor in Japan's modernisation and democratisation. He also took up numerous lifestyle themes, lamenting the lack of appreciation in Japan of the importance of architecture and urban culture.

Needless to say, as a successful governor in Japan he also worked hard at attracting investment and industry to his predominantly agricultural prefecture, especially in high-tech industries. He also cultivated the 'charismatic' style of a popular US governor. He promoted the image of his own personality. Good-looking, fit and a successful sportsman, he did things like participating in a national ski competition on behalf of Kumamoto.

But Hosokowa was also seriously ambitious and although he enjoyed being a 'chief executive' politician in Kumamoto, in Japan the real action in politics is in Tokyo. Hosokowa went back there in 1991 when he resigned as governor and was appointed to the Council for the Promotion of Administrative Reform. Hosokowa was increasingly concerned with the effects of financial corruption on Japan's political culture. However, his council's recommendation for the setting up of an ongoing and independent watchdog agency was rejected by the ruling party and the bureaucracy. In 1989 the LDP for the first time in a very long time lost outright control of the Upper House. This had led many serious players in Japanese politics to start thinking the unthinkable, that there might be a better way than working within the LDP for reform. Unhappy with the rejection of the council's recommendations, hugely impatient with both the LDP and the general political scene, Hosokowa, in 1992, led a small walkout from the LDP and formed the Japan New Party.

At the time this was not regarded as an earth-shattering event in Japanese politics, because Hosokowa's standing was not yet high enough to make it such, but it was significant. It also accelerated the trend for other LDP dissidents and even party mandarins who had simply lost faith in the old structures to start contemplating moving away from the LDP. In July 1992 Hosokowa returned to Japan's national Upper House, leading the Japan New Party to a respectable result in which it won 8 per cent of the vote and four seats. Hosokowa's platform reflected the concerns of his adult life. He wanted to bring more women into politics. Courageously, he favoured liberalising the rice trade to allow foreigners into the Japanese rice market. He proposed general deregulation and liberalisation of the Japanese economy. He wanted to assert political control over the bureaucracy, again a ridiculously moderate suggestion in most countries, a quite revolutionary proposition in Japan. Above all else, he proposed political reform, campaign funding reform and electoral reform designed to promote a contest of policies rather than of wealthy personalities.

Of course, a vote of 8 per cent is hardly overwhelming, but given the short time in which he had organised the new party, and the general ferment in Japanese politics at the time, it was a significant result. In June 1993 Hosokowa's party won 20 seats in the Tokyo Metropolitan Assembly.

In the meantime, the giants of Japanese politics had been making their own desperate and decisive power plays. Tsutomu Hata, a senior Cabinet minister, led a walkout of 30 LDP members protesting at the continued corruption within the political system. Japanese politics were thrown into crisis and turmoil. The LDP lost its working majority in the Lower House. On 18 June a motion of no confidence was passed in Kiichi Miyazawa's government. Miyazawa was forced to dissolve parliament and call national elections. Hata founded the Renewal Party, one of several short-lived parties which were to form and re-form in the next turbulent few years of Japanese politics.

In the national election of July the LDP failed to gain a

majority. Some eight parties won seats from the LDP. Hata's group ended up with 55 Lower House seats. Hosokowa's party scored 35. Seven of the 'non-LDP' parties came together in a coalition. There was intense horse-trading over the prime ministership. The socialists were regarded as incapable of providing a prime minister. Hata was favoured because of the good result his party had got in the election. But he was eventually seen as too recently and too intimately a part of the LDP culture and the coalition opted instead for the cleanskin and popular Hosokowa.

Hosokowa has subsequently been criticised for effectively making the price of his party's participation in the coalition the prime ministership itself, that this was too overweening a sign of self-regard and ambition. But a politician without ambition is no politician at all. Moreover, Hosokowa was basically successful. He stitched together a coalition and he actually got things done. He accomplished change. Furthermore, it was obvious that the Japanese people, as well as the international community, wanted and expected change. As it turned out, we all probably underestimated the strength of the forces resisting change in Japan, among them powerful sections of the bureaucracy and of the political establishment. And by this I mean not just the LDP but the socialists as well. When they left Hosokowa's coalition government and climbed into bed with the LDP they got a temporary occupancy of the prime ministership, but to do this they had to abandon all their longstanding policy positions and basically act as electoral cover for the LDP to take over again. This was bizarre and at the time inherently unpredictable. So was the scandal which ultimately claimed Hosokowa's resignation. But the new government began with a sense of excitement and seductive, limitless possibility.

Some who would minimise Hoskowa's role also claim that the real force in his government was Ichiro Ozawa, a former secretary-general and super heavyweight power broker of the LDP, who later went on to become Opposition leader in 1996. Undoubtedly Ozawa played a hugely significant role. Undoubtedly he was a more ruthless and, behind the scenes at least, more effective political manipulator than Hosokowa. But the assessment of Hosokowa as nothing more than Ozawa's puppet seems wrong on at least two counts. First, Hosokowa's actions were consistent with the philosophy and broad policy approach which he had been espousing for much of his adult life. He took the decision to leave the LDP and set up his own party without involving Ozawa. He was used to leadership from his time as a prefectural governor. There is too much in Hosokowa's record of independent and fairly consistent political action to allow him to be convincingly portrayed as nothing more than an Ozawa stooge. Moreover, political parties, and certainly governments, need a variety of types of political figures and political authority. Ozawa was a fixer, but Hosokowa offered his own unique assets to the governing coalition, among them a very high level of popularity which Ozawa certainly did not possess. Popularity in a democratic system is a form of power in itself. Hosokowa's government could have done with all the high-powered support available. Ozawa was an asset to the government, notwithstanding his past as an LDP fixer, and so was Hosokowa. They were complementary. There is no need to denigrate Hosokowa by exaggerating Ozawa's role.

When it came to Hosokowa's actually assuming the prime ministership the Liberal Democratic Party seemed for a time unable to cope with the idea that it was going to be out of office. It engaged in a range of stalling tactics but finally Hosokowa was voted in as prime minister by a parliamentary resolution by 262 votes to 224, on August 6, 1993. At 55 he was the youngest prime minister since his grandfather had held the post at 48 years of age. Hata became his deputy prime minister and foreign minister.

Hosokowa started well, making public efforts to lessen the degree of conflict over trade between the US and Japan, although in the end refusing to accept American numerical targets for trade deals because they breached the principle of free trade and constituted managed trade. In the end Hosokowa, despite the press drawing superficial parallels between him and Clinton, was not able to prevent a worsening of acrimony between Japan and the US over trade. It is not the least of the irresponsibilities of the Clinton administration that it put so much pressure, in such a destructive and negative fashion, on the government most likely to enact serious reform which Japan had seen.

He also moved to express more fully than any previous prime minister regret and apology for Japan's actions in the Second World War. This was a process carried further still by Hosokowa's successor, Tomiichi Murayama. But Hosokowa's efforts represented a new benchmark for their time and can be seen as part of the historical process of Japan reassuring its neighbours and of the ever-so-slow process of putting the past truly behind it. On August 23, 1993, in his first speech to the parliament, Hosokowa said: 'I would like to take this opportunity to express our profound remorse and apologies for the fact that Japan's actions, including acts of aggression and colonial rule, caused unbearable suffering and sorrow for so many people.' Hosokowa's words, like Murayama's, would not satisfy Japan's critics but they did signal a new stage in the process. They also signalled the generally liberal direction Hosokowa was trying to take. This was further reinforced in September of that year when Hosokowa addressed the General Assembly of the United Nations and committed Japan to an indefinite extension of the Nuclear Non-Proliferation Treaty, under which Japan, and most other nations, forswear the development, possession, proliferation or use of nuclear weapons, in exchange for the declared nuclear powers (the US, Russia, China, France and Britain) making efforts towards ultimate nuclear disarmament.

He also introduced an economic stimulus package, something that Japanese governments have been doing all through the 1990s. It consisted of the usual things—increased public works, special concessionary interest rates on loans to home buyers, cheaper money for small business and government aid for areas hit by natural calamities such as earthquakes and floods.

Most importantly, he introduced a political reform package. It included a ban on corporate donations to individual politicians. However, its most important feature was a change to the system of electoral representation such that the multi-member constituencies would give way to single-member constituencies. Hosokowa underlined the seriousness of his commitment to this package by saying that if it was not passed by the end of the year he would resign. Ultimately a watered-down version of what he wanted was passed, early in the new year. It combined an element of proportional representation with the single-member constituencies, as well as limited campaign finance reform and a lessening of the gerrymander in favour of rural electorates, which had been extremely averse to change. This reform package may yet transform the culture of Japanese politics and may turn out to be Hosokowa's single greatest contribution to Japanese history.

Under the old multiple-member constituencies politicians from the same party would effectively be running against each other, as well as their opponents from other parties, in a single seat. Because there was more than one member to be elected from each seat there was more than one candidate running from each of the parties. This meant that electors were very much voting for the individual candidates rather than the parties, and party platforms, they represented. This was a significant factor in stultifying serious policy competition, and therefore serious policy discussion, in Japanese elections. It also meant there was enormous concentration on the individual personalities of the individual candidates. It was a recipe for money politics. In future Japanese elections there will be a single LDP candidate, a single socialist, and single representatives of various other parties which run. People will be more inclined to vote for a party and its program, or even perhaps its leader, than for the local gift-giving, vote-buying array of LDP candidates battling it out with each other.

Hosokowa used his first speech as prime minister to parliament to stress the overriding importance of political reform. He said:

> At this major turning point, Japan needs political leadership
> more than at any time since the end of the war. It is vital that
> a political establishment which is trusted by the Japanese
> people be reinstated as soon as possible. Previous Cabinets have
> pursued political reform as the foremost issue on their agendas,
> but we have not yet seen any reforms take shape. This delay in
> enacting political reforms is the source of the popular mistrust
> of politicians and represents a lack of political leadership. These
> conditions of political lethargy have in turn hindered action on
> many key issues, including policies for improving the economy,
> and I am seriously concerned that they will have a serious and
> adverse effect on Japan's future. The precious opportunity to
> realise political reform which we were given by the Japanese
> people in the previous election must not be squandered. I

consider the achievement of political reform during this year to
be the first and foremost issue for my Cabinet.

Hosokowa also tried to deregulate Japanese society, and particularly the economy. This was more clearly a failure and one
which demonstrated the enormous conservative, blocking power
of the Japanese bureaucracy. He asked the government departments to nominate lists of regulations which they could expunge.
Of course no bureaucracy responds well to a request like that.
To provide a substantial list is an admission that much previous
activity has been useless or counterproductive. It is also a recipe
for declining power and cuts in numbers and budgets. Some
things about government bureaucracies translate across virtually
all national cultures. They do not cut themselves. They are not
into self-immolation. They also dislike self-mutilation and are
averse to weight reduction programs. Naturally, the lists the
departments provided of regulations to be expunged were pitiful.
In any event it was a fairly naive way to approach such a task.
It is not surprising that it failed. Some specific deregulation
measures—such as lifting sales restrictions on cellular phones and
abolishing restrictions on the sizes of breweries—were passed and
these were useful but modest.

But Hosokowa was already facing more serious difficulties.
The internal contradictions of his coalition were evident in
numerous policy areas. The socialists were opposed to his support
for having Japanese troops participate in United Nations peacekeeping efforts. They were also greatly distressed by his courageous move, in the context of the Uruguay Round of the GATT
trade negotiations, to allow foreign rice to be sold into Japan. It
is impossible to think of a constructive contribution the socialists
made in Japan in this period (or in any other for that matter).
Their ultimate recalcitrance led them eventually into a bizarre
embrace of their old foes, the LDP. They eventually destroyed
the most promising reform government in Japan's history, which
is not the least of the sins for which they will be weighed in
long-term assessments of Japanese politics. Their future, happily
for Japan and its partners, looks bleak.

When I met Hosokowa in November, 1993, he was perhaps
at the height of his powers. He was handsome, personable, looked
young and extremely fit. Two aspects of the interview were

slightly disconcerting, however. One was that he made a small factual error in the course of what he said about APEC. He mixed up the number of working groups looking at manpower issues with the number of working groups altogether. It was a small error. Straight after the interview some of the officials present button holed the journalists and told them that the prime minister had misspoken and meant to say something else. It was a small incident but it was interesting that the bureaucrats were absolutely unhesitant in correcting their boss after he had spoken. The other slightly odd aspect of it was that at that stage Hosokowa was answering written questions submitted in advance and one would have thought that he would have had the lines down pat.

Second, and rather disappointingly, he stuck rigidly to a very formal, pre-scripted format for the interview. This was particularly disappointing because Hosokowa has written and spoken much of his desire to get rid of needless formality in Japanese life, especially political life. Most East Asian leaders require a list of written questions in advance of an interview but virtually none ever makes you stick to that list. The aides of President Kim Young-sam of South Korea, for example, requested the written list of questions, to which they furnished a written list of replies, but then the interview was free to range over any questions I cared to ask. With Hosokowa the written pre-submitted list of questions was read out one by one and Hosokowa answered them, then only for a few moments at the end of the session was a more spontaneous discussion allowed.

When I met him Hosokowa was just about to go, in a few days, to the first APEC summit, and naturally he talked a lot about APEC. Of course, at first he accepted our congratulations for the passage of the political reform bill and you could see it was a wrench to take his mind away from that triumphant subject. But eventually he turned to international affairs and his first message was to make sure that everyone understood the depth of Japan's commitment to APEC.

APEC does indeed offer a great deal to the Japanese. It offers them a way to keep the United States productively tied to East Asia, it offers them a forum, especially through the regular APEC summits, of presenting East Asian economic dynamism to American audiences in a positive light, it offers them a chance to 'multilateralise' their trade disputes with the US and thus take some of the venom out of them. It also offers them a de-ethnicised version of regional organisation, which, given the inclusion of the United States and Australia, is not based on any racial identity or racial exclusivism. It also gives them another, substantial international push for trade liberalisation, which among other things they can use to convince their own electorate that they have to liberalise their economy as part of the entry fee to the modern global economy. It also gives them a good vehicle to use to pressure the always recalcitrant Europeans about liberalising international trade.

Hosokowa wanted his own endorsement of APEC made plain. He described it to me as 'the core of regional cooperation in the Asia–Pacific'. APEC, he said, should and would become the global model for 'inclusive regionalism'. It had the primary task of strengthening and implementing the GATT: 'APEC should augment and complement GATT. The economic development of the Asia–Pacific was built on the multilateral trading system.'

However, he rejected a suggestion by Australia's then prime minister, Paul Keating, that APEC should be turned into the Asia Pacific Economic Community. This rejection was probably out of consideration for the feelings of Southeast Asian nations who were more cautious about APEC than either Japan or Australia.

Hosokowa was also insistent that APEC remain true to its vision of 'open regionalism'. Through the '90s there was a debate about whether APEC should become a preferential trade bloc like NAFTA or the European Union, that is, a bloc in which member nations lowered tariffs to each other but not to the outside world. The competing vision was that APEC should liberalise trade on a Most Favoured Nation basis, that is, with the benefits of liberalisation open to the whole world. Hosokowa's view was strongly in favour of the second option, as part of his broader commitment to the GATT process. He specifically rejected recommendations from the APEC Eminent Persons' Group which would have turned APEC into a free trade area.

An APEC free trade area, he said, 'is not the direction which would be desirable'. APEC, he said, should always be complementary to GATT: 'It should not and could not be a substitute for GATT.' He also believed the forthcoming APEC summit would be important in ratcheting up the international political will to complete the Uruguay Round of the GATT. That is exactly what did happen, so Hosokowa's ambition was well founded. He also said Japan would do everything it could, and everything that was necessary, to complete the Round before the end of the year. That was a clear reference to liberalisation of the rice market, which was another of Hosokowa's most important reforms.

I spoke to Hosokowa the day before the American Congress was to vote on the NAFTA deal. The Japanese, like most Asians, inherently did not like NAFTA because it discriminated against them. However, the forces against NAFTA in the United States were not opposing it because it was discriminatory. They were full-blown protectionists who opposed NAFTA because it involved some trade liberalisation. They would have used a victory on NAFTA to attack GATT and APEC. Thus, although NAFTA itself was not good trade policy, people who supported trade liberalisation around the Asia–Pacific offered it qualified support.

Hosokowa gave a qualified endorsement to NAFTA when I spoke to him. He said he was interested in seeing NAFTA become a framework for open, regional cooperation: 'If that is the case NAFTA will contribute to the economic revitalisation of North America. That will be a positive factor for the Asia–Pacific region and also useful in upholding the multilateral trade system.'

It is more than noteworthy that Hosokowa was willing to offer political support to Clinton for something which in the immediate sense went against Japanese interests because of a sensible understanding of the long-term issues involved. It is equally noteworthy that at no stage during Hosokowa's brief and critical prime ministership did he get similar support from Clinton, who made things as difficult for his Japanese counterpart as he could at every turn.

Hosokowa did however object to the cynical use that was being made of Japan by both sides of the NAFTA debate within the US. The American opponents of NAFTA said, totally inaccurately, that it was another example of America giving away special benefits to other nations, in this case Mexico, with no regard for the consequences for American workers. In fact, while American leadership of the liberal international trading order after the Second World War was of historic importance, very little in the way of American trade liberalisation was non-reciprocal, that is, given away without getting corresponding benefits for America.

However, the proponents of NAFTA, among them President Bill Clinton, were even more dishonest in their use of Japan as a tool in the rhetoric of debate. With complete irresponsibility, and a more or less total disregard for the truth, they argued that America needed NAFTA because its chief trade competitors, in particular the Europeans and the Japanese, had similar deals which gave them similar advantages in their regions. While this is true of Europe, it is completely untrue of Japan, which has not relied on discriminatory, preferential deals anywhere, and least of all in its region of East Asia, to gain market access.

Hosokowa also spoke that day of the grave challenge presented to Japan's security by North Korea. He wanted to emphasise to me that he was against sanctions against North Korea [because of its nuclear program] at that stage, although he did not absolutely rule out Japanese support for them in the future. At that stage, however, he wanted to continue the diplomatic dialogue with North Korea. North Korea had recently prevented International Atomic Energy Agency inspectors from carrying out inspections of its nuclear facilities. Hosokowa said:

> That certainly is a problem. And we are very much concerned
> that this problem seems to be becoming a reality now. How
> long to wait—well that is a very difficult question. All we can
> say is—and I am sure the Americans and the South Koreans
> would be in the same position—we should continue to make
> efforts as much as possible for diplomatic and political dialogue.

Hosokowa was then engaged in an effort to get Pyongyang to resume diplomatic talks with Tokyo. These fitful efforts of Japan to have a meaningful dialogue with North Korea have occasionally annoyed South Korea, but in truth they have never added up to all that much of consequence.

Hosokowa also displayed his instinctive caution and sense of responsibility on security matters by saying he did not think Northeast Asia needed any new collective security arrangements. There had been much talk of the possibility of setting up a security dialogue body for Northeast Asia, designed to embrace basically China, Korea, Japan, the US and possibly Russia. Either alongside this, or possibly as some kind of evolution out of it, there was talk of some new collective security arrangement for the region. But Japan under Hosokowa, while it was challenging many orthodoxies, was basically comfortable with its security alliance with America, and with the web of separate but connected bilateral alliances which a number of countries in the region, notably Japan and South Korea, had with the US. This was a practical and hard-headed view. Given the scars on the Korean psyche from Japan's behaviour in the past, it is all but impossible to imagine South Korea and Japan entering into a formal alliance with each other. Yet each is a military ally of the United States, and American bases in Japan would probably be used to help defend South Korea, if hostilities broke out on the Korean peninsula, just as American bases in Korea could be used to help defend Japan if that was ever necessary. For both Asian powers it was best, politically and militarily, to let these contradictions be resolved by separate alliances for each with the US. There is an unhealthy element here in both Japan and Korea of not quite facing reality—especially the reality of how intermingled Japan and Korea's security interests really are, but the bottom line, of supporting the US alliance, was a practical way forward for both nations.

Hosokowa told me that he thought Northeast Asia did not need any new collective security arrangements: 'It is neither necessary nor realistic to have a collective security set-up like NATO for the region.' Similarly, he said he did not think APEC should embrace security questions, nor had he discussed security matters in an APEC context. It is occasionally suggested, sometimes by powerful Americans, that APEC should have a security role. Hosokowa prudently supported the traditional Japanese preference for keeping security structures separate from economic-dialogue structures.

The months after I met Hosokowa were ones of unaccustomedly vigorous government for Japan. In February 1994, Hosokowa introduced a substantial tax reform package centred on a big tax cut. Later in the same month he went to Washington for a forlorn and fruitless summit with President Clinton. Hosokowa strongly restated his commitment to resisting Washington's demands for numerical targets in trade. Clinton, for his part, in the face of continued escalation of the bilateral trade deficit, claimed that the market-opening mechanisms Hosokowa was offering 'simply do not meet the standards agreed to' earlier by Clinton and Hosokowa's predecessor, former prime minister Miyazawa. As usual the Clinton White House threatened all kinds of doom against Japan, in part of what came to be part ritual, part fiasco, in the bilateral relationship.

Tragically a corruption scandal was to claim Hosokowa's scalp and destroy his government, although it is likely that the socialists, who in many ways had even more to fear from reform than the LDP, would eventually have left the governing coalition even if Hosokowa had remained prime minister. The particular allegation was that Hosokowa had accepted a $1 million bribe from a delivery company, Sagawa Kyubin, in his time as governor of Kumamoto. He claimed that the money had been a loan and he had repaid it but he was unable to prove this claim. These allegations were all the LDP needed to bring down a prime minister who had been regarded as a cleanskin and who had done so much to combat the culture of corruption. Whatever the precise facts in Hosokowa's case, in some ways what happened to him is representative of a trap which often snares authentically reformist leaders operating in a political culture which has condoned corruption, or 'money politics' more generally, for a lengthy period. To have become figures of significance within that system they must have participated to some extent in the old practices. This is so even if their instincts are honest and their motivation generally good and their desire one of real public service. When the system is starting to break down these figures are the ones who try to institutionalise reform. But their past participation in the old system is used against them. A slightly similar situation arose for President Kim Young-sam towards the end of his term as president of South Korea. He was accused of having received money from former President Roh Tae-woo's slush fund. Kim strenuously denied that he had ever taken any money for himself but his spokesmen admitted that he had received funds with which to run the party, as was inescapable under the old dispensation. In Hosokowa's case it was truly tragic that the political leader who did more than any other to fight corruption should have had his prime ministership so brutally terminated.

Of course, the allegations were sufficient for the LDP to virtually bring parliament to a halt. Hosokowa felt he had to resign, which he did on April 8, although he remained active in politics and continued to deny that he had done anything wrong. He could still emerge as a decisive figure in the future. After Hosokowa's departure Hata briefly headed the government. He was prime minister for only 59 days and saw the socialists, and another party, defect from his coalition. On June 25 he lost a vote of no confidence in his government and had no alternative but to resign. The socialists went into government in coalition with their old enemy, the LDP. As part of the deal their leader, Tomiichi Murayama, became prime minister. The idea of a socialist prime minister would once have seemed revolutionary but Murayama's government was extraordinarily timid and conservative, at a time when Japan was crying out for decent and decisive reform-minded leadership.

It is easy and in some circles fashionable to dismiss Hosokowa as a political lightweight who got out of his depth in the prime ministership. But Hosokowa truly broke the mould in Japanese politics. As I have argued in this chapter, he oversaw substantial change himself—in leading the first non-LDP government in nearly four decades, in liberalising the rice market, in taking the process of apology and reconciliation for the Second World War further than had been done before, and above all in political reform. He also provided an alternative style, a sense that there were new possibilities in Japanese politics. If he never does anything else, he will have earned a commendable place in Japanese history for these achievements, and his countrymen will have a greater range of choices as a result of his efforts.

11

LEE TENG-HUI AND THE PROMISE OF CHINESE DEMOCRACY: STAND TALL, FELLOW TAIWANESE

The Taiwan State Guest House is a palatial though sombre building, dating from the days of Japanese colonial rule. It is surrounded by lush gardens and rests in the heart of noisy, polluted, downtown Taipei. One Saturday night, late in 1992, the joint was hopping. A lavish cocktail party to celebrate the 81st anniversary of the founding of the Republic of China saw hundreds of dinner-suited potentates in attendance. There were Cabinet ministers, business tycoons, diplomats, government officials and a goodly number of international journalistic hacks.

There was one star: Taiwan's president, Lee Teng-hui, beaming with pride at his and his nation's achievement, strolling among the guests in the company of his good friend the president of Panama.

The word for the night was glamour. The main house and garden danced with multicoloured fairy lights, jazz music played in the background. There was a distinct sprinkling of very beautiful women, including a number of recent Miss Taiwans, wearing their victory sashes. The night was balmy, the drink flowed (though no one was drunk), the limousines queued up as far as you could see. 'This,' one old China hand remarked to me, 'is what Shanghai must have been like when the Kuomintang ran it.'

The Kuomintang, the Nationalist Party which rules Taiwan,

294

has not run any part of mainland China since 1949, when it lost the civil war to its great historic rival, the Chinese Communist Party. And Shanghai under the KMT, while it may have been glamorous in isolated parts, was more generally characterised by squalor, poverty, filth and corruption. But history gave the KMT a second chance and the KMT has made a much better fist of running Taiwan than ever it did of running Shanghai. So much so that Taiwan is now one of the wealthiest nations in the world, with a per capita income of more than $US12 000 and rising rapidly, and consistently one of the largest levels of international reserves, generally hovering around the $US90 billion level or more.

More than that, Taiwan is now an authentic democracy. In a decade it has gone from being something like a military dictatorship to being a pretty full democracy—the first in 5000 years of Chinese civilisation. As such it is of huge importance to the whole world. More than one-fifth of the human race is Chinese. Some, notably the mainland Chinese leadership, argue that Chinese culture, in particular as expressed in Confucian values, is inherently hostile or unsuited to democracy. The idea is that Confucian societies value harmony, social stability and reverence for authority and leaders and these values are allegedly antithetical to the dialectical processes of democracy, the search for truth through the free and public clash of differing opinions. Yet the paradox of democracy is that it is generally more stable than any other political system, especially if it is combined with a tolerable economic performance. Democracy confers unique legitimacy on political authority and thus promotes stability.

Of course, you still need decent leadership, and this, in recent years, Taiwan has had. Taiwan in 1996 held a virtual festival of democracy, when Lee Teng-hui submitted himself to a direct election for the presidency. It was the first such election in Chinese history. The international consequences were vast. American public opinion warmed to Lee and to Taiwan's democratic experiment. Although Taiwan had had a fully democratically elected parliament since 1992, the symbolism of a directly elected president was powerful. It made Taiwanese democracy more accessible, more understandable, especially to American opinion.

It also greatly vexed the mainland Chinese leadership, who

have displayed in recent years an exceptional clumsiness in dealing with public opinion anywhere—be it Hong Kong, Taiwan, the United States, or the west generally. There is a droll irony of history at play here. When the mainland Chinese were at their absolute worst, pursuing policies not only harsh and undemocratic but semi-genocidal in their impact, during the cultural revolution and other spasms of insanity, they managed western public opinion pretty well. Now that they have undertaken promising economic reform, (which, while there has not been accompanying political reform, has markedly increased the political space available to the average Chinese)—in other words, now that they have a moderately positive story to tell, they have totally lost the ability to deal effectively with the western media, or with western public opinion generally. This may be because China now is much more open to the outside world. It is much harder to romanticise China, much harder for the regime to control foreign impressions of China.

But this is not a wholly satisfactory explanation of Beijing's recent brutishness and clumsiness. Much is a result of the uncertain leadership transition after Deng Xiaoping. Much, too, is the result of China's recent economic success, and the realisation that China is destined to be a great power. This is a circumstance no one, including the leaders in Beijing, is accustomed to dealing with.

Oddly, perhaps, the most adept handlers of the new situation have been the leaders in Taiwan, particularly Lee Teng-hui himself. Lee is a very distinctive individual. He embodies all of the major, and extremely diverse, influences on Taiwan's modern destiny. Despite the attention paid in recent times to its security spat with mainland China, Taiwan is generally misunderstood in international opinion. It is regarded as a plucky little Chinese society which is part of the East Asian economic miracle and has recently become a democracy. This is fair enough so far as it goes, but the extreme complexity of Taiwan's modern history is too little understood. It is, and always has been, a very, very different society from mainland China. Taiwan is better understood in its own terms as a unique Asian society heavily influenced by three great powers—the United States, Japan and China, rather than as an offshore Chinese society, or, in the mainland's own preposterous terminology, a 'renegade province' of mainland China itself.

Before the twentieth century the island of Formosa was the subject of only fitful attention from the mainland and underwent periods of European colonial rule. From 1895 to 1945 Taiwan was ruled by Japan. This rule was relatively benign. Taiwan is one of the few Asian societies to have some positive memories of Japanese colonial rule. It would be too much to say Taiwan has a love–hate relationship with Japan. Both words would be too strong, but the Japanese influence in Taiwan is very great. From 1946 to 1949 Taiwan was ruled from Beijing by the KMT who basically looted and pillaged the island. While the end of Japanese rule, and the return to China, had been welcomed on Taiwan in 1946, the experience of the KMT carpetbaggers was profoundly disillusioning. The period 1946 to 1949 was corrupt, brutal and disillusioning for Taiwanese. After 1949 Taiwan was ruled by the exiled KMT losers in the Chinese Civil War, under the leadership of Generalissimo Chiang Kai-shek. The KMT brought with it more than a million mainland refugees and a whole leadership infrastructure which was imposed on the society of Taiwan. Native Taiwanese, as opposed to mainlanders, were severely discriminated against.

But under strong American tutelage, the KMT did enact sensible economic reforms, beginning with land reform and followed by industrialisation, which gradually produced an economic success story. America's role, political, military and economic, was critical. So, later, in the economic sphere, was Japan's. From the mid-1980s, Chiang's son, Chiang Ching-kuo, began liberalising politically. This was partly at America's urging, partly at the urging of Taiwan's new middle class. Now Taiwan is prosperous, democratic, a combination of western and traditional Chinese influences, independent in everything but name and more than a little fearful of its giant neighbour, China.

Lee Teng-hui draws together all of these influences in his own story. He is an amalgam of the forces which have shaped modern Taiwan. These forces include China, Japan, the US, Christianity and Confucianism. Lee was born in Puping village near Shanchih on January 15, 1923. Shanchih was a small rural town, of perhaps a hundred households, in northern Taiwan, near Tamsui, which is now a suburb of Taipei. His parents were farmers, not very well off, and the young Lee would journey with his grandfather into nearby Taipei city to sell the produce from his family's rice and tea farm. Later he would make his career as an agriculturalist. At the time Lee was born, the land, ownership of the land, the reliability of the harvest, the kindness of nature—these were the factors which determined wealth and poverty, life and death, for the vast majority of Chinese. Lee's grandfather ran the farm; his father started out farming but discovered a yen for politics and ran successfully for the Taipei City Council.

Lee was born into stable and long-standing Japanese rule and for some part at least of his life considered himself Japanese. For a time he was known by a Japanese name, Masao Iwasato. Although he later said he hated the colonial system, he also found much to admire in Japanese rule. Some claim that even today Lee speaks better Japanese than Mandarin Chinese (the Chinese dialect spoken in his home as a child was not Mandarin). Some sources have claimed to have heard him speak Japanese in private conversation with his wife. In his early days Lee was impressed with the strength of Japanese power. All of this is important. Lee's sense of Chineseness, certainly of mainland-Chineseness, was attenuated. Also, he saw clearly that an Asian power could be a great power.

It would be wrong of course to idealise Japanese rule on Taiwan. As in most cases of colonial rule there was great discrimination against the locals compared with the colonisers. The Japanese on the island were unquestionably the elite. But the Japanese did also bring economic modernisation to Taiwan, modernisation which most analysts agree was central to Taiwan's subsequent emergence as a tiger economy.

Young Lee was a bright student from an early age. The Japanese administrators recognised talent and made use of it. Lee was thus granted admission to a Japanese high school. He was one of only a handful of Chinese to be allowed into the school, following competitive examinations. He suffered what you might call the normal existential dilemmas of a Chinese child in that situation but concentrated on making a success of his studies. There is no doubt that intellectually Lee was, and is, very impressive. He was so bright that the Japanese took him to Japan to study at the Kyoto Imperial University.

His time in Japan even involved service in the Japanese armed forces. Kyoto, the historic city of beautiful temples and special religious significance, was spared Allied bombing during the Second World War. At the end of the war Lee returned to Taiwan and continued his studies at the National Taiwan University. He completed his degree there in agricultural economics and began a career as an academic at the same university. In 1949 he married Tseng Wen-fui, who came from the same village as Lee, and whose family had been friends of Lee's family across three generations.

In 1951 Lee won a scholarship to Iowa State University in the United States. This began a profoundly important association for Lee (as for so many of East Asia's best and brightest) with America, which became, to Lee—as to so many others—teacher, friend, patron and strategic guarantor of last resort.

By 1953 he had an MA from Iowa and a taste for American life. He returned to Taiwan and re-entered academic life as a teacher at his old university. The key career development for Lee came in the late 1950s when he became professionally involved in the United States–Republic of China Joint Commission on Rural Reconstruction. This was important for Lee in two ways. It deepened his association with the American technocrats who were so important in providing policy advice to Taiwan's government, and it got Lee directly involved in what was to become one of the great achievements of the Taiwan government—namely land reform and the huge increase in productivity and output from the rural sector. Not only did this broaden the benefits of economic success, and broaden the access to land, it provided an economic surplus from agriculture which was able to be used for industrialisation.

Throughout the 1960s Lee consistently won promotion at JCRR. In the mid-'60s came another crucial break, the chance to go to Cornell University, in Ithaca, New York, in the US, and study for a doctorate in his field of agricultural economics. His doctoral thesis was later awarded the prize for the best dissertation for 1968 by the American Association for Agricultural Economics. The title of his thesis was, 'Intersectoral Capital Flows in the Economic Development of Taiwan'. It became a work of some importance in development studies. Interestingly it had plenty of positive things to say about Japanese administration of Taiwan.

While it can be presumed that Lee worked hard on his prize-winning doctorate, it was really the greater exposure to American life that was most important from his time at Cornell. He was a leader there among the substantial Taiwanese community and even came under suspicion of holding radical views by the Taiwan secret police, although nothing ever came of these suspicions. He would later recall that watching the Vietnam protests and the whole episode of 1960s American university radicalism was important to the development of his political views. It was not that the conservative Lee was sympathetic to the views of the radical students but rather that he saw how the United States allowed every shade of opinion full expression and how the society did not collapse as a result, but in some ways became stronger. Lee himself has said that the type of democracy he is building on Taiwan is a mixture of Confucian and western values and the western element of that certainly came from the United States.

In 1970 Lee became head of the JCRR's Rural Economy Division. He first encountered Taiwan's political leadership in that capacity, when he presented a report to Chiang Ching-kuo, then deputy premier, in 1971. It was a propitious meeting. A year later, at Chiang Ching-kuo's urging (Chiang Ching-kuo's father, Chiang Kai-shek, was still president at this stage), Lee was appointed a minister of state. He was the youngest person ever appointed to such a rank and, as a native Taiwanese, an important symbol of greater inclusion in what was still then a government dominated by mainland Chinese.

Lee was certainly achieving rapid promotion and proving himself a distinguished technocrat. But there was nothing at this stage of his career to indicate the future political deftness and self-confidence which would characterise his presidency. In 1978, Lee was appointed mayor of Taipei, which was a big political break. It gave him high public visibility and he used the office to hone his reputation as a moderate reformer. In particular, he widened the mechanisms of public consultation, foreshadowing the direction Taiwanese politics generally would take in the '80s of pursuing a more representative political system.

Like many other East Asian leaders, he delivered modest but earnest homilies to his people, urging them, for example, to take up jogging in the mornings, in what was almost an echo of the healthy-lifestyle advice so beloved of Lee's Singapore namesake, Lee Kuan Yew. Lee Teng-hui himself had a love of the violin, and a modest competence at the instrument. He launched an annual music festival and attempted to broaden the focus of Taipei life beyond the traditional emphasis on economic success.

In 1981 he was appointed governor of Taiwan province, an anomalous but by no means powerless position which derived from the then fiction of Taiwan's government that it was the legitimate government of all China and Taiwan was merely a province of China. During this period he again focused on agricultural reform, although agriculture was by then a far smaller component of the Taiwanese economy. Throughout the technocrat and early political phase of his career Lee showed himself progressive but not radical. The great changes which Lee would introduce as president of Taiwan were not really on the agenda at that time, and Lee extended the agenda progressively, but incrementally. He appeared progressive but not dangerous and as such was especially useful to a KMT seeking to modernise itself, particularly given that he was a native Taiwanese as well.

It was during this period that Lee suffered the worst personal tragedy of his life. His beloved only son died of cancer in 1982. It was a devastating blow to the family-minded Lee, who has become very devoted to his grand-daughter, the child of his dead son. It was a time in some ways of personal crisis. Lee coped in part through the strengthening of his Christian faith. Lee is a Presbyterian. He takes an ecumenical view of religion in his political role, encouraging and patronising all the major faiths. But his own beliefs are clear and orthodox Christian beliefs. Even these days he occasionally acts as a lay preacher. At the time of his son's death, regular Bible-meetings and prayer groups, and the human solidarity to be found in such traditional Christian gatherings, helped sustain him through the dark passages.

In 1984 Lee was selected by the National Assembly to be Chiang Ching-kuo's vice-president, following the death of Chiang the elder and the assumption of the presidency by Chiang Ching-kuo. This was a surprise decision and represented a new political high for a native-born Taiwanese. Central to the appointment, of course, was his relationship with Chiang Ching-kuo. But his reputation as a cleanskin native Taiwanese was attractive to the KMT mandarins. The KMT was coming under pressure by this point from dissident elements within Taiwan. In particular, it was not credible for the KMT to continue with only mainlanders in its highest political positions. Although it was theoretically the National Assembly which chose Lee to be vice-president, in truth the choice was based on his close relationship with Chiang Ching-kuo and Chiang's shrewd appreciation of the need for political change. Some 85 per cent of Taiwan's population was native born, and Lee's elevation was a recognition of their role in Taiwanese life.

As vice-president Lee was 100 per cent loyal to Chiang. He was sent, like all vice-presidents, on numerous overseas trips. But in Taiwan's case in those days a vice-president could only go to those countries with which Taiwan had diplomatic relations, so Lee made the rounds of South Africa and a number of impoverished Latin American nations which benefited financially from having diplomatic relations with Taiwan, namely Guatemala, Costa Rica, Paraguay, Uruguay and Panama. It was not the most scintillating life but Lee was a heartbeat away from the presidency

Lee was also chosen for the vice-presidency because he had no independent political power base and could not possibly be a threat to Chiang. Lee never had occasion to oppose his mentor but some of the KMT mandarins who had agreed to his elevation would have cause to regret their under-estimation of Lee's political skills. Chiang, with Lee as his vice-president, began the process of liberalising and democratising Taiwan. Chiang allowed Taiwanese citizens to visit the mainland, he began the lifting of the martial law under which Taiwan had been ruled since 1949 and he permitted the formation of an Opposition political party, the Democratic Progressive Party.

Chiang died suddenly on January 13, 1988, and the mainland KMT dynasty died with him. As vice-president, Lee's succession, at least for the short term, was automatic and he became president on the same day, being sworn in on the evening of

Chiang's death. Lee's early months in the presidency were highly uncertain. The KMT was deeply factionalised. Conservatives in the ruling party, and some members of the Chiang dynasty, were keen to exert authority over Lee, to stamp his presidency as belonging to them. In the early days it was by no means clear that Lee was going to be the KMT's candidate to succeed Chiang, after serving out the rest of Chiang's uncompleted term. The National Assembly would choose a new president in 1990. Lee's candidacy was fiercely opposed by the late Chiang's stepmother, a redoubtable woman and a formidable player in the upper echelons of Taiwan politics.

Before 1990, he was a president on probation. It was during this period that Lee began to exhibit real political skill of the highest order, masterfully using the institutional advantages of incumbency to reward potential supporters and isolate and diminish enemies. In the early days of his presidency, before his power was consolidated, Lee maintained a studied ambiguity about how far he was going to take the process of reform in Taiwan.

One of his most effective manoeuvres concerned his potential rival for power, Hau Pei-tsun. Hau was a deeply conservative military man. Hau was a haughty and very old-fashioned KMT stalwart. Lee promoted him to the position of premier and then in effect gave him the job of defending the government's cautious but slowly accelerating reform program against the raucous opposition leaders and student demonstrators. It was a task Hau was almost uniquely ill-equipped to perform. He was not particularly keen on the reforms anyway and he was temperamentally unsuited to promoting and defending them in the rude dialectics of democratic forums. The Opposition forces always preferred Lee to Hau and Lee used this preference effectively, while maintaining his base in the KMT itself. Eventually Hau resigned in 1992.

To reformers Lee offered hope, which was after all the official KMT line, to conservatives he offered some measure of reassurance. No one was confronted with immediate, radical change. The continuation of current policies was promised. In this Lee benefited greatly from the fact that the reform process had been well and truly initiated by Chiang Ching-kuo. Reform had Chiang's imprimatur, as powerful in death as it had been in life.

Chiang had died of a heart attack in January 1988. Lee's first test came within six months. Some ultra-conservatives within the KMT tried to block his election as party chairman. But the KMT itself had changed. Many of its members, including all of its younger members, had been born on Taiwan. Lee's position was stronger than it looked. On July 8, 1988, as part of the party's 13th congress, Lee was elected chairman of the KMT.

Partly to reassure the conservatives, partly because it was sensible to move slowly, he initially reaffirmed the conservative policy of no official contact with mainland China. However, he also promised to work towards eventual peaceful reunification with mainland China (provided this involved no question of communist rule) and, more importantly, to continue the path of economic reform within Taiwan.

In Lee's early months as pesident there were rowdy street protests and demonstrations by forces smpathetic to the DPP, demanding a more representative government system for Taiwan. Although these demonstrators were often roughly handled by Taiwan's police, and although they were often highly critical of Lee's rule, they in fact strengthened his hand against party conservatives. The demand for reform was obviously strong. And Lee did enough to win respect from some reformers, appointing more native-born Taiwanese to senior positions within the KMT.

Gradually Lee implemented what would come to be known as 'pragmatic diplomacy', that is, an attempt by Taiwan to win greater informal and semi-formal diplomatic recognition for itself, to increase the amount of international space it could operate in. Lee's government sought to participate in international bodies it had previously boycotted because they admitted mainland China. The diplomatic fallout from the Tiananmen massacre in Beijing in 1989 greatly assisted Lee in this. More countries were reluctant to give in to Beijing's bullying about not dealing with Taiwan after the massacre. The sight of the butchers of Beijing dictating to the international community that it must not deal with an increasingly democratic Taiwan was repugnant to many people. In 1989 Lee was able to have Taiwan represented at the Asian Development Bank meeting in Beijing. At the same time he began to scale down Taipei's unrealistic claims of sovereignty over all of China. He adopted a formula of 'one China, two equal governments', which was a significant departure from Taiwan's previous stance.

Lee undertook his famous 'golf' diplomacy. This began with a trip to Singapore in 1989. Sensibly and pragmatically leaving aside any necessity to be afforded the normal courtesies of a head of state, Lee began undertaking various vacation or golf trips to countries which did not have diplomatic relations with Taiwan. Most countries did not have diplomatic relations with Taiwan because Beijing made non-recognition of Taiwan a condition of having diplomatic relations with mainland China. In this process Lee sacrificed a tiny bit of face at one level—not being treated formally like a head of government—in order to win face at another level, the level of real substance for Taiwan's relations. During his vacations or golf trips Lee would of course have 'private' meetings with the government leaders of the countries involved. Lee's pragmatic diplomacy substantially raised Taiwan's international profile and was hugely popular with the Taiwan public.

In March 1990, Lee was elected unopposed by the National Assembly as president in his own right. But the Opposition groups were outraged that the election had not been a direct, popular election and there were more protests and demonstrations. In 1991 Lee ended the state of emergency under which Taiwan had been ruled since 1949. Opposition parties had also been allowed to run candidates in local elections for the first time in 1989. But naturally they were deeply dissatisfied with the composition of the National Assembly, which was still dominated by ancient mainlanders, elected before 1949 and allegedly representing mainland provinces. Finally, at the end of 1991, there were full and free democratic elections for the National Assembly, and next year for the National Parliament.

To visit Taiwan in those days, as I did frequently, was to be caught up in the whirl of change and the sense of possibility, of excitement, that anything was possible on this island. In truth Taiwan's democracy dates from then, but, for reasons already mentioned, the direct presidential election of 1996 was the symbolic point for America, and for much of the international community.

Lee continued the momentum of democratic reform by championing the cause of direct presidential elections, which were finally accepted in 1994 and took place in 1996. All this democratic change was exhilarating not only inside Taiwan but for Taiwan's standing internationally. The equation between Taiwan and China was changed fundamentally. No longer were there two repressive Chinese societies with one just happening to be an ally of the US from the days when mainland China was aligned with the Soviet Union in the Cold War. Now there was one democratic Taiwan and one authoritarian China. More than that, the end of the Cold War removed the strategic imperative which had driven China–US cooperation and which had limited what either of them would do in respect of Taiwan.

Before all the fallout of the Beijing–Washington split had played itself out Lee had presided over seemingly rapid warming of relations between Taiwan and China. In one of the most significant moves of all, in 1990 China, Taiwan and Hong Kong had all simultaneously joined the Asia Pacific Economic Cooperation forum which had been set up by Australia in the previous year. Negotiating their simultaneous entry was a feat of considerable diplomatic magnitude, in which both Australia and the Republic of Korea played key roles. High-level bilateral talks between Taiwan and mainland China took place in 1993. Under Lee's pragmatic encouragement, Taiwan began to play an important role, as an investor and design-and-management centre, in the mainland Chinese economy, both in Guangdong province and in Fukkien, just across from Taiwan on the mainland.

Lee's pragmatic diplomacy led to unprecedented recognition for Taiwan. On allegedly 'private' visits he famously went to Thailand and met the king, and went to Indonesia and played a round of golf with President Suharto. Beijing did not react strongly to these developments and the world, certainly the East Asian region, began to be lulled into a false sense of security that Taiwan and China could work out an effective *modus vivendi* as two de facto independent but closely related neighbours. All this was to be shattered, however, by Beijing's determination, which has so far been unsuccessful, to bring Taiwan to heel.

The occasion, if not necessarily the cause, of Beijing's reaction against Lee's pragmatic diplomacy was his visit in June 1995 to his alma mater, Cornell University, to accept a distinguished-

alumnus award. The matter was as usual comprehensively mis-
handled by the Clinton administration. I recount the sequence
of events in the chapter in this book on Bill Clinton's leadership.
Suffice to say that the Clinton administration first reassured its
Beijing interlocutors that Lee would not be given a visa, because
to do so would be to breach their 'one-China' policy. Then, after
Congressional resolutions in support of a Lee visit, the Clinton
administration as usual adopted the line of least resistance and
allowed Lee to visit.

At first there was reason to believe that Beijing might. react
with commonsense. Lee's visit was announced in May. Following
the announcement a senior mainland delegation visited Taiwan.
Everything seemed normal. But then in June the nature of
Beijing's reaction changed altogether. The Chinese ambassador
was withdrawn from Washington. A campaign of personal denunciation of Lee in the mainland Chinese press became truly
hysterical. Lee was labelled the 'harlot of history', a gangster, a
criminal and a collaborator with the Japanese. China also began
firing allegedly 'test' missiles near Taiwanese waters.

Lee himself made a few rhetorical outbursts against the communists, calling them 'blockheads' and 'dead brains'. He also told
them 'my meat is tasty', which broadly translates as 'Don't come
too close, buddy, or you're in deep trouble'. But Lee's rhetoric
was clearly a reaction to Beijing's campaign and in any event was
not remotely comparable in ferocity or sustained venom with the
campaign Beijing ran against him.

Beijing's actions were pretty scary for the people of Taiwan,
and the region. Lee, having secured such an international victory
as the visit to the United States represented, had to keep his
nerve. His visit to Cornell became a great celebration of Taiwanese democracy. He was feted by many senior congressmen, especially but not exclusively Republicans. Virtually since 1949 the
Taiwanese have displayed a beautiful sense of how to play to an
American audience, how to influence American public, corporate
and above all congressional opinion. It has been one of the great
historic accomplishments of the KMT and ought to be studied
by other Asian nations who are far less influential in Washington.

Lee's address at Cornell was perfectly titled 'Always in My
Heart', pitched just right to appeal to that deep strain of

sentimentality in the American character, a sentimentality which is especially strong when it takes the form of gallantry towards the 'plucky little guy'. His speech is worth quoting at a little length both for its substance, and for what its style says about the Taiwanese mastery of the American political idiom.

There were frequent references to Taiwan's debt—spiritual, political, military and economic—to the United States. Lee closed his speech in stirring style:

> The United States was extremely helpful in the early stages of Taiwan's economic development. We have never forgotten America's helping hand in our hour of adversity, so your nation occupies a special place in our hearts . . .
>
> As I have spoken to you today I have done so with the people in my heart. I know that what my people would like to say to you now can be expressed by this simple message:
>
> The people of the Republic of China on Taiwan are deter-mined to play a peaceful and constructive role among the family of nations.
>
> We say to friends in this country and around the world:
>
> We are here to stay;
>
> We stand ready to help;
>
> And we look forward to sharing the fruits of our demo-cratic triumph.
>
> The people are in my heart every moment of the day. I know that they would like me to say to you that on behalf of the 21 million people of the Republic of China on Taiwan, we are eternally grateful for the support—spiritual, intellectual and material—that each of you has given to sustain our efforts to build a better tomorrow for our nation and the world. In clos-ing, I say God bless you, God bless Cornell University, God bless the United States of America and God bless the Republic of China.

To non-American western ears this passage might sound a little corny. There is of course no reason to doubt Lee's sincerity in uttering those words. But corny or not they certainly played perfectly to an American audience. Throughout his speech Lee returned again and again to a central motif, almost a musical phrase running repeatedly and melodiously through the larger symphony he was creating: Taiwan is a democracy, this is our legitimacy.

He said:

> I believe that the precept of democracy and the benchmark of
> human rights should never vary anywhere in the world,
> regardless of race or region. In fact, the Confucian belief that
> only the ruler who provides for the needs of his people is given
> the mandate to rule is consistent with the modern concept of
> democracy. This is also the basis for my philosophy of respect
> for individual free will and popular sovereignty.

Again, undeniably the strongest part of Taiwan's case—its
democracy—was framed in a universal context perfectly designed
to appeal to American listeners.

Lee also made an overt bid for greater formal international
recognition:

> When a president carefully listens to his people the hardest
> things to bear are the unfulfilled yearnings he hears. Taiwan
> has peacefully transformed itself into a democracy. At the same
> time, its international economic activities have exerted a
> significant influence on its relations with nations with which it
> has no diplomatic ties. These are no minor accomplishments
> for any nation, yet the Republic of China on Taiwan does not
> enjoy the diplomatic recognition that is due from the
> international community. This has caused many to
> underestimate the international dimension of the Taiwan
> experience. Frankly, our people are not happy with the status
> accorded our nation by the international community.

Did Lee miscalculate, with his visit to Cornell and his brilliant
address? Did he provoke China unnecessarily and thereby endan-
ger his people? I don't think so, although a lot of analysts do.
Lee was certainly pushing at the diplomatic boundaries imposed
on Taiwan by China and perhaps it was inevitable that he would
crash into those boundaries at some point. But before considering
the pragmatic questions it is worth pointing out that Lee's
position is unassailable in principle. Mainland China has ruled
Taiwan for three years in the last hundred. Communist China
has never ruled Taiwan. Since 1949 Taiwan has been completely
independent in everything but name. In that time Taiwan has
developed as a peaceful, prosperous and democratic society which
threatens no one, covets no neighbour's territory, exerts no
untoward military pressure, and respects its own and everyone

else's human rights. Beijing cannot convince the people of Taiwan to reunite with the mainland under Communist Party leadership. If the principle of self-determination and respect for human rights were to be applied, Taiwan's de facto independence would be recognised. It is only the crude threat of Chinese force, the threat, let's be plain, to murder and maim tens, perhaps hundreds, of thousands of people, which makes unification of any kind even an issue.

But alas, principle counts for little in international relations. Judged pragmatically, were Lee's actions irresponsible or counter-productive? Again, the argument seems to be with Lee. After his visit to Cornell, Beijing ran a continuous and hysterical campaign against him. This did not really end until the presidential election in March 1996. Lee scored here perhaps the greatest single triumph of his life. In a four-way race he won well over 50 per cent of the vote and finished more than 30 per cent ahead of his nearest rival. During the election campaign Beijing's campaign of denunciation against Lee intensified. Beijing also fired live missiles within tens of kilometres of Taiwan's coastline and some of its busy cities. It massed troops on the mainland near Taiwan. Towards the end of the missile firings it admitted that they were an attempt to influence the election in Taiwan. Lee's huge electoral victory was a thorough repudiation by the Taiwanese electorate of Beijing's attempted intimidation. Thus at one level of pragmatism the answer about Lee's behaviour is clear. It was successful in that it was overwhelmingly endorsed by his elector-ate.

Was Taiwan's security imperilled by Lee's actions? The first point to make here is that it is the Chinese politburo, not Lee, who responded excessively and took military action without the slightest justification. But a shrewd leader must take account of the irrational or merely aggresive behaviour of his country's neighbours. However, on this score Lee also emerges well. The Americans, after the Chinese had begun their live missile firings, sent two aircraft-carrier battle groups to the waters near Taiwan to support Taiwan. This was the most powerful armada the United States had assembled in Asia since the end of the Vietnam War. Its deployment was a decisive move, which shored up Taiwan, reassured American allies around Asia and forced Beijing, which is in no position to contemplate military conflict with America, to calm down.

There were more important results for Taiwan even than this. Before the naval deployment the Clinton administration had pursued a preposterous policy of 'strategic ambiguity' over whether or not it would respond to Chinese military moves across the Taiwan Straits, including eventually perhaps an attack on Taiwan. Yet ambiguity has often been the unwitting trip wire for war. In the lead-up to the Korean War, and in the Gulf War, American spokesmen made statements which led the aggressors to believe that the territory they coveted did not represent a vital American interest and would not be defended by American arms. Strategic ambiguity in this case was meant to make the Chinese uncertain but it probably emboldened them.

In fact, American law, and a number of international agreements to which America is party, commit the US to the maintenance of Taiwan's security. The key documents are the Shanghai Communique of 1972, issued by Richard Nixon and Chou En-lai, the joint communique issued by Beijing and Washington when Jimmy Carter established formal diplomatic relations with mainland China in 1979, the Taiwan Relations Act passed by the US Congress in 1979 and the joint communique and exchange of letters between Ronald Reagan and Chinese premier, Zhao Ziyang, issued on the 10th anniversary of the Shanghai Communique in 1982.

American officials, when they finally decided to take action to protect Taiwan, argued that such action was consistent with all the documents listed above. In the original Shanghai Communique both sides committed themselves to normalising diplomatic relations. Premier Chou En-lai declared that:

> The Taiwan question is the crucial question obstructing the
> normalisation of relations between China and the United
> States; the government of the People's Republic of China is the
> sole legal government of China; Taiwan is a province of China
> . . . the liberation of Taiwan is China's internal affair . . . all
> US forces and military installations must be withdrawn from
> Taiwan. The Chinese government firmly opposes 'two Chinas'
> and 'independent Taiwan'.

The US acknowledged that Chinese on both sides of the Taiwan

Straits accepted that there was one China and Taiwan was part of China. The US said it 'does not challenge that position'. The next sentence in the US declaration is crucial: 'It [the US] reaffirms its interest in a peaceful settlement of the Taiwan question by the Chinese themselves.'

US spokesmen have since said that everything the US has done on Taiwan is predicated on the peaceful settlement of the Taiwan question. Thus, if Beijing uses force against the Taiwanese, it breaks the agreement. This was certainly not explicit in the documents, but was widely accepted at the time. The US also promised to reduce its forces on Taiwan 'as the tension in the area diminishes'. In the 1979 joint communique establishing diplomatic relations President Jimmy Carter acknowledged Beijing's position that 'there is but one China and Taiwan is part of China'. But he also declared: 'The United States continues to have an interest in the peaceful resolution of the Taiwan issue and expects that the Taiwan issue will be peacefully settled by the Chinese themselves.' These sentences form the continuing US commitment to rejecting the use of force across the Taiwan Straits. However, the US Congress, which has always loved Taiwan and felt guilty about suggestions that Washington was abandoning it, wanted more. There was a strong feeling then that Carter could have got more formal recognition of Taiwan's right to exist if he had been tougher with the Chinese.

Congress fixed the matter up by passing the Taiwan Relations Act, which the president signed into law, and which governs US relations with Taiwan to this day. The Act declared that it is the policy of the United States 'to consider any effort to determine the future of Taiwan by other than peaceful means, including boycotts or embargoes, a threat to the peace and security of the western Pacific area and of grave concern to the US; to provide Taiwan with arms of a defensive character; and to maintain the capacity of the US to resist any resort to force or other forms of coercion that would jeopardise the security, or the social or economic system, of the people on Taiwan.' Thus, from the moment that Act was signed by the president, the US has had a security obligation to Taiwan. In full knowledge that this was American policy, indeed that American administrations were bound by law to follow this policy, China's premier, Zhao Ziyang, issued a joint communique with Ronald Reagan in August 1982.

In that communique the Chinese leader said that China's 'fundamental policy' was to 'strive for a peaceful resolution of the Taiwan question'. American spokesmen later said that the American intention to gradually reduce the arms it supplied to Taiwan was premised on that commitment. In other words, China was meant to seduce Taiwan into eventual reunification, not rape it at gunpoint. The problem for the Taiwanese, and for the government that Lee led, was that the years of relative quiet between Taiwan and China had allowed the meaning of these documents to drift into uncertainty, promoted, as I've argued, by the Clinton administration's ridiculous embrace of strategic ambiguity.

If Lee is to be regarded as precipitating the tensions with China, both by his Cornell University visit and his campaign to have Taiwan admitted as a member of the United Nations, then he should also be credited with the significant improvement of Taiwan's overall security situation that paradoxically came about as a result of these tensions. By constantly playing to Taiwan's strength, its democracy, he built up an irresistible momentum of goodwill in the United States which Clinton could not ignore. As a result, at the end of the imbroglio there was far less strategic ambiguity about America's commitment to Taiwan's security than there had been at the start. This in itself constituted a substantial gain for Taiwan's overall security outlook. Of course the Americans and the Japanese were also telling Lee privately to try to calm things down after the election, that Taiwan would not get military support if it stepped beyond the accepted if artificial bounds on its behaviour, such as by declaring formal independence.

Lee's inauguration speech in May 1996 was a model of restraint and he probably did not need American or Japanese advice to achieve this restraint. He offered to go on a 'journey of peace' to Beijing to negotiate with his mainland counterparts. He did not stress, indeed has hardly publicly mentioned, Taiwan's quest for a UN seat. He did of course defend, boldly proclaim even, Taiwan's democracy but he eschewed any harsh criticism of the mainland. He declared:

Today the existence and development of the Republic of China on Taiwan has won international recognition and respect. In the new international order of today, such basic tenets as democracy, human rights, peace and renunciation of force are universally adhered to; they are in full accord with the ideals upon which our country was founded. We will continue to promote pragmatic diplomacy in compliance with the principles of goodwill and reciprocity. By doing so we will secure for our 21.3 million people enough room for existence and development as well as the respect and treatment they deserve in the international arena.

In truth Lee had played a difficult hand to perfection.

Probably, even if it had wanted to, Beijing could not in 1996 have launched a successful invasion of Taiwan. The Taiwan Straits are 160 km wide at their narrowest point, but defence analysts believe the topography of the respective coastlines means that the invasion route would be 200 km to 320 km. China's forces could not support more than one major beachhead on Taiwan. Given the limitations of its amphibious fleet it would fall prey to Taiwan's aircraft, missiles, submarines, artillery and surface combatants. Short of nuclear devastation, China could not conclusively subdue Taiwan by force, which means that the eight-month campaign of military intimidation, from June 1995 to March 1996, was basically a psychological battle. If Lee had faltered the consequences for his nation could have been dire. Although China could not have invaded and subdued Taiwan, it could have done other things, perhaps at great cost to itself, which would have had a serious impact on Taiwan, things such as blockading its ports or firing artillery at it. Weakness on Lee's part, or a failure to get the Americans to do the right thing, could have had calamitous consequences, leading Taiwan into a forced negotiation with the odds very much against it. Leaders can only be judged by the results they produce. Lee stood firm against the mainland Chinese, and managed the delicate and complex relationship with the Americans, while not overplaying his hand. It was an effective performance.

In May 1996 I went to Taiwan to attend Lee's inauguration as the elected president of the Republic of China on Taiwan. Again it was a festive place to be, although a certain amount of relief at the relaxation of tension with the mainland, and still an undercurrent of apprehension, were discernible.

The election itself had been dominated by the mainland campaign against Lee, to the great disadvantage of his opponents. The DPP ran the veteran of the independence movement, Peng Ming-min. The DPP knew that the people of Taiwan were not prepared to risk a war with the mainland in order to pursue the symbols of independence, when they already had all the substance. The DPP therefore tried to fudge its position on independence, saying it supported independence but there would be no need for a formal declaration of independence, because Taiwan was already independent in everything but name. Nonetheless, if Beijing damaged anybody in the election it was the DPP. These tensions were evident in the subsequent internal tensions and splits within the DPP.

Two candidates ran who were associated with the New Party. This is a breakaway from the KMT which stresses old-fashioned Chinese nationalism. Although fiercely anti-communist, and supportive of Taiwan's new democracy, it is often believed to be preferred by Beijing because it most strongly emphasises Chinese cultural unity and the need for eventual reunification with the mainland. Neither of the two candidates associated with the New Party did well. Nonetheless the emergence of the New Party has been an important structural change in Taiwanese politics. It gives voters an alternative to the KMT other than the DPP. It represents a conservative pressure group and allows the KMT to position itself as a centrist ruling party.

Lee benefited from the splits among his opponents, as well as the vilification of him by Beijing, the gravitas of long incumbency and the huge membership and fabulous wealth of the KMT, including its close links with the television networks.

In May 1996, I spoke to a range of Taiwanese opinion makers and found, even among Lee's critics, a grudging admiration for his part in the achievement of democracy on Taiwan. Diane Ying, the publisher of the business magazine, *Common Wealth*, gives Lee high marks for democratising Taiwan, but still regards her society as a 'crippled democracy', citing corruption, violence and the lack of a fully independent judiciary as limits on Taiwanese democracy. Antonio Chiang, publisher of *The Journalist* magazine, delivers a similar judgment: 'President Lee did liberate us from the martial law system. That is his great contribution. He changed the KMT from an authoritarian party to a chaotic party. His weakness is he doesn't know how to institutionalise the new system.'

Vincent Siew, one of Lee's senior Cabinet ministers and closest colleagues, who managed Lee's presidential campaign, says Lee is a natural politician who loves campaigning and that the KMT owes its modernisation to Lee. He also thinks any possible reunification with China is a very long way away:

> Economically we [Taiwan and China] are quite advanced, politically we are a democracy, socially we are open and free. Unification can only occur without pain if the gap is narrowed. Whether mainland China can continue to reform towards a market economy and a free society is unclear.

There is no doubt that Lee has transformed Taiwan into a democracy, but he still benefits from the remaining authoritarian touches of the island's political culture. The manner of the celebration of the inauguration was in its way an odd event for a democracy. There were 50 000 invited guests to the event in a stadium in Taoyuan, about an hour's drive south of Taipei. It was the sort of mass rally the mainland communists themselves love and democratic societies normally eschew. Taiwan flags were issued to all the thousands of foreign and local dignitaries who were all expected to wave on cue to provide the mock-spontaneous images of joy beamed around the world. Such choreographed displays of political enthusiasm would be neither needed nor welcomed in a more mature, more settled, democracy and if anything they detract from rather than augment Lee's genuine achievement (although they were certainly remarkable as spectacle).

Later, in a vast congratulatory series of courtesy calls, hundreds upon hundreds of locals and foreigners, all carefully chosen, many flown in at the government's expense, trooped in one by one to shake hands and offer ten seconds of individual congratulations to Lee. It was rather like meeting the pope. You get the feeling that the more established Taiwan democracy becomes the less people will have a taste for this pomp and circumstance.

But it would be churlish to criticise Lee's celebration too much. He earned it. He is one of that small breed of leaders who has overseen and driven a transition to democracy in his nation, and then gone on to lead a successful administration. He also maintained Taiwan's security at a time of tension and challenge from the biggest nation in the world. Similarly, he has presided over a government which has pursued economic policies which have given Taiwan some of the fastest economic growth rates in the world. Democracy, security, prosperity—this is a pretty good compact for a leader to make with his people. Lee is a serious figure, but for a Chinese leader he smiles readily and his grin is broad and sometimes seems a little self-satisifed. But then, as they say, winners are grinners.

The American touches in Lee are evident. It is right that America honour its commitments to Taiwan, for Taiwan has honoured its commitments, to its own people and to the broader stream of humanity who have an interest in the fate of the Chinese people. Another famous address of Lee's, in April 1995, was entitled 'Stand Tall, Fellow Chinese'.

Sensibly Lee has abandoned claims to speak on behalf of all Chinese, though in one magazine interview in 1996 he did compare himself with Moses. Taiwan may not be the promised land exactly, but it is a free, democratic, decent place to live. All of this is due in no small part to Lee Teng-hui.

And these days his people do stand tall, much taller than before.

Index

318